THE HUMAN CLONING DEBATE

3rd Edition

edited by
GLENN MCGEE, PH.D.

BERKELEY HILLS BOOKS
Berkeley California

Published by Berkeley Hills Books
P.O. Box 9877, Berkeley California 94709
(510)848-7303 fax (510)525-2948
www.berkeleyhills.com

ISBN 1-893163-41-5

Permissions: See pages 304–305, which are an extension of the
copyright page.

Cover design by Elysium Design, San Francisco.

Library of Congress Cataloging-in-Publication Data

The human cloning debate / edited by Glenn McGee.— 3rd ed.
   p. ; cm.
Includes bibliographical references.
  ISBN 1-893163-41-5 (alk. paper)
  1. Human cloning—Moral and ethical aspects.
  [DNLM: 1. Cloning, Organism. 2. Bioethical Issues. 3. Religion. QH
442.2 H9178 2002] I. McGee, Glenn, 1967-
√ QH442.2 .H85 2002
   174'.25—dc21
                                        2002008680

CONTENTS

Part Six — God and the Clone

Glenn McGee

Introduction

If it ever thrived, the *Leave it to Beaver* family is fading into the millennium. Ward, June, Wally and Beaver Cleaver and their functional, "nuclear" family, are being replaced by dozens of other kinds of families. The political football "family values" is also being replaced, as society gets used to a world of divorce, changing working conditions, and new kinds of reproduction. To be sure, some artifacts of the *Beaver* model persist. My mother, and perhaps yours, is still sanguine about the ideals of her parents and her parents' parents–ideals of the 20th century. But in the new millennium, how we understand the family is changing, and changing fast. Shortly before his death Benjamin Spock struggled with the task of re-writing his classic book about childcare, noting on American television that "I don't know who the audience is anymore." For families it has become an era of bioethics.

Family courts, clergy, employers, and society at large struggle to make sense of the myriad new kinds of families. Divorce creates a custody battle for frozen embryos, or the thawing of abandoned frozen embryos brings a request from the Vatican to place, gestate and adopt, wholesale, thousands of little potential orphans. Single adults, homosexual couples, and couples in their 50s request adoption, ask friends to donate gametes, or arrange for a gestational carrier. Recently widowed women, sisters, or mothers request that children be made from sperm harvested post-mortem from their recently deceased male relatives. Couples who use assisted reproduction offer their extra embryos to other couples through "adoption" arrangements, and college students sell their gametes on the open market, through web pages, making children they hope never to meet and plan to exclude from their estate. Lots of people still have sex, get married, buy houses, and settle in quaint suburbs. But most of them are eventually divorced, turning then to lawyers and courts to help figure out how to make of their new lives a "family." So, eventually, whether through adoption, infertility treatment, or divorce most children of our era will have more than one set of "parents." And for even the most ordinary pregnancies a flood of new choices has entered the picture about how to shape a baby so as to prevent deadly hereditary disease, or to enhance the child's future.

We have begun making babies the modern way, into new families and through new technologies. No matter how bewildering the context, we continue to acquire and embrace new methods for finding, having, and making babies. Take 1997. International child acquisition increased more than 200% as adoption of those from war-torn nations and China became almost commonplace, despite concerns about the "exporting" of children with HIV + status. The state of Washington elected again to be the only state in the nation where adoption may be arranged without any court or state review of any kind. This facilitated a rush to arrange "abortion alternative" facilities in Seattle that would provide children for the childless with no waiting in line.

We were not expecting many of the reproductive technological advances of the past half-decade. It was discovered, by accident, that infertility treatments leading to gestation might be possible for post-menopausal women of advanced age. 63-year-old Arceli Keh brought a fake I.D. to a University of Southern California reproduction clinic, claimed to be 53, and was able to successfully carry a fetus to term, giving birth to a child. Ethicists wondered whether or not menopause should be a barrier for gestation, and some speculated that elder pregnancy might be a moral problem since the parent is unlikely to live past the child's adolescence. Others, though, argued that elder males have families with some frequency and that if safety turns out not to be an issue there should be no age barrier. In a related conversation, researchers at the University of Pennsylvania revealed that the use of post-mortem retrieval of sperm from recently deceased men has suddenly come into the clinical mainstream, with requests for such retrieval now common. Ought women or others to be allowed to determine in the emergency room what is to be done with the sperm of their deceased friends, relatives, or mates? Can children be made from such processes? Ought 24-year-old urology residents to be making policy on the fly for the next generation of reproductive technology?

When one young infertile couple in Atlanta was unable to conceive and unable to afford more reproductive services, their infertility practitioner saw the opportunity and offered to provide them an entire battery of experimental infertility experiments free of charge. In exchange, the couple would agree to enroll in a new program that had significant risks. The program involved using a frozen oocyte, or human egg. Until 1997 animal studies had showed troubling results that could easily have translated into birth defects for the first human couple, if they were successful at all in becoming pregnant. Miraculously, a successful birth was achieved, and overnight women began to discuss the potential for egg banking programs that would allow women to delay gestation so that pregnancy could come after the critical career-building years of the 30s and 40s.

Another accident resulted in the birth of septuplets to the McCaughey family in Iowa. Shortly after their infertility treatment resulted in multiple gestations, a common result of such treatment, the family announced that they would not "selectively reduce" the number of fetuses but instead attempt to carry seven to term. Although this had never before been recorded, the children were born uneventfully and given critical care in an Iowa hospital. Many supported the family, as the governor of Iowa donated a house and a food company donated a year's baby food. However, the medical costs for the family were expected to top $5 million in the first year, prompting many to ask at what cost to society will risky infertility treatments be provided. Thousands of quadruplets and quintuplets asked why novelty should pay for a house. A black couple in Houston gave birth to eight children and found no such warm reception.

Ironically, costs and success rates of U.S. in vitro fertilization (IVF) programs have become more controversial too, as the U.S. Centers for Disease Control and Prevention released a major report on the success rates for assisted reproduction. The report, located on the web, showed success rates in some programs as low as 8% per IVF "cycle." At an average cost of $7,000 per cycle, our national expenditure for assisted reproduction has exceeded $2 billion. At what cost should parents struggle against such bad odds to make genetically similar children?

The new options are myriad: hyperovulation for egg donation, sperm donation from friends, eggs seemingly auctioned by models on the Internet, then desperate couples offering $50,000, $60,000 and finally $100,000 for the right donor. Sperm donation on the web now dominates that practice, making old news of the "genius bank" at California's Repository for Germinal Choice. Families are being created in all sorts of new combinations: gestational carrying of embryos made from gametes of parents or gametes of donors for other parents, frozen embryo storage and adoption, the harvesting, freezing and use of sperm from dead men, and various combinations of the above.

It is widely argued that there is insufficient regulation of unorthodox pregnancy. Ethicists have called reproductive technology a "wild west" field of medicine in which anyone can do anything to make a baby. Hollywood and clergy decry the attempt to have "perfect babies" even as clinical medicine ramps up its arguments for public funding to find more ways to solve "the infertility crisis."

You would guess that this entire debate about making babies in new ways is changing things. You would be wrong. Remarkably, ethical discussion about the use of new reproductive techniques has not resulted in any substantial change in the training of physicians, clergy, genetic counselors or scientists, nor have bioethics debates changed the law. And three years after the cloning of Dolly no real national law about reproduction or cloning exists, with only the occasional and poorly crafted state statute in its stead. The debate in America, unlike the rest of the world, is motivated by bursts of fear and enthusiasm, and increasingly by the stock market's search for growth and discovery.

Dr. Spock, Meet Dolly

And then came Dolly, a sheep made from the fusion of a black sheep's egg and DNA extracted from a mammary cell of a white sheep. The first cloned mammal was created in a sleepy Scottish village by a team of fairly even-tempered scientists, the leader of whom had adopted his own children. Dolly was named for a country music singer and displayed on the Today Show. Dolly was clearly born into a scientific class of her own, as you will read in essays by Potter Wickware and others. But our changing understanding of family and the changing ways we make families set the context for a debate about human cloning. Before Ian Wilmut and Keith Campbell at the Roslin Institute made the landmark discovery debated in these pages, couples and churches and physicians and everyone else were already beginning to struggle with the larger debate about making babies the modern way.

In the wake of the announcement in February 1997 that an adult sheep had been cloned, some otherwise sedate journalists, policymakers, clinicians and ethicists began to spin wild tales of the grand possibilities and profound dangers that could emerge from human applications for cloning. The Center in which I teach all but shut down that March as, one by one, the faculty moved into "uplink studios" for dozens of interviews with harried, almost frantic journalists. The proposals to which we would respond were as absurd and fantastic as any in science fiction: families would seek to replace dying children with cloned copies, clones engineered to have an ablated cerebral cortex would provide precisely matched transplant organs for their sick "siblings," and clones bred for their roles would take over Wall Street and or the "bad jobs" down at the Public Works.

As Arthur Caplan notes in these pages, worldwide legislative furor and U.S. Presidential declarations on human cloning followed in the weeks after Dolly's birth. President Clinton convened the National Bioethics Advisory Commission (NBAC), which issued a fairly predictable call for a temporary ban on human cloning. In July of 2001, the House of Representatives voted in favor of a ban on the creation of cloned human embryos for any purpose; at the time of this writing, the Senate has yet to take up the measure. Things had almost died down when Advanced Cell Technology—a small biotech firm in Massachusetts—announced in October of 2001 that they had created the first cloned human embryos. The significance of the event was doubtful: ACT's intention was to produce stem cells for therapeutic cloning, not bring the cloned embryo to term. And the experiment fell short of even that more modest goal, since the embryo had only reached the six-cell stage before ceasing to divide—well shy of the "blastocyst" stage of development, when the embryo has grown to around 150 cells and stem cells can begin to be harvested. The development nevertheless prompted President George W. Bush to appoint his own Council on Bioethics (chaired by Leon Kass), which, not surprisingly, supported the President's opposition to all kinds of human cloning, reproductive as well as therapeutic. While the prospect of reproductive cloning in the U.S. looks doubtful, that has not affected plans to undertake it elsewhere. A team of fertility doctors led by Severino Antinori, an Italian, and Panos Zavos, an American, has repeatedly voiced their intention to get an infertile couple pregnant with a cloned human embryo, at a site somewhere in Europe or Asia; in May 2002 Zavos told a House subcommittee that it would happen within the year. However that may be, cloning seems certain to remain a political hot button issue, the symbolic fulcrum of discussions about infertility medicine and embryo research.

The Technology

Potter Wickware describes in detail in Chapter One how Wilmut's team successfully transplanted chromosomes harvested from an adult white sheep's somatic cell into an enucleated egg from a brown sheep. The egg, carrying its new nucleus, was literally shocked into behaving as though it had been fertilized. In a few of the 280 attempts made by Wilmut, eggs began cell division, and were implanted as "embryos" into the uterus of a sheep. The birth of Dolly signals that somatic cell DNA might be used in creating a variety of animals who would share many traits and a high degree of DNA similarity with their source animals. Veterinary geneticists and agricultural biotechnology experts all share a high degree of confidence that cloning in animals will be an important part of research on animals—and perhaps even reinvent the way we make some kinds of animals. The promise of animal cloning ranges from bizarre website-based projects dedicated to cloning dogs and cats, to projects in several universities on the use of cloning technologies for beefing up endangered species populations and collections in zoological parks. Cloning can also make a significant step forward in the race to integrate DNA synthesis and new reproductive technologies; perhaps the most important result of cloning in animals will be the ways in which it advances not cloning but the creation of cloning-based cellular transplants. These are fascinating possibilities and their use alone poses interesting technological issues. However, perhaps the toughest debate for the next years will be the one we take up today: cloning in human families.

Prior and subsequent experiments with embryonic primates, cattle and humans[1] suggest that at least some of the recent advances in veterinary gene transfer, cloning, and twinning might be utilized in humans, as John Robertson notes in Chapter Two. The technologies that one might describe as "human cloning" are myriad. Definitions of cloning are, frankly, subjective. There is no obvious way to define a clone and there are as yet no techniques that would allow one to determine in any objective way whether or not a particular organism is in fact "truly" a clone. The working definition of cloned organism in genetics is an organism produced with DNA that is transferred from another single organism, though there is conceptual confusion and debate about even this.

Those who would substitute the moniker "nuclear transplantation" for cloning point out that not all organisms who receive DNA from a single organism can correctly be grouped together as "clones." And beyond the transfer of DNA, there are other genetic and environmental components of a "cloned" embryo. This means that it is very troubling to call a cloned embryo "identical" or a "copy" of its DNA source. Human applications of these technologies might create a child with somatic cell-derived chromosomes from one person and maternal egg, egg-wall DNA, mitochondrial DNA, and gestation with another. Each of these pieces of the resulting "cloned embryo," however, could be contributed by a different person, with the net whole still called a clone. Such a child could have DNA from a "father-donor," who would technically be the person "cloned." The child would also, though, receive some genetic information from the donors of the DNA in the mitochondria and the egg wall. The "mother-gestator" would substantially influence it in subtle and sometimes not-so-subtle ways as the maternal environment role in activates gene expression and brain development. Who is the mother? Who is the father? Who the grandparents? These are difficult issues that matter for policy as well as ethics.

There are many ways in which adults (or even children) will play the biological role of parent to a clone. More than one parent can donate the genes, since there is genetic information in both the egg and the mitochondria. The egg donor may determine limits on height or other traits without donating DNA. Even the cytoplasm seems to have some important effects on development. All of these can be donated. Gestation too creates a context that will be influential in the phenotype of the organism. For example, smoking in pregnancy has been clearly linked to abnormalities in offspring.

The upshot of all this is that the chromosomal information that determines genotype will not be the only genetic role in making a clone. But this does not mean that the clone is "ordinary" or simply a "delayed identical twin," as others have claimed. A clone is the product of an odd, high-tech confederation of donors of various biological products, which produces offspring that is "identical" to none of the donors. All of this ends up involving much more intervention into pregnancy than has ever been seen before.

A Context for Cloning

In addition to technological distinctions between clones and babies of more ordinary origin, there would obviously be important distinctions between the social and parental roles of those who "make" clones, and those who parent other babies. "Strictly" speaking, it was argued early in the debate, the female donor of DNA to a clone (who gives that clone her chromosomes) is not the mother but a twin, and the father not a father but brother-in-law. This has bearing not only on the social but also legal meanings of parenthood, e.g., would the clone inherit from the father or the grandfather? In slightly more complex cloning arrangements, such as a woman using her own chromosomal information but not her own egg (e.g., to avoid transmitting mitochondrial disorders), the donor of the mitochondria and egg is in a completely new situation. As several of the contributors to our theological debate note, cloning in the family seems a Pandora's box. One the one hand, parents or individuals might try to use cloning to make a child who is almost entirely the creation of one person, overly restricting the meaning of childhood or the freedom of the child. On the other hand, parents who utilize cloning will create a child whose involvement with physicians, scientists, multiple possible genetic and social parents will give new meaning to the expression that "it takes a village" to raise a child. Cloning, it has been fairly claimed, challenges the very meaning of parenthood.[2]

The present volume takes up the challenge of a genuine debate about ethical issues in human cloning, from the perspective of the family and society. Our focus is not on whether or not Fidel Castro or H. Ross Perot could make an army of clones, or on headless clones as organ donors. In these pages no attention is devoted to the military and international law implications of cloning, e.g. whether "offshore," cloning is a threat to the United Nations. These questions are in some small measure interesting. The purpose of *The Human Cloning Debate*, however, is to examine the human implications of cloning within their real context: new reproductive technology for families.

The third edition of *The Human Cloning Debate* is organized into six sections, covering the background of the cloning debate, the relationship between personal and communal rights to control cloning, the emergence of revulsion about cloning and equally rapid emergence of bioethics to deal with fears and policy, the social and moral problems with choosing clones, the right to cloning treatments for the infertile, the rights of cloned offspring, and the role of religion.

In the following chapter, Potter Wickware addresses the scientific dimensions of the cloning debate, raising in the process some central questions about how we set the debate in motion.

John Robertson and Arthur Caplan, prominent scholars of reproductive ethics, then take on the debate in earnest. Robertson makes a clear case for reproductive rights, arguing that decisions about some kinds of cloning technology might best be left to parents and individuals. Arthur Caplan rejects the arguments of Robertson, Lee Silver, Greg Pence and others that reproductive genetic engineering ought not be thoroughly regulated, and argues that human cloning represents the best test case for bioethics as an institution.

Bioethics as an institution is on trial in the public debate, and in the third section the institutions spawned by the cloning debate come under fire. Leon Kass, responding to the "thin gruel" of bioethics, argues that our collective reticence about cloning technology ought to be granted more credence. His claim that our thoughtless embrace of technology might literally bear fruit in cloning figures prominently in many arguments in favor of a cloning ban. Ronald Bailey responds from the American political right wing that cloning may be an appropriate technology if utilized in accord with the free market. Susan Wolf pens the most careful and direct critique of the efforts of the National Bioethics Advisory Commission, and Sherwin Nuland argues that beyond institutions to stop cloning is the question of social maturity, which, in his view, Americans clearly lack.

While the National Bioethics Advisory Commission report on a ban for cloning contains some discussion of the rights of children, and makes reference to children's rights to "an open future," the meaning of reproductive technology for children and families has not received much careful attention. In a section devoted to the meaning of "wanting" a cloning, Philip Kitcher advances the argument that it is the motivation of parents that shapes children's worlds, and thus that distinctions between ethical and unethical cloning requests can be made on the basis of knowing the motivations. Richard Lewontin sees the failure of the cloning debate in terms of our inability to integrate religion and knowledge of the environment into our debates about what sort of families and children should be tolerated. Leon Eisenberg compares the techniques that create sheep to the ideas that create human families.

As human cloning becomes available, many will seek it as an infertility treatment. Carson Strong and Timothy Murphy debate the idea that cloning is a reasonable or obligatory treatment for male or female infertility, and if so in which cases. At stake is one's right to compel society to help one have a clone.

The discussion then turns to what rights the clone has, and whether an unborn or even unimplanted clone can even be said to have interests, and if so what interests. Ian Wilmut and I argue that the best model for understanding cloning and new reproductive technologies might be that of adoption, requiring couples to clear their intentions for cloning with a family court, and ensuring that society will support both the children of cloning and the families that it creates through this new technology. Justine Burley and John Harris argue that the entire notion of a child having rights before it is created, or at least special rights entitling it to protection from cloning, is impossible to justify.

The arguments of a number of theologians and spokespersons for religious groups are presented in the final section. While these vary dramatically in shape and size, each shares the conviction of the others that cloning is an issue of deep religious significance requiring a new orientation to theological and religious texts.

The Human Cloning Debate is designed to reconstruct the debate so that both dialogue and consensus are possible on some important issues about the meaning of the family in a new world of reproductive technology. It is also an attempt to bring together the voices of those who have brought the most creative, imaginative approaches to the problem, and those who have spent significant time reflecting and writing about reproduction during the past decades. It is for that reason that I have chosen to omit the rigorous but arcane work of many prominent philosophers who have distilled the problems of cloning down to an unrecognizable puzzle. For that reason as well, I have chosen to omit the significant number of new laws and policies passed since the cloning of Dolly, as almost all are identical "short-term bans" which appeal to the desirability of "waiting a while" for the conversation to start. I hope that this introduction to the human cloning debate will help as you begin a new conversation with friends, in institutions, at home, and even on the Internet. Reflection on the meaning of love, children and family represents the best use of time one can imagine.

Acknowledgements:

My colleagues and I have in no small measure benefited from the generous commitment to bioethics that our institutions have made in recent years. The work that led to the present collaboration was funded in part by a grant to the University of Pennsylvania from the Greenwall Foundation for the study of social issues in bioethics. My work was funded in part by the British government in the form of the 2000 Atlantic Fellowship in Public Policy. The commitment of Berkeley Hills Books to develop books that facilitate public debate about bioethics made this project possible, and a pleasure. The careful hand of publisher Robert Dobbin, and his team accomplished much of the work.

In the assembly of the Third Edition, thanks to colleagues and staff at the Center for Bioethics of the University of Pennsylvania, in particular to Arthur Caplan, Director, who made it possible for me to devote time to a significant revision, and to my secretary Deborah Putnam Thomas and the Staff of the Centre for Medical Ethics and Law at the Kings College London School of Law. Thanks, too, to my family, and in particular my amazing wife Monica Arruda McGee.

London, England

Notes

[1] The 1993 experiments at George Washington University utilizing artificial zonal coverings of the embryo to allow the "twinning" of an embryo are the singular example in the recorded record to date of human cloning experimentation.

[2] President Clinton makes this claim in his charge letter to the National Bioethics Advisory Commission.

Potter Wickware

History and Technique of Cloning

> Whereas ordinary mortals are content to imitate others,
> creative geniuses are condemned to plagiarize them-
> selves.
> — Vladimir Nabokov, *Ada, or Ardor* (1979)

Nabokov's reflection strangely illuminates today's debate about human cloning, which commenced after
an historic announcement by Ian Wilmut, a Scottish
cell biologist, in February 1997. In the international
science journal *Nature,* Wilmut described how his
group had succeeded in producing Dolly, a genetic
clone of a ewe that had died six years earlier, from the
animal's breast tissue cells, which had been preserved
in a freezer. Initial doubts that she was a genuine clone
were allayed by tests reported in mid-1998. By Spring,
2002, the nuclear transfer method used to produce
Dolly has yielded cloned mice, cattle, swine, and domestic cats. A cloned dog is in the works, and at least

two groups on the scientific fringe have declared their intent to clone a human being.

Despite the carnival atmosphere that is beginning to attach to the technology, Dolly represents a genuine and substantial advance for basic biology and medicine. Physicians are eager to develop the promise that it seems to hold for such things as cloning modified pigs whose organs and cells could be successfully transplanted into humans—a possible solution to the widespread shortage of transplant organs—or even of growing replacement organs starting from a patient's own cells, a process known as tissue engineering. Scientists are elated at the discovery that there are cells in adults that are not irreversibly altered by differentiation—which had been almost an article of dogma in developmental biology—and which can direct development of a clone. From this already much has been discovered about how DNA is activated and how cells—and by extension tissues and organisms—develop.

But in contrast to the excitement of biomedical scientists, response from the public tends to be marked by a more fearful tone. There's a sense that even if cloning animals may be acceptable, humans are categorically different and are not to be tampered with. Churchmen have condemned human cloning as an offense against human dignity and a violation of God's law. In Europe and elsewhere the Green lobby holds up the prospect of human cloning as a risky, unethical abuse by a biotechnology industry concerned only with profit. Legislation banning it has been enacted in the US, as it has been in Japan and most countries in Europe.

Since the middle of the last century advances in bioscience have occurred with breathtaking—some might say frightening—speed. To the genetic engineers of the

1970s the idea that it would have been possible to clone
an entire genome and raise a viable animal from an
adult body cell would have been unimaginable, as indeed it was to the vast majority of the scientific community prior to 1997. Yet the intellectual velocity of
the present is likely to hold steady or even increase in
the future, causing startling new choices to manifest
themselves in years ahead. In this sense cloning can
be thought of as just another in a series of challenges
to conventional thinking in biology that commenced
perhaps with the publication of Darwin's *Origin of Species* nearly 150 years ago. Thus, in coming to terms
with the problems and promises presented to us by
mammalian cloning technology, it's important to begin by understanding what the technology is, where it
came from, and how it works. The rest of this chapter
gives a broad, nontechnical overview of these points.

Cloning defined

An identical twin is a clone. So is a potato. So are Dolly
and the now numerous band of animals that have been
brought to life via nuclear transfer. But cell lines and
gene libraries used in medical research are also clones.
In nature reproduction by cloning occurs in many
plants, in honeybees and wasps, in some lizards. What
these disparate entities have in common is that all are
genetic xerox copies, made from a previously existing
template or master without the agency of sex. All come
into being without the reshuffling and reordering of
hereditary material that takes place when two parents
mingle their genes in their offspring, giving rise to
unpredictable combinations, such as a child with its
father's nose and its mother's personality. While it may
seem strange to say that an identical twin originates

without sex, in fact it is the sexless fission of the early embryonic clump of cells into two clumps that gives rise to a twin. That origin may be only one cell division away from the sexual event, but that single division, with its identical rather than reshuffled duplication of genes is, in reproductive terms, a yawning gulf of separation. For the potato, some time in the indeterminate past there a sexual event occurred, which was followed by many rounds of clonal, or vegetative, duplication, so that a potato is about as sexless a creature as one can conceive of. As for Dolly, she was six years and forty or so rounds of cell divisions away from the sexual event that gave rise to her genetic identity.

Biology primer

To understand cloning it's necessary to grasp a handful of underlying biological fundamentals: DNA and heredity, proteins and chromosomes.

DNA is a polymer, chemically not unlike rayon or hair. It consists of fantastically long and prolific strands punctuated by regularly occurring projections called bases, which stick out sideways from a long backbone piece, like pickets from the rail of a fence. Two strands fit together joined by their bases, so that the duplex resembles a railroad track, with crossties corresponding to paired bases. Human cells contain about 3 billion bases; scaled up to railroad track size the DNA in each cell would be about 20 million miles long. In one respect, being long and monotonous, DNA is a boring molecule, but from another perspective it has a most remarkable property. During the brief period when cells divide, the double-stranded DNA comes apart down the middle, like an enormously long zipper. Then down each half-track comes DNA polymerase—a protein that challenges the writer for adequate superlatives—rather like a repair locomotive, and duplicates each missing half. The synthesis is a close to perfect one-to-one matching of base for base. Thus one strand becomes two, with the rest of the cellular material growing and dividing in concert. The DNA in the proliferating cells becomes the track that guides the individual through its lifetime, and its progeny down through the generations.

There are four kinds of DNA bases, A, C, T and G, named for the first letter of their respective chemical names. They occur in any order and make up a code that goes on interminably something like this: ... GAGATTTAACCGA ... A small percentage of the stream contains stretches called genes, which at the right time and under the proper circumstances the body is able to decode and translate into proteins.

There's a wonderful passage in Homer where the demi-god Proteus, in an effort to escape from the hero Odysseus, becomes first a lion, then a boar, a serpent, a wave, a tree. Proteins' protean nature allows them to carry out functions of structure, control, signaling, metabolism, transport, chemical breaking down and building up. Among the four categories of life molecules—the others being carbohydrates (i.e., sugars), lipids (i.e., fats) and nucleic acids (i.e., DNA and its relative RNA)—proteins are the sleight-of-hand artists, the producers, the movers and shakers of the body.

DNA has to be organized. Imagine a film archive without reels, with the film strewn about in tangles underfoot, with no systematic way for playing it back. The chromosome is DNA's reel and shelving system. The DNA strands are complexed with proteins that serve as spools. The spooling is dynamic, so that the DNA is practically all put away when the cell is dividing—as though it were moving day at the film archive— while during the normal activity cycle of the cell filaments of the chromosome are partially unraveled and float out into the nucleoplasm, exposing the genes relevant for activity in a given cell at a given time, and the ones which are not are folded up and suppressed. A chromosome with an expression loop is like a tape cassette that has been "eaten" by the tape player, with a long rolled-out portion connected to a nearby wrapped-up one. For example, genes that code for proteins that produce the complex sugars collectively known as mucus are highly active in the cells of the gut, but not at all in the cochlear cells of the ear. Chromosomes come in pairs, one from mom, one from pop. Humans have 23 pairs of chromosomes, sheep 26, mice 20, cattle 30, swine 19. During the embryonic and fetal stages of development chromosomes are highly active, but with complete differentiation in the adult up to 90% of genes in any given cell type are apt to be permanently turned off.

Fig. 1. Human chromosomes in "metaphase spread" (Potter Wickware)

In this image of a "metaphase chromosome" the ant-like shapes are DNA from one of the author's white blood cells. The DNA is fully condensed, with all genes turned off and the chromosomes bundled up in preparation for cell division.

Now that we have mastered the essentials of molecular and cell biology, we're ready to return to cloning.

Cloning and sex

Despite its patina of modernity and association with a perhaps suspect scientific invention, cloning in nature probably predates sex as a reproductive mode. The cost of sex is considerable. In flowering plants, for example, it entails the production of flowers and seeds—as potentially risky and expensive a proposition for them as are the mating activities of humans. Specialized sexual organs, the flowers, must be produced, along with bright pigments, scents, and food sources to attract pollinators. Then follows the process of fumbling and groping by insect palps, bird beaks, and bat tongues in their tenderest and most intimate regions. For all the enticing excitement of these events, consider the cost in energy and resources to produce the structures, and don't forget the possible hazards: disease, injury, predation, death. For all its plodding predictability, cloning is a more straightforward and economical way to accomplish the same result.

But cloning fails as a strategy during times of environmental challenge, for example when too-successful organisms outrun their range, or when some global catastrophe— an asteroid impact, an epoch of volcanism, a shift in the chemistry of the atmosphere— strikes. Then creatures must adapt if they are to survive. That happens by sex. Sex produces offspring which are genetically different from the parent, with genetic resources which give them possibilities of response and behavior not available to the previous generation. According to the Darwinian principle, among the variable offspring will be some individuals better suited than others to changes brought about by an unpredictable environment. The more fit individuals have a better chance of surviving long enough to pass along their survival traits to their progeny. The process continues down through time, with species, families, and orders waxing and waning according to the ease with which they are able to respond with new genetic combinations to changes in the environment.

A creature that lives in a steady-state environment need not play the sexual game of chance and jeopardize a winning combination with needless recombination. This is not to say that plants, or anything else, can jettison sex altogether. Sex at least has to be held as a reserve strategy. Sooner or later just about everything that lives has to have sex. Even bacteria practice a form of it. But for much of the time, for many of the creatures that we share this globe with, sex need not be the common or preferred mode of reproduction.

Cloning and agriculture

Domestication of plants and animals changed humans from hunter-gatherers to farmers, and improvement in domesticated plant and animal stock— defined as ever more closely determined and predictable phenotype—has followed through the millennia. The idea of cloning is thus latent in the set of agricultural techniques that are identified with the development of civilization itself.

Cloning in plants was recognized by early agronomists and put to practical use in the process of plant grafting, particularly in the production of orchard crops. The production of elite animals by selective breeding also has a long history and has led to artificial insemination, IVF, the collection of eggs and storage of embryos. By the early 60's, livestock clones were first produced from early embryos, and eventually, after many abortive attempts, by Wilmut from fully differentiated adult cells. With the exception of cloning, all these techniques have been successfully extended to humans.

Cloning by separation of early embryos is a time-tested method in animal husbandry. An egg is fertilized in a culture dish and the first few cell divisions are allowed to occur. When the embryo has attained a mass of eight or so cells—a barely visible speck to the naked eye—a technician with a microscope and micromanipulator intervenes. Mimicking the natural process of twinning she delicately teases apart the ball-shaped early embryo (morula) to yield eight or more single cells (blastomeres), each of which is then implanted in a receptive female. In the uterine environment each of these single cells behaves like a newly fertilized zygote, instead of a cell that is actually two or three or more divisions away from conception. In this way eight or more genetically identical animals can be produced, where before there would have been only one. This technique has become important in producing uniform livestock that have some desired natural trait such as increased milk production or improved quality of wool. In early 2000 scientists at Oregon Health Sciences University cloned rhesus monkeys for medical research by the same method. Within the last decade or so the technique has been significantly broadened by the addition of genetic engineering the early embryonic cells of mammals. Research animals, typically mice and rats, and now pigs and goats as well, with some of their own genes "knocked out," or with foreign genes inserted, have proven invaluable to medical scientists as they strive to work out the molecular details of many diseases, including Alzheimer's, diabetes, drug addiction, schizophrenia and many others.

Cloning by embryo separation only works for very early embryos, however. Soon after cell division commences the cells individually lose the power to generate an entire organism. They begin to specialize, to "differentiate," with whole regions of their DNA not relevant to their final function beginning permanently to shut down. The number of clones obtainable from embryo separation is thus limited to the small number of cells that retain universal development potential during the earliest rounds of cell division. By contrast, nuclear transfer from fully differentiated adult somatic cells, the technique that gave rise to Dolly, could theoretically produce clones in unlimited numbers.

Cloning and biotechnology

By the 1960s the explosion of knowledge about life at the cellular and molecular levels thrust cloning into the mainstream of life sciences research. There are three kinds of lab-based cloning, all quite different in technique and outcome, but the same in that identical copies of DNA are produced without sexual recombination. They are molecular cloning, cellular cloning, and cloning by nuclear transfer.

Boyer, Cohen and the other successors of Watson and Crick, who solved the structure of DNA in 1952, discovered that (with a few unimportant exceptions) DNA comprises the same alphabet and the same language in all organisms. From the discovery of the commonality of DNA it followed that it could be swapped from one organism to another, and that the source of the DNA—human white blood cells, for example—often made no difference whatever to the new host. Thus *E. coli* bacteria or yeast could be made to take up the human gene coding for insulin or Factor VIII, the clotting factor that is lacking in persons who have hemophilia, and treat it as if it were its own. Today these valuable drugs are produced by microbial clones whose DNA has been "recombined" in this way. Even more startling combinations are possible. In 1986, for example, a Japanese scientist, in an effort to produce a "reporter gene" for tracking inserts in gene transfer experiments, extracted the gene coding for the luciferase protein from firefly and inserted it in tobacco. When provided with luciferin, a chemical that emits light when acted on by luciferase, the tobacco plant glowed in the dark. Green Fluorescent Protein, derived from jellyfish, is another popular reporter, used in research to light up a protein of interest so that it can be tracked through an experiment in rat, fruit fly, human or some other cell type.

The amplification and expression of DNA through molecular cloning in the above examples is limited to comparatively short stretches of DNA making up the one or few genes that are of interest. The bacteria or yeast replicates its entire complement of DNA—its genome—some number of times, and the stitched-in insert goes along for the ride. When the desired production is attained, the scientist somewhat ungratefully gives the yeast or bacteria a shot of lye to kill it, then snips out the now-abundant insert DNA, discards the rest, and proceeds to the next steps of research or drug development. Using this approach the genes involved in cystic fibrosis, muscular dystrophy, hemophilia, dwarfism and many other diseases have been discovered over the last 25 years.

But molecular cloning stops far short of cloning an entire mammalian genome, consisting of tens of thousands of genes, as was done with Dolly. It might be thought of as running off copies of some small number of documents on a copy machine, while Ian Wilmut's achievement with Dolly was like duplicating the entire Library of Congress. But in essence the two processes are the same in that in both cases the molecule of heredity—DNA—is reproduced without sexual recombination.

With the important exceptions of sperm and egg cells, all the cells in our bodies are clones, and the process of cloning is one that goes on continually. For example, skin cells and the cells that line the gut turn over rapidly, and identical copies—clones—are produced to replace the ones that wear out. Similarly, when activated by a pathogen previously seen by the body, B memory cells, which produce antibodies, quickly go into production and churn out identical clone armies to swamp the invader.

Cellular cloning is merely the mimicking of these natural processes in a culture dish. The recombinant microbes that produce drugs in bulk are cellular clones. Research for cancer, inherited diseases, and many other areas of basic science and clinical need depends on the many specialized cell lines that have been developed using the same recombinant technology.

Cloning by nuclear transfer

Surprisingly, Dolly turns out not to have been the first

mammalian clone. In 1995 Wilmut and his colleagues used nuclear transfer of cell nuclei—with their cargo of DNA—from early embryo cells to produce two viable lambs, Megan and Morag. These earlier lambs represented the true breakthrough, and it was probably because of a school massacre in Scotland the week of the announcement that the world's attention was diverted from them. Incremental improvements in technique followed, first nuclei from later stage fetal cells, and then from adult tissue, which gave rise to Dolly. Wilmut's innovation, the culmination of twenty-five years' work which let him succeed where others had failed, was to synchronize the cell cycle of donor and recipient material through serum starvation before bringing the two together. The cellular bread and water diet—a thin broth with minimal nutrients, vitamins and growth factors—slowed down the normally active donor DNA and allowed DNA replication and cell division to proceed in the usual way after donor nucleus was joined with recipient egg. In previous efforts, the overactive donor and recipient were out of synchrony with each other, and mistakes in cell divisions soon resulted in nonviable embryos.

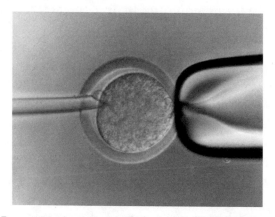

Fig. 2 Egg cell being microinjected (credit: PPL Therapeutics)

The recipient—an unfertilized egg—was prepared by drawing out its DNA-containing nucleus, but leaving the outer membranes and the yolk—its accumulated store of nutrients. Micropipettes are used at this stage of the work: tiny glass tubes, thinner than hairs, a blunt-ended holding pipette to grasp the cell by a mild suction, and the much thinner and sharply pointed insertion pipette for the drawing out and placing in. A donor cell—in Dolly's case a cell from mammary gland of a six-year-old Finn Dorset ewe—is prepared by the inverse process: the nucleus is saved and the rest of the cell is discarded.

Finally the serum-starved cell parts are brought together. The donor is placed by pipette between the outer region of the egg known as the zona pellucida and the plasma membrane. (Think of a hard-boiled egg: the shell is the zona pellucida and the plasma membrane is the white film that lines the inside of the shell.) The cells are now in intimate proximity, like two soap bubbles with a common interface, but not yet fused. Wilmut used bursts of voltage—an AC pulse to perforate the nuclear membrane of the donor and the inner membrane of the egg, followed by DC pulses to fuse them. In Wilmut's method fusion and activation occur simultaneously. The tiny electric shocks mimic the natural acrosomal process of fertilization, initiated by a burst of calcium in the head of a sperm that stimulates enzymatic activity which dissolves away the egg's protective zona and culminates in the fusion of the two cells and the beginning of embryonic growth. After a few passages in culture, the now multicell embryo was implanted in a surrogate ewe—a blackface, not a Finn Dorset, so that it would be plain that Dolly was not the result of a surreptitious mating. Patiently Wilmut and his team repeated the process over and over again. Out of 277 attempts, 34 (12%) achieved the blastocyst stage. Of these, eight (3%) achieved the fetus stage. Of these, five (2%) became live lambs. Of these, only Dolly (0.4%) survived.

Teruhiko Wakayama, at Japan's Riken Institute, who cloned mice in 1999, improved the success rate by refining Wilmut's method by separating fusion and activation in time. First, with a very fine needle, the donor nucleus was placed inside the yolk sac of the recipient. Then, one to six hours later, activation was induced by putting the clone-to-be in a chemical bath that mimicked the acrosomal milieu of fertilization. This time delay, during which reprogramming (see below) presumably takes place, combined with a scrupulous prevention of any mingling between donor and recipient cytoplasm during the transfer step, probably explains his lab's better than 2% success rate.

But 2% is still low compared with the real thing. Moreover, worries about the long-term health of cloned animals have now cropped up. In 2002 a retrospective look at the health histories of cloned mice showed that most die prematurely, and seem to be more prone than their normal counterparts to health problems such as liver damage, tumors, and pneumonia, suggestive of an immune system impairment. Similarly, a high rate of abortion and stillbirth in cloned cattle has been noted. Dolly herself has turned up with arthritis in a hind leg, although at the age of 5½ she is well into middle age, and the aches and pains she may be suffering are impossible to connect with cloning. A less than perfect process does seem to be implicated in the case of the mice and cattle, however. Damage to egg or nucleus may occur at various points: extraction of donor nucleus, injection into recipient, and the timing of the different steps. Presumably, further practice and refinement as the technique transits from art to science will bring the trouble spots into better focus and enable improvements to be made.

Metaphysics of cloning

Do Dolly and company have parents? The animal born as a result of conventional fertilization manifestly has both mother and father. But the cloned animal is born by a female which could be its mother—that is, the female that produced the egg into which the donor nucleus was inserted—but in practice usually is carried by a surrogate. The important point is that motherhood, as defined by the female that donated a set of haploid chromosomes, in the clone's case happened in a previous generation. Similarly, the father is normally defined as the male that not only donated its set of haploid chromosomes, but whose sperm in the moment of penetrating the surface of the egg activated it and initiated the chemical reactions that culminates with the birth of the offspring. In producing the clone, though, the sperm is absent, its vitalizing role taken over by a scientist armed with tiny glass pipettes, a micromanipulating machine, and a jolt of voltage or chemical bath, which the egg mistakes for a sperm head battering its way through the coat of the zona pellucida. And as for the male's portion of haploid DNA, as with the female's, it too was produced in a previous generation. So while the clone may be said to have grandparents, it does not have parents in the familiar sense of the word.

How old is a clone? In the naturally fertilized creature it's easy to assign the beginning of life: it's that moment of fertilization when the creature obtains its full genetic complement, and begins to grow and differentiate. Egg and sperm don't live long unless and until they are united. At that moment the great transformation occurs and DNA from mother and father is joined and a new hand is dealt and everything commences with new parts. It's easy to register a new identity to the zygote that originates at this moment. In the clone growth and differentiation follow the same time line, but as for its genetic identity, that was determined in a different cell in a different animal, at some time in the past. Obviously, the cloned creature's organs and tissues, and the proteins, fats, and carbohydrates they are made of are all new, but the code that governs it is not. So in the sense that what the clone is made of is coded for by old DNA, the clone is not new. But what does "new" mean in this context? Is a reissue of *David Copperfield* using the original 1850 plates new or old? A sharp, even hair-splitting set of definitions needs to be brought to bear on questions that for the naturally fertilized creature are completely commonplace. After all, the donor mammary gland cell that was used to create Dolly came from a six-year-old sheep. When she was born she was zero years old at the organismal level, but her DNA was six years old.

Reprogramming

The apparent and astonishing result of cloning from a fully differentiated adult cell contradicts research in embryology and development going back to the 50's, which seemed to show that the farther along a cell was in its association with an organism—the more committed it was to a specialized function (liver, retina, skin, nerve, etc.)—the less capable it was of going back to universal potential. Differentiated cells have their own suites of genes that are active and inactive, so that genes coding for eye color are never active in liver cells, for example. That a clone was created from adult cellular material showed that cells could go backward after all, in the sense of being able to pick up functions that they had apparently lost—to be capable of "retrodifferentiating," or of being "reprogrammed." So somewhere between the beginning and the end of the nuclear transfer process the clone DNA becomes deprogrammed, losing its memory of life in mammary or cumulus cell, and learns to function like meiotic DNA. In the little universe of the egg the adult donor DNA becomes infantilized, apparently losing memory of its former life. How and where this transformation occurred is an intense area of research interest. For now we can make some educated guesses.

DNA programming is accomplished by means of expression loops on the chromosomes. Chromatin proteins embedded in the chromosome hold out some loops and hold others down. DNA programming in a given cell type does change over time; for example, aging cells have different expression patterns from young cells. But for chromatin to jump backward in time, as it were, and be reset to its condition at the time of conception is very surprising. What could be responsible for it? Several lines of investigation—starting with John Gurdon's basic research in embryology forty years ago—suggested that unknown substances present in the cytoplasm of egg and early embryo cells were able to retrodifferentiate the DNA in specialized cells. Soon after the genetic code was deciphered the question arose as to why the activity of DNA diminished as the cell specialized following some number of divisions. In eggs the DNA does everything: it is "totipotent." But the more developed the cell—the more fully characterized as tissue or organ—the less of its

DNA was active. Gurdon saw two possible explanations: either DNA was deleted, somehow going away from the cell, or else it stayed in the cell but was turned off. Gross observations among dividing cells seemed to show that the chromosomes were still all there, but the metaphase spread is in effect a view from 30,000 feet. And many mature cells such as neurons rarely if ever divide, so no spreads could be observed in them in any case.

To answer the question Gurdon and his followers undertook a series of experiments. They began with a fertilized frog egg and irradiated it to kill its nucleus. (DNA is sensitive to radiation, while proteins are more robust and can withstand the energy.) Next, using micropipettes, they took a cell from frog gut, a cell whose destiny was already set, and fused it with the enucleated egg cell. The single fused egg went on to produce an entire tadpole and sometimes beyond to produce an adult. The result showed not only that the DNA was all still present in the later stage cells, but that something in the cytoplasm of the egg enabled the differentiated DNA to become totipotent again.

What might these substances be? In addition to nutrients—glucose, vitamins, amino acids—the essential components in serum include certain proteins called growth factors, substances with names like Platelet-Derived Growth Factor, Insulin-Like Growth Factor and Transforming Growth Factor-beta. They number about fifty in all, each with a corresponding receptor in the cell. Present in very scanty concentrations, these substances contain immense, almost Grail-like energy, with the power to nourish, heal, wound, and strike down, to influence the cell's decision to live, grow, and be active, and to guide it at each branch point along the developmental path. When the growth factor docks with its receptor the cell is activated to respond in some specific way. At the molecular level, the machinery in charge of DNA synthesis is activated, and the highly precise operation (not one mistake allowed in a billion moves) proceeds. The copying of the DNA is followed by profound changes in the nucleus and other cell structures, the condensation of chromosomes, the formation of the spindle apparatus, the division of the cytoplasm, and the other activities that culminate in the symphony of mitosis, or cell division.

Another substance likely to be involved with reprogramming is telomerase, a protein that acts on the part of the chromosome known as the telomere (Greek, the part at the end), a specialized region at the tip of the chromosome that serves both as "molecular bookend" and cellular clock. It is made from DNA patched together in a pattern of repeats, or "stutters" (in the pattern TTAGGG), which fold to form the structure that defines the boundary of the chromosome. Because of the way that DNA polymerase operates, a bit of it is lost with every cell division. When the telomere is gone, that's it for the cell. But in certain aggressive tumors, such as ovarian tumors, far from declining in length telomeres not only retain their length but even get longer. This endows them with more than the normal number of cell divisions. The agent responsible for rebuilding telomeres is the enzyme telomerase; normally it operates only in germ cells and in other cells is turned off. In ovarian tumors and many other cancers, though, it's inappropriately activated.

When Wilmut and his colleagues produced Dolly there was worry that her cells, being derived from an adult animal which had already used up some of the allotted divisions, would condemn her to a restricted lifespan. When in 1998 it was shown that she did indeed have shorter than normal telomeres, gloom set in. Pity for the lamb herself was overshadowed by concerns that the cloning technique would turn out to be useless for purposes such as engineering replacement cells for patients suffering from diseases like diabetes or Parkinson's disease. Subsequent research with cloned calves showed that telomere rebuilding occurs during embryonic development.

Cloning and tissue engineering are connected, both beginning with healthy adult cells as starting material. But—to look ahead ten years or so—tissue engineering would not aim for an entire animal, only part of one. Instead of implanting the egg in a surrogate mother, as was done with Dolly, the job would be confined to the culture dish, using growth factors to guide and limit development to a needed part, such as pancreatic islets, or neurons, for patients whose own starting material is worn-out or defective. Growth factors would be used to accurately control and limit the process.

Animal clones fulfill the ambition of generating uniform, predictable stock, with market advantage for both farmer and food processor. Cloned animals might also be improved in some other desirable way to secrete some useful protein in their milk, blood, or urine. Sheep—including animals at Wilmut's own Roslin Institute—as well as pigs and goats have already been engineered to carry human genes for alpha-antitrypsin, the protein which is missing or defective in persons with emphysema; lactoferrin, present in the milk of nursing mothers and which helps provide iron to babies and fight infections; hemoglobin; human monoclonal antibodies used in cancer treatment; human insulin and growth hormone; beta interferon (used for treating multiple sclerosis); t-PA (used for treating heart attacks); and human blood plasma fractions for treating coronary bypass grafts, among other purposes. Although the animals produce in bulk these proteins which would be difficult, impossible, or risky to obtain using older methods, it is difficult and expensive to produce the animals themselves. Gene targeting, a technique analogous to genetic engineering, combined with cloning by nuclear transfer, would make it possible to create a herd of genetically identical transgenic animals that would produce therapeutic proteins in any desired amount.

From a scientific perspective, cloned mice are probably more valuable than the Roslin Institute's herd animals, because they have short gestation periods and well-characterized genetics, and their embryos are much easier to manipulate than those of larger animals. It is from them rather than sheep that understanding of the genome, and the gigantic set of crossing and overlapping chemical reactions (including the all-important ones involved in reprogramming) that it encodes, are likely to originate. Cloning research would feed into development of future technologies such as tissues in piglets in which the violent rejection factors have been engineered out.

But does not a feeling of uneasiness nag at us as we blithely go about making adjustments to familiar domestic creatures? Sex generates diversity. Cloning suppresses it. Natural systems are built on the basis of diversity, because the environment changes, and genetic recombination arose to deal with this unpredictability. The environment tomorrow may produce conditions that puts today's fittest creature at a disadvantage, favoring that organism which has a strange and possibly—under other circumstances—lethal gene-expression pattern. There's no way to see into the future, says the logic of nature, and no way to prepare in advance for its onslaughts. What to do? Evolution solves the problem by generating vast numbers of possible combinations, profligately, indiscriminately, with no respect for any particular individual. "A single death is a tragedy. A million deaths is a statistic," Stalin is supposed to have said. Nature is as pitilessly totalitarian. Throughout life most creatures that are born are doomed to die without reproducing themselves, because nature's solution to the problem of an unpredictable world is to produce all possible genetic combinations, from which the unknown circumstances of the future will sift out the viable organism. It's a card game in which each hand represents a new organism with a new genetic combination. That nature makes no assumptions about the future may be good, bad, or irrelevant for the individual. It may or may not be a good thing that the naturally fertilized creature is unique. It may be unique by virtue of an unpleasant temperament, or disease susceptibility. Nature doesn't know, doesn't care. All that's certain is that circumstances will change, and what's a liability in the here and now could be a lifesaver in the there and then.

Certain human genetic diseases illustrate this point. Sickle cell disease, a form of anemia in persons of African and Mediterranean descent, confers protection against malaria, and so it is a health advantage to carry a copy of this "disease" gene in malaria country. Similarly, cystic fibrosis, a choking disease of the lung that is relatively common among Caucasians, is thought to have conferred protection against the severe diarrhea that afflicted the people who lived in the filthy settlements of pre-modern Europe. Other genetically determined conditions such as color blindness or albinism have no known benefit, and afflicted persons' lives are to some extent impaired. Too bad for them, but conceivably the environment could change in some way in which these traits could be advantageous. Were that to occur, the individuals bearing them would survive and pass them along to their offspring, while those with what we deem normal skin pigment and vision would die out.

Cloning completely upsets this logic. Indeed we can see into the future, says the cloner, and as far as the clone and its environment are concerned we predict it will look exactly as it does now. Furthermore, the cloner has regard for the individual and rejects the group, with all the broad combination of possibilities created by random gene shuffling. Cloning is a complete reversal of the natural condition. It's as though you as the clone are playing a card game in which the same hand is repeatedly re-dealt. But it's a scheme that only works in the artificial and protected world of the farmyard or research lab. In the larger card game of life you as a clone might have won the pot in the last hand with a full house, but this time around the fellow sitting across from you might have four of a kind.

This brings us to the final point, that a clone, despite its genetic identity, can never be identical as an individual to its progenitor unless an impossible condition is satisfied: it must be raised in an identical environment. Small stimuli at the embryonic stage result in large outcomes for the adult. From the very beginning the chemical environment in one uterus varies from that of another. The immune systems of identical twins differ from one another; CC ("Copy Cat"), the house cat cloned in 2001, has a different coat pattern from her genetic parent. But even though through this reasoning we might persuade ourselves that a cloned Jack the Ripper could turn out to be a great philanthropist, and a cloned Einstein a hopeless dunce, it's inescapable that these clones would have a smaller range of possibilities open to them than humans who attained their lives in the conventional way. These are some of the contradictions and complexities we face as we decide if we should welcome, tolerate, or forbid the further development of cloning technology.

Acknowledgements

Michael A. Goldman, Ph.D., Professor of Biology, San Francisco State University. Thanks for reviewing the manuscript and making helpful suggestions.

David Ayares, Ph.D., VP of Research and Development, PPL Therapeutics. Thanks for helpful discussion about Dolly and cloning technology, and for the image of nuclear transfer in Fig. 2.

John Robertson

Cloning as a Reproductive Right

A proper assessment of human cloning requires that it be viewed in light of how it might be actually used once it is shown to be safe and effective. The most likely uses would involve extending current reproductive and genetic selection technologies. Several plausible uses can be articulated, quite different from the horrific scenarios currently imagined. The question becomes: Do these uses fall within mainstream understandings of why procreative freedom warrants special respect as one of our fundamental liberties? Investigation of this question will set the stage for examining what public policy toward human cloning ought to be.

The Demand for Human Cloning

Legitimate, family-centered uses of cloning are likely precisely because cloning is above all a commitment to have and rear a child. It will involve obtaining eggs, acquiring the DNA to be cloned, transfer of that DNA to a denucleated egg, placement of the activated embryo in a uterus, gestation, and the nurturing and rearing that the birth of any child requires. In addition, it will require a psychological commitment and ability to deal with the novelty of raising a child whose genome has been chosen, and who may be the later-born identical twin of another person, living or dead.

The most bizarre or horrific scenarios of cloning conveniently overlook the basic reality that human cloning requires a gestating uterus and a commitment to rear. The gestating mother is eliminated through the idea of total laboratory gestation as imagined in Huxley's *Brave New World*, or through high-tech surgery as in the movie *Multiplicity*. In others scenarios, it is thought that an evildoer can hire several women to gestate copies, with little thought given to how they would be reared or molded to be like the clone source. Nearly all of them overlook the impact of environmental influences on the cloned child, and the duties and burdens that rearing any child requires. They also overlook the extent to which the cloned child is not the property or slave of the initiator, but a person in her own right with all the rights and duties of other persons.

Because cloning is first and foremost the commitment to have and rear a child, it is most likely to appeal to those who wish to have a family but cannot easily do so by ordinary coital means. In some cases, they would turn to cloning because of the advantages that it offers over other assisted reproductive techniques. Or they would choose cloning because they have a need to exercise genetic choice over offspring, as in the desire for a healthy child or for a child to serve as a tissue donor. Given the desire to have healthy children, it is unlikely that couples will be interested in cloning unless they have good reason for thinking that the procedure is safe and effective, and that only healthy children will be born.

The question for moral, legal, and policy analysis is to assess the needs that such uses serve—both those expected to be typical and those that seem more bizarre—and their importance relative to other reproductive and genetic selection endeavors. Can cloning be used responsibly to help a couple achieve legitimate reproductive or family formation goals? If so, are these uses properly characterized as falling within the procreative liberty of individuals, and thus not subject to state restriction without proof of compelling harm?

To assess these questions, we must first investigate the meaning of procreative liberty, and then ask whether uses of cloning to enhance fertility, substitute for a gamete or embryo donor, produce organs or tissue for transplant, or pick a particular genome fall within common understandings of that liberty.

Human Cloning and Procreative Liberty

Procreative liberty is the freedom to decide whether or not to have offspring. It is a deeply accepted moral value, and pervades many of our social practices.[1] Its importance stems from the impact which having or not having offspring has in our lives. This is evident in the case of a choice to avoid reproduction. Because reproduction imposes enormous physical burdens for the woman, as well as social, psychological, and emotional burdens on both men and women, it is widely thought that people should not have to bear those burdens unless they voluntarily choose to.

But the desire to reproduce is also important. It connects people with nature and the next generation, gives them a sense of immortality, and enables them to rear and parent children. Depriving a person of the ability or opportunity to reproduce is a major burden and also should not occur without their consent.

Reproductive freedom—the freedom to decide whether or not to have offspring—is generally thought to be an important instance of personal liberty. Indeed, given its great impact on a person, it is considered a fundamental personal liberty. In recent years the emergence of assisted reproduction, noncoital means of conception, and prebirth genetic selection has also raised controversies about the limits of procreative freedom. The question of whether cloning is part of procreative liberty is a serious one only if noncoital, assisted reproduction and genetic selection are themselves part of that liberty. A strong argument exists that the moral right to reproduce does include the right to use noncoital or assisted means of reproduction. Infertile couples have the same interests in reproducing as coitally fertile couples, and the same abilities to rear children. That they are coitally infertile should no more bar them from reproducing with technical assistance than visual blindness should bar a person from reading with Braille or the aid of a reader. It thus follows that married couples (and arguably single persons as well) have a moral right to use noncoital assisted reproductive techniques, such as in vitro fertilization (IVF) and artificial insemination with spouse or partner's sperm, to beget biologically related offspring for rearing. It should also follow—though this is more controversial— that the infertile couple would have the right to use gamete donors, gestational surrogates, and even embryo donors if necessary. Although third-party collaborative reproduction does not replicate exactly the genes, gestation, and rearing unity that ordinarily arises in coital reproduction, they come very close and should be treated accordingly. Each of them, with varying degrees of closeness, enables the couple to have or rear children biologically related to at least one of them.

Some right to engage in genetic selection would also seem to follow from the right to decide whether or not to procreate.[2] People make decisions to reproduce or not because of the package of experiences that they think reproduction or its absence would bring. In many cases, they would not reproduce if it would lead to a packet of experiences X, but they would if it would produce packet Y. Since the makeup of the packet will determine whether or not they reproduce, a right to make reproductive decisions based on that packet should follow. Some right to choose characteristics, either by negative exclusion or positive selection, should follow as well, for the decision to reproduce may often depend upon whether the child will have the characteristics of concern.

If most current forms of assisted reproduction and genetic selection fall within prevailing notions of procreative freedom, then a strong argument exists that some forms of cloning are aspects of procreative liberty as well. For cloning shares many features with assisted reproduction and genetic selection, though there are also important differences. For example, the most likely uses of cloning would enable a married couple, usually infertile, to have healthy, biologically related children for rearing.[3] Or it would enable them to obtain a source of tissue for transplant to enable an existing child to live.

Cloning, however, is also different in important respects. Unlike the various forms of assisted reproduction, cloning is concerned not merely with producing a child, but rather with the genes that the resulting child will have. Many prebirth genetic selection techniques are now in wide use, but they operate negatively by excluding undesirable genetic characteristics, rather than positively, as cloning does. Moreover, none of them are able to select the entire nuclear genome of a child as cloning does.[4]

DNA Sources and Procreative Liberty

To assess whether cloning is protected as part of a married couple's procreative liberty, we must examine the several situations in which they might use nuclear transfer cloning to form a family. This will require addressing both the reasons or motivations driving a couple to clone, and the source of the DNA that they select for replication. It argues that cloning embryos, children, third parties, self, mate, or parents is an activity so similar to coital and noncoital forms of reproduction and family formation that they should be treated equivalently.

a. Cloning a couple's embryos. Cloning embryos, either by embryo splitting or nuclear transfer, would appear to be closely connected to procreative liberty. It is intended to enable a couple to rear a child biologically related to each, either by increasing the number of embryos available for transfer or by reducing the need to go through later IVF cycles.[5] Its reproductive status is clear whether the motivation for transfer of cloned embryos to the wife's uterus is simply to have another child or to replace a child who has died. In either case, transfer leads to the birth of a child from the couple's egg and sperm that they will rear.

Eventually, couples might seek to clone embryos, not to produce a child for rearing, but to produce an embryo from which tissue stem cells can be obtained for an existing child. In that case, cloning will not lead to the birth of another child. However, it involves use of their reproductive capacity. It may also enable existing children to live. It too should be found to be within the procreative or family autonomy of the couple.

b. Cloning one's children. The use of DNA from existing children to produce another child would also seem to fall within a couple's procreative liberty. This action is directly procreative because it leads to birth of a child who is formed from the egg and sperm of each spouse, even though it occurs asexually with the DNA of an existing child and not from a new union of egg and sperm.[6] Although it is novel to create a twin after one has already been born, it is still reproductive for the couple. The distinctly reproductive nature of their action is reinforced by the fact that they will gestate and rear the child that they clone.

The idea of cloning any existing child is plausibly foreseeable in several circumstances. One is where the parents want another child, and are so delighted with the existing one, that they simply want to create a twin of her, rather than take a chance on the genetic lottery.[7] A second is where an existing child might need an organ or tissue transplant. A third scenario would be to clone an existing child who has died, so that it might continue to live in another form with the parents.

The parental motivations in these cases are similar to parental motivations in coital reproduction. No one condemn parents who reproduce because they wanted a child as lovely as the first, they thought that a new child might be a tissue source for an existing child, or because they wanted another child after an earlier one had died. Given that the new child is cloned from the DNA of one of their own children, cloning one's own embryos or children to achieve those goals should also be regarded as an exercise of procreative liberty that deserves the special respect usually accorded to procreative choice.

c. Cloning third parties. A couple that seeks to use the DNA of a third party should also be viewed as forming a family in a way similar to family formation through coital conception. The DNA of another might be sought in lieu of gamete or embryo donation, though it could be chosen because of the source's characteristics or special meaning for the couple. The idea of "procreating" with the DNA of another raises several questions about the meaning and scope of procreative liberty that requires a more extended analysis. I begin with the initiating couple's rights or interests, and then ask whether the DNA source or her parents also have procreative interests and rights at stake.

(i) The initiating couple's cloning rights. We now ask whether the rights of procreation and family formation of a couple seeking to clone another's DNA would extend to use of a third party's DNA to create a child. Whether rearing is also intended turns out to be a key distinction. Let us first consider the situation where rearing is intended, and then the situation where no rearing is intended.

A strong case for a right to clone another person (assuming that that person and her parents have consented) is where a married couple seeks to clone in order to have a child to rear. Stronger still is the case in which the wife will gestate the resulting embryo and commits to rearing the child. Is this an exercise of their procreative liberty that deserves the special protection that procreative choice generally receives?

The most likely requests to clone a third party would arise from couples that are not reasonably able to reproduce in other ways. A common situation would be where the couple both lack viable gametes, though the wife can gestate, and thus are candidates for embryo donation. Rather than obtain an embryo generated by an unknown infertile couple, through cloning they could choose the genotype of the child they will carry and rear.

Whose DNA might they choose? The DNA could be

obtained from a friend or family member, although parents pose a problem. It could come from a sperm, egg, or DNA bank that provides DNA for a fee. Perhaps famous people would be willing to part with their DNA, in the same way that a sperm bank from Nobel Prize winners was once created. Rather than choose themselves, the couple might delegate the task of choosing the genome to their doctor or to some other party.

A strong argument exists that a couple using the DNA of a third party in lieu of embryo donation is engaged in a legitimate exercise of procreative liberty. The argument rests on the view that embryo donation is a protected part of that liberty. That view rests in turn on the recognition of the right of infertile couples to use gamete donation to form a family. As we have seen, coital infertility alone does not deprive one of the right to reproduce. Infertile persons have the same interests in having and rearing offspring and are as well equipped to rear as fertile couples. If that is so, the state could not ban infertile couples from using noncoital techniques to have children without a showing of tangible or compelling harm.

The preceding discussion is premised on the initiating couple's willingness to raise the cloned child. If no rearing is intended, however, their claim to clone the DNA of another should not be recognized as part of their procreative liberty, whether or not they have other means to reproduce. In this scenario an initiator procures the DNA and denucleated eggs, has embryos created from the DNA, and then either sells or provides the embryos to others, or commissions surrogates to gestate the embryos. The resulting children are then reared by others.

The crucial difference here is absence of intention to rear. If one is not intending to rear, then one's claim to be exercising procreative choice is much less persuasive. One is not directly reproducing because one's genes are not involved—they are not even being replicated. Nor is one gestating or rearing. Indeed, such a practice has many of the characteristics that made human cloning initially appear to be such a frightening proposition. It seems to treat children like fungible commodities produced for profit without regard to their well-being. It should not be deemed part of the initiating couple's procreative liberty.

(ii) The clone source's right to be cloned. Mention of the procreative rights of the person providing the DNA to be cloned is also relevant. I will assume that the clone source has consented to use of their DNA. If so, does she independently have the right to have a later-born genetic twin, such that a ban on cloning would violate her procreative rights as well?

The fact that she will not be rearing the child is crucial. Her claim to be cloned then is simply a claim to have another person exist in the world with her DNA (and note that if anonymity holds, she may never learn that her clone was born, much less ever meet her). If so, the only interest at stake is her interest in possibly having her DNA replicated without her gestation, rearing, or even perhaps her knowledge that a twin has been born. It is difficult to argue that this is a strong procreative interest, if it is a procreative interest at all. Thus, unless she undertook to rear the resulting child, the clone source would not have a fundamental right to be cloned.

But this assumes that being cloned is not itself reproduction. One could argue that cloning is quintessentially reproductive for the clone source because her entire genome is replicated. In providing the DNA for another child, she will be continuing her DNA into another generation. Given that the goal of sexual and asexual reproduction is the same—the continuation of one's DNA—and that individuals who are cloned might find or view it as a way of maintaining continuity with nature, we could plausibly choose to consider it a form of reproduction.

But even if we view the clone source as fully and clearly reproducing, she still is not rearing. Her claim of a right to be cloned is still a claim of a right to reproduction *tout court*—the barest and least protected form of reproduction.[8] If there is no rearing or gestation her claim merely to have her genes replicated will not qualify for moral or legal rights protection. If the clone source has a right here to be cloned, it would have to be derivative of the initiators' right to select source DNA for the child whom they will rear.

d. Cloning oneself. Another likely cloning scenario will involve cloning oneself. A strong case can be made that the use of one's own DNA to have and rear a child should be protected by procreative liberty.

As we have just seen, the right to clone oneself is weakest if rearing is not intended. Even if we grant that self-cloning is in some sense truly reproductive, rather than merely replicative, it would still be reproduction *tout court*, the minimal and least protected form of reproduction. Thus cloning oneself with no rearing intended would have no independent claim to be an exercise of procreative liberty. If it is protected at all, it would be derivative of the couple who then gestate and rear the cloned child.

The claim of a right to clone oneself is different if one plans to gestate and rear the resulting child. The situation is best viewed as a joint endeavor of the couple. As in embryo donation, the couple would gestate and rear. In this case, however, there would be a genetic relation between one of the rearing partners and the child—the relation of later-born identical twin.

The idea of a right to parent one's own later-born sibling is also plausibly viewed as a variation on the right to use a gamete donor. If such a right exists, it plausibly follows that that they would have the right to choose the gametes or gamete source they wish to use. A right to use their own DNA to have a child whom they then rear should follow. Using their own DNA has distinct advantages over the gametes purchased from commercial sperm banks or paid egg donors. One is more clearly continuing her own genetic line, one knows the gene source, and one is not buying gametes. Some persons might plausibly insist that they would have a family only if they could clone one of themselves because they are leery of the gametes of anonymous strangers.[9]

One might also argue for a right to have and rear one's own identical twin—the right to clone oneself—as a direct exercise of the right to reproduce. If one is free to reproduce, then one should also have the right to be cloned, because the genetic replication involved in cloning is directly and quintessentially reproductive. Duplicating one's entire DNA by nuclear cell transfer enables a person to survive longer than if cloning did not occur. To use Richard Dawkins' evocative term, the selfish gene wants to survive as long as possible, and will settle for cloning if that will do the job.[10] If rearing is intended, a person's procreative liberty should include the right to clone oneself. Only tangible harm to the child or others would then justify restrictions on self-cloning.

Constituting Procreative Liberty

The analysis has produced plausible arguments for finding that cloning is directly involved with procreative liberty in situations where the couple initiating the cloning intends to rear the resulting child. This protected interest is perhaps clearest when they are splitting embryos or using DNA from their own embryos or children, but it also holds when one of the rearing partner's DNA is used. Using the DNA of another person is less directly reproductive, but still maintains a gestational connection between the cloned child and its rearing parents, as now occurs in embryo donation.

In considering the relation between cloning and procreative liberty, we see once again how blurred the meanings of reproduction, family, parenting, and children become as we move away from sexual reproduction involving a couple's egg and sperm. Blurred meanings, however, can be clarified. The test must be how closely the marginal or deviant case is connected with the core. On this test, several plausible cases of a couple seeking to clone the DNA of embryos, children, themselves, or consenting third parties, can be articulated. In all instances they will be seeking a child whom they will gestate and rear. We do no great violence to prevailing understandings of procreative choice when we recognize DNA cloning to produce children whom we will rear as a legitimate form of family or procreative choice. Unless all selection is to be removed from reproduction, their interest in selecting the genes of their children deserves the same protection accorded other reproductive choices.

Public Policy

Having discussed the scientific questions and social controversies surrounding cloning, and the likely demand for it once it is shown to be safe and effective, we are now in a position to discuss public policy for human cloning. In formulating policy, however, we must take account of the state of the cloning art. One set of policy options applies when human applications are still in the research and development or experimental stage. Another set exists when research shows that human cloning is safe and effective. The birth of a sheep clone after 277 tries at somatic cell nuclear transfer has shown that much more research is needed before somatic cell cloning by nuclear transfer will be routinely available in sheep and other species, much less in humans. But an important set of policy issues will arise if animal and laboratory research shows that cloning is safe and effective in humans. Should all cloning then be permitted? Should some types of cloning be prohibited? What regulations will minimize the harms that cloning could cause?

Based on the analysis in this article, a ban on all human cloning, including the family-centered uses described above, is overbroad. But we must also ask if some uses of cloning should be forbidden and whether some regulation of permitted uses is desirable once human cloning becomes medically safe and feasible.

No cloning without rearing. A ban on human cloning unless the parties requesting the cloning will also rear is a much better policy than a ban on all cloning. The requirement of having to rear the clone addresses the worse abuses of cloning. It prevents a person from creating clones to be used as subjects or workers without regard for their own interests. For example, situations like that in *Boys from Brazil* or *Brave New World* would be prohibited, because the initiator is not rearing. This rule will assure the child a two-parent rearing situation—a prime determinant of a child's welfare. Furthermore, the rule would not violate the initiator's procreative liberty because merely producing children for others to rear is not an exercise of that liberty.

Ensuring that the initiating couple rears the child given the DNA of another prevents some risks to the child, but still leaves open the threats to individuality, autonomy, and kinship that many persons think that cloning presents. I have argued that parents who intend to have and rear a healthy child might not be as prey to those concerns as feared, yet some cloning situations, because of the novelty of choosing a genome, might still produce social or psychological problems.

Those risks should be addressed in terms of the situations most likely to generate them, and the regulations, short of prohibition, that might minimize their occurrence. It hardly follows that all cloning should be banned, because some undesirable cloning situations might occur. Like other slippery slope arguments, there is no showing that the bad uses are so likely to occur, or that if they did, their bad effects would so clearly outweigh the good, that one is justified in suffering the loss of the good to prevent the bad.

Notes

[1] The moral and legal arguments for procreative liberty are presented in John A. Robertson, *Children of Choice: Freedom and the New Reproductive Technologies* (Princeton 1994), pp. 22–42.

[2] For elaboration of this argument, see John A. Robertson, "Genetic Selection of Offspring Characteristics," 76 *B.U.L. Rev.* 421, 424–432 (1996).

[3] The article emphasizes the rights of married couples because they will be perceived as having a stronger claim to have children than unmarried persons. If their rights to clone are recognized, then the claims of unmarried persons to clone might follow.

[4] Since only nuclear DNA is transferred in cloning, DNA contained in the egg's cytoplasm in the form of mitochondria is not cloned or replicated (it is in the case of cloning by embryo splitting). The resulting child is thus not a true clone, for its mitochondrial DNA will have come from the egg source, who will not usually also be providing the nucleus for transfer. Mitochondrial DNA is only a small portion of total DNA, perhaps 5%. However, malfunctions in it can still cause serious disease. See Douglas C. Wallace, "Mitochondrial DNA in Aging and Disease," 277 *Scientific American* 40 (August 1997).

[5] It might also be done to provide an embryo or child from whom tissue or organs for transplant for an existing child.

[6] Again, it might be used to create an embryo or child from whom tissue or organs for transplant into an existing child might be obtained.

[7] I am grateful to my colleague Charles Silver for this suggestion. However, other colleagues with children inform me that they would not clone an existing child, because they would want to see how the next child would differ.

[8] Reproduction *tout court* (without more) refers to genetic transmission without any rearing rights or duties in the resulting child, and in some cases, not even knowledge that a child has been born. The courts have not yet determined whether engaging in or avoiding reproduction *tout court* deserves the same protection that more robust or involved forms of reproduction have. For further discussion, see *Children of Choice*, pp. 108–109.

[9] Of course, this means that the other partner will have no DNA connection with the child she rears, unless she also provides the egg and mitochondria.

[10] In the long run, cloning might not be adaptive, because genetic diversity is needed. However, if the alternative is no genetic continuation at all—say because no reproduction occurs, or a gamete donor is chosen—then cloning increases the chance of long-term survival of the cloned DNA more than no cloning at all. Richard Dawkins would clone himself purely out of curiosity: "I find it a personally riveting thought that I could watch a small copy of myself nurtured through the early decades of the twenty-first century." (Peter Steinfels, "Beliefs," *New York Times*, July 12, 1997, p. A8).

Arthur Caplan

If Ethics Won't Work Here, Where?

Why Take Ethics Seriously?

What does human cloning have to do with ethics? Or, more accurately, why should human cloning have anything to do with ethics? Once the initial frenzy over the cloning of Dolly the sheep had abated, a large number of people began to express skepticism or even outright hostility to the idea that ethics had anything of value to say about human cloning. Biologist Lee Silver spoke for many when he wrote, "[I]n a society that values individual freedom above all else, it is hard to find any legitimate basis for restricting the use of reprogenetics [Silver's term for genetic engineering including cloning and assisted reproductive technologies]" (Silver 1997, p. 9).

The skeptics found a basis for their skepticism in three areas. Cloning had taken on a life of its own and had powerful supporters who were committed to seeing human cloning advance to serve their own agendas (Adler

1997, Powers 1998). Cloning should advance unhindered because every American has a fundamental and constitutionally guaranteed right to reproduce (Robertson 1994, Silver 1997, Wolf 1997). Human cloning should advance because science must always be free to go where it wishes to go (Stolberg 1998, Kolata 1998).

None of these arguments is especially persuasive as a reason against trying to think about the ethics of human cloning. The fact that some may want to pursue their own agenda or their own self-interest is in fact a very good reason for thinking about the ethics of human cloning especially since cloning involves the creation of new persons. The fact that persons do have a liberty right to reproduce says nothing about their right to an entitlement to technological aid in having children, or whether it makes sense to limit that right if the mode used for the creation of children is not in the child's best interest (NBAC 1997, Davis 1997, Caplan 1998). And it is simply not true that science and biomedical research enjoy open-ended, unbounded liberty when it comes to the pursuit of new knowledge. Anyone who has submitted a grant for peer-review knows that the right to inquiry is almost always limited by the ability to command the support of the community to pay for it.

The strongest reason for skepticism about the relevance of ethics to human cloning was that a large number of people in positions of authority doubted that ethics would make any difference to the pace or path that cloning took. This form of skepticism is present in the commonly voiced concern of politicians, policy makers and scholars that ethics seems always to trail behind the latest scientific or medical breakthroughs (Fox and Swazey 1992, Silver 1997), and that there is no reason to presume ethics will prove more potent with respect to human cloning then it has in curbing, modifying or stopping any technology in biomedicine in the years since the Second World War.

The phenomenon of the 'ethics lag' has been accepted by many commentators on cloning as a fact (Adler 1997, Silver 1997). All one need do to see the depth of this belief is track any story about the ethics of any major new breakthrough in biology or medicine. It will not be many paragraphs before the writer notes either that ethics always seems to be lagging behind scientific advances or that biomedicine has outstripped the capacity of ethics and the law to keep pace. The 'ethics lag' is a powerful presumption in American, European and Japanese assessments of the future of biomedicine (Adler 1997, Weiss 1998).

One way to respond to the worry that ethics cannot keep up was to call for bans on human cloning (NBAC 1997). The President of the United States moved quickly to ban the use of Federal moneys to support research into human cloning. This was followed by many calls for Congress to enact legislation banning human cloning. More then twenty states were considering bills to ban cloning by the summer of 1998. Many nations such as Germany, Britain and France quickly banned human cloning as did the European Parliament, the Council of Europe and the World Health Organization. But there was and remains a great degree of doubt that even bans will work (Wolf 1997, Kolata 1998).

Many people believe that it is a simple matter to evade a ban and conduct human cloning research secretly or in a third world location. Some believe not only that it is simple but that it is inevitable. This is the only way to explain the elevation of Dr. Richard Seed—a retired Chicago physicist who announced at a conference in Chicago on December 5 1997 that he intended to clone human beings—from obscurity to a figure capable of inspiring national anxiety. Seed was a pathetic figure who had absolutely no hope of cloning anyone or anything at any time. Still, his elevation for a few months early in 1998 to a national nightmare was the most obvious manifestation of the belief in the ethics lag. But there were many other manifestations of doubt that ethics would make any difference whatsoever to the future of the genetic revolution in evidence in the months after the birth of Dolly in Scotland became public knowledge.

Commentators and pundits went bonkers over the appearance of Dolly. Some fretted about the national security risk posed by clone armies in the hands of rogue regimes. Others wrung their hands over the use of cloning to create hordes of clones that might be mined to supply tissues and organs to those in need of transplants. A few commentators speculated on the societal implications of immortality achieved by means of cloning oneself sequentially. These sorts of speculations made little scientific sense but they did reflect deep public doubt and mistrust of advances in the realm of genetics and genetic engineering (Caplan 1998).

One legislator who spoke out vociferously about human cloning on the basis of the Dolly experiment was Senator Tom Harkin of Iowa. In hearings on cloning he expressed the view that once science had started down the path toward new knowledge there was nothing anyone could do to stop its progress. He ventured the opinion that no law, or moral rule or set of values had ever deterred biomedicine from doing anything, and that the best the world could hope for was that those working on cloning chose to do so in an ethical fashion (Lane 1997, NBC News 1997).

The view that biomedicine cannot be stopped, shaped or changed by ethics might well be called Harkinism. The position holds that biomedical progress moves under its own momentum. It advances a supremely fatalistic and skeptical view about ethics: Once science has made a key breakthrough and gets rolling there is nothing anyone can do to stop it.

There is something terrifying about Harkinism. If accepted it means that there is really no point in debating or arguing about the ethics of any biomedical advance. The future will be what it will be and there is nothing anyone can do about it. Worse still, if the unscrupulous or the crazy get their hands on biomedical advances, if a competent and rich Dr. Seed were to seek the sponsorship of a renegade regime to start his cloning company, there is nothing anyone can do to deter or stop this sort of thing. The only problem with both the invocation of the ethics lag and with Harkinism is that they are both wrong.

Has ethics or bioethics ever stopped anything in medicine?

Many years ago, in the late 1970s, when I was a graduate student just beginning a position at the Hastings Center, the nation's most influential private bioethics institute located just north of New York City, Daniel Callahan, then the Director, and I had a standing bet. We would ask the various scholars, physicians and researchers who came to the Center to give talks or participate in seminars to name a single technology that had been stymied, blocked or destroyed as a result of a bioethical objection or argument. Our bet was that no one would be able to do so. We agreed to provide a free lunch for all staff if someone ever came up with a single case of a technology that had been stopped because of ethical concerns or reservations. No one ever did.

Dan and I would use the inability to identify any scientific application or technology that had ever foundered on the rocks of ethics as a way to calm the worries of physicians and researchers that if they even talked about ethics they might somehow wind up being responsible for hindering inquiry. No act could have been seen as more treasonous, more incompatible with being a member of the biomedical community, than to permanently hinder scientific progress for ethical reasons. Reassured that they could not do permanent damage to their own research programs or those of colleagues, the visitors would then almost always dig in for a dialogue on bioethics, since they felt certain that talk of ethics would not really put the practice of science at any risk.

I have come to think that Daniel Callahan and I were wrong about the power of ethics. The problem was that when we asked for case examples we were looking for instances in the very recent past where someone's bright idea had gone down in smoke forever due to ethical worries. However, seeing the impact of ethics on science is more akin to detecting the processes of evolutionary change, being aware of barometric pressure, or being alert to the presence of gravity.

Evolution is a phenomenon that is difficult to observe because it goes on very slowly all around us. It is hard for anyone to be aware of the weight of air or the pull of gravity because they are present in our lives at all times. These forces are a part of our environment. We adjust to them. It is only in their absence, when humans travel into space or deep into the sea, that we realize the powerful force that they constantly exert upon us.

Similarly, ethics is most noticeable with respect to the role it plays in shaping science when it is not present or present in a very different form. The inhumane experiments conducted in the German and Japanese concentration camps by competent scientists and physicians and public health officials during the Second World War show how very different scientific behavior is in the absence of the normal ethical restraints that dominate the practice of science and medicine. Research conducted in the United States and other nations in the 19th century on serfs and slaves—who were not seen as persons or even as human—or on animals in the 18th and early 19th centuries, give more tragic evidence of the role played by ethics in biomedical research today (Caplan 1998).

It is simply not true that ethics has not had or cannot have an impact on what biomedicine does, or what biomedicine becomes. While the influence is not always obvious, once one looks closely it can be detected.

For example, we presume that doctors will reveal to potential subjects the nature of experiments they might want them to serve in, and that they will obtain their permission before studying them. The requirement of informed consent in recruiting subjects to biomedical research is, however, a relatively recent innovation. As recently as the 1930s and 40s subjects were routinely lied to or deceived about the nature of human experimentation, and consent was often not sought.

Prohibitions on research on retarded children living in institutions and upon fetuses except when it might be for their benefit have been in effect for decades, as have prohibitions against embryo research and fetal tissue transplantation. These moral bans have had the effect of almost bringing these areas of inquiry to a complete halt. Research on the total artificial heart and the use of animals as sources of organs for transplants was halted for more then a decade as a result of moral objections. The inclusion of women in clinical trials is a direct response to moral criticism. The decision in the 1970s to halt research involving recombinant DNA work until sufficient oversight could be applied to experiments was fueled by moral doubts on the part of scientists about the safety of early research with recombinant DNA (Singer 1977). It is hard to maintain a strong allegiance to either the ethics lag or Harkinism once one takes a close look at the history of biomedical research.

True, ethics cannot always restrain or curb biomedicine's drive to know. Nor can it always provide a reliable safeguard against the actions of a fiend or a nut. But the fact that ethics is not omnipotent should not mislead us into believing that it is impotent, either.

The power of ethics in steering and even prohibiting certain kinds of conduct is not always easy to see. Just as Jane Goodall spent fifteen years observing chimpanzees without seeing them engage in killing before an all-out war broke out in the groups she had known and described as peaceable, so ethics may not be much in evidence until a true conflict of interest or scandal sends everyone scrambling for their code of ethics.

Should Ethics Guide Human Cloning?

Well, if there is no prima facie reason to doubt that human cloning does raise key ethical issues, and if it is not ridiculous to suggest that ethics might actually succeed in steering the direction of future research and application of knowledge about cloning to humans, then what are the reasons for ethical concern about cloning?

The reasons are simple—safety and the best interest of someone who might be cloned. There is almost no verified knowledge available about the safety of cloning involving DNA obtained from adult cells. There is more knowledge about cloning involving DNA from fetal cells and the splitting of embryos to create clones (a subject that has drawn almost no moral commentary even though it is probably the form of cloning most within our reach).

To create a human clone based on the experience of cloning one sheep from adult cell DNA would be blatantly immoral. The clone could be born deformed, dying or prematurely aging. There would be no basis for taking such risk unless there was some overwhelmingly powerful reason to clone someone. Safety alone in the earliest stages of human cloning justifies moral concern in the form of clarifying the ethics of human experimentation. At what point will enough data from animals be on hand to justify a human trial? At what point would the risks involved still permit someone to try cloning, and who, and for what reasons? People of good will can and do disagree about the answers to these questions, but the very fact that disagreement exists shows the centrality of ethics to the enterprise of human cloning.

The other reason ethics is very relevant to human cloning is that it is not clear that cloning is a good way to make a person. If someone feels burdened by having a very close resemblance to one parent, if they feel that their future is not their own because they were made to conform to someone else's expectations and dreams (Davis 1997), if a clone feel overwhelmed by the burden of knowing too much about their biological destiny because it is written in the body and appearance of the parent from which they came, if a human clone elicits inappropriate or hostile reactions from parents and others—then it may prove to be too burdensome to ask someone to go through their life as a clone. It is not clear that cloning is too burdensome. But it is far from clear that it is not. Until that issue has been debated then there is no reason to think that ethics should be excused if it lags in any way behind the science of cloning.

References

Adler, Eric, "As Dolly, the first clone of an adult mammal, made her debut last week, a skeptical and doubting public asked... What's next? Technology inspires wonder and worry," *The Kansas City Star*, March 2, 1997, pp. A1, 5–6.

Caplan, Arthur L., *Am I My Brother's Keeper?* (Bloomington 1998).

Davis, D. "Genetic Dilemmas and the Child's Right to an Open Future." *Hastings Center Report* 26, 1997, pp. 6–9.

Fox, R.C. and J.P. Swazey, *Spare Parts* (New York 1992).

Kolata, Gina, "With an eye on the public, scientists choose their words." *The New York Times*, January 6, 1998 v147, pp. B12, F4.

Lane, Earl, Senator, "Human Clones Ok/But scientists tell panel: for animals only," *Newsday*, March 13, 1997, p. A08.

National Bioethics Advisory Commission. *Cloning Human Beings* (Rockville MD, June 1997).

NBC News Transcripts, *TODAY*, March 13, 1997, Senator Tom Harkin discusses his views on human cloning.

Powers, William, "A Slant on cloning," *National Journal*, January 10, 1998, v30 n2, p. 58(6).

Robertson, J.A., Children *of Choice* (Princeton 1994).

Silver, L., *Remaking Eden: Cloning and Beyond in a Brave New World* (New York 1997).

Singer, Maxine, "Historical Perspectives on Research with Recombinant DNA," in *Research with Recombinant DNA* (Washington DC 1977).

Weiss, Rick, "Fertility Innovation or Exploitation? Regulatory Void Allows for Trial—and Error—Without Patient Disclosure Rules," *The Washington Post*, February 09, 1998, pp. A1, 16.

Wolf, S. "Ban Cloning? Why NBAC is Wrong," Chapter Six below.

Leon Kass

The Wisdom of Repugnance: Why We Should Ban the Cloning of Humans

Our habit of delighting in news of scientific and technological breakthroughs has been sorely challenged by the birth announcement of a sheep named Dolly. Though Dolly shares with previous sheep the "softest clothing, woolly, bright," William Blake's question, "Little Lamb, who made thee?" has for her a radically different answer: Dolly was, quite literally, made. She is the work not of nature or nature's God but of man, a British man, Ian Wilmut, and his fellow scientists. What's more, Dolly came into being not only asexually—ironically, just like "He [who] calls Himself a Lamb"—but also as the genetically identical copy (and the perfect incarnation of the form or blueprint) of a mature ewe, of whom she is a clone. This long-awaited yet not quite expected success in cloning a mammal raised immediately the prospect—

68

and the specter—of cloning human beings: "I a child and Thou a lamb," despite our differences, have always been equal candidates for creative making, only now, by means of cloning, we may both spring from the hand of man playing at being God.

After an initial flurry of expert comment and public consternation, with opinion polls showing overwhelming opposition to cloning human beings, President Clinton ordered a ban on all federal support for human cloning research (even though none was being supported) and charged the National Bioethics Advisory Commission to report in ninety days on the ethics of human cloning research. The commission (an eighteen-member panel, evenly balanced between scientists and nonscientists, appointed by the president and reporting to the National Science and Technology Council) invited testimony from scientists, religious thinkers and bioethicists, as well as from the general public. It is now deliberating about what it should recommend, both as a matter of ethics and as a matter of public policy.

Congress is awaiting the commission's report, and is poised to act. Bills to prohibit the use of federal funds for human cloning research have been introduced in the House of Representatives and the Senate; and another bill, in the House, would make it illegal "for any person to use a human somatic cell for the process of producing a human clone." A fateful decision is at hand. To clone or not to clone a human being is no longer an academic question.

Taking Cloning Seriously, Then and Now

Cloning first came to public attention roughly thirty years ago, following the successful asexual production, in England, of a clutch of tadpole clones by the technique of

nuclear transplantation. The individual largely responsible for bringing the prospect and promise of human
cloning to public notice was Joshua Lederberg, a Nobel
Laureate geneticist and a man of large vision. In 1966,
Lederberg wrote a remarkable article in The
American Naturalist detailing the eugenic advantages
of human cloning and other forms of genetic engineering, and the following year he devoted a column in The
Washington Post, where he wrote regularly on science
and society, to the prospect of human cloning. He suggested that cloning could help us overcome the unpredictable variety that still rules human reproduction, and
allow us to benefit from perpetuating superior genetic
endowments. These writings sparked a small public debate in which I became a participant. At the time a young
researcher in molecular biology at the National Institutes
of Health (NIH), I wrote a reply to the Post, arguing
against Lederberg's amoral treatment of this morally
weighty subject and insisting on the urgency of confront-
ing a series of questions and objections, culminating in
the suggestion that "the programmed reproduction of man
will, in fact, dehumanize him."

Much has happened in the intervening years. It has
become harder, not easier, to discern the true meaning
of human cloning. We have in some sense been softened
up to the idea—through movies, cartoons, jokes and in-
termittent commentary in the mass media, some serious, most lighthearted. We have become accustomed to
new practices in human reproduction: not just in vitro
fertilization, but also embryo manipulation, embryo donation and surrogate pregnancy. Animal biotechnology
has yielded transgenic animals and a burgeoning science
of genetic engineering, easily and soon to be transferable to humans.

Even more important, changes in the broader culture

make it now vastly more difficult to express a common and respectful understanding of sexuality, procreation, nascent life, family, and the meaning of motherhood, fatherhood and the links between the generations. Twenty-five years ago, abortion was still largely illegal and thought to be immoral, the sexual revolution (made possible by the extramarital use of the pill) was still in its infancy, and few had yet heard about the reproductive rights of single women, homosexual men and lesbians. (Never mind shameless memoirs about one's own incest!) Then one could argue, without embarrassment, that the new technologies of human reproduction—babies without sex—and their confounding of normal kin relations—who's the mother: the egg donor, the surrogate who carries and delivers, or the one who rears?—would "undermine the justification and support that biological parenthood gives to the monogamous marriage." Today, defenders of stable, monogamous marriage risk charges of giving offense to those adults who are living in "new family forms" or to those children who, even without the benefit of assisted reproduction, have acquired either three or four parents or one or none at all. Today, one must even apologize for voicing opinions that twenty-five years ago were nearly universally regarded as the core of our culture's wisdom on these matters. In a world whose once-given natural boundaries are blurred by technological change and whose moral boundaries are seemingly up for grabs, it is much more difficult to make persuasive the still compelling case against cloning human beings. As Raskolnikov put it, "man gets used to everything—the beast!"

Indeed, perhaps the most depressing feature of the discussions that immediately followed the news about Dolly was their ironical tone, their genial cynicism, their moral fatigue: "an udder way of making lambs" (*Nature*), "who will cash in on breakthrough in cloning?" (*The Wall Street Journal*), "is cloning baaaaaaaad?" (*The Chicago Tribune*). Gone from the scene are the wise and courageous voices of Theodosius Dobzhansky (genetics), Hans Jonas (philosophy) and Paul Ramsey (theology) who, only twenty-five years ago, all made powerful moral arguments against ever cloning a human being. We are now too sophisticated for such argumentation; we wouldn't be caught in public with a strong moral stance, never mind an absolutist one. We are all, or almost all, post-modernists now.

Cloning turns out to be the perfect embodiment of the ruling opinions of our new age. Thanks to the sexual revolution, we are able to deny in practice, and increasingly in thought, the inherent procreative teleology of sexuality itself. But, if sex has no intrinsic connection to generating babies, babies need have no necessary connection to sex. Thanks to feminism and the gay rights movement, we are increasingly encouraged to treat the natural heterosexual difference and its preeminence as a matter of "cultural construction." But if male and female are not normatively complementary and generatively significant, babies need not come from male and female complementarity. Thanks to the prominence and the acceptability of divorce and out-of-wedlock births, stable, monogamous marriage as the ideal home for procreation is no longer the agreed-upon cultural norm. For this new dispensation, the clone is the ideal emblem: the ultimate "single-parent child."

Thanks to our belief that all children should be wanted children (the more high-minded principle we use to justify contraception and abortion), sooner or later only those children who fulfill our wants will be fully acceptable. Through cloning, we can work our wants and wills on the very identity of our children, exercising control as never before. Thanks to modern notions of individualism and the rate of cultural change, we see ourselves not as linked to ancestors and defined by traditions, but as projects for our own self-creation, not only as self-made men but also man-made selves; and self-cloning is simply an extension of such rootless and narcissistic self-re-creation.

Unwilling to acknowledge our debt to the past and unwilling to embrace the uncertainties and the limitations of the future, we have a false relation to both: cloning personifies our desire fully to control the future, while being subject to no controls ourselves. Enchanted and enslaved by the glamour of technology, we have lost our awe and wonder before the deep mysteries of nature and of life. We cheerfully take our own beginnings in our hands and, like the last man, we blink.

Part of the blame for our complacency lies, sadly, with the field of bioethics itself, and its claim to expertise in these moral matters. Bioethics was founded by people who understood that the new biology touched and threatened the deepest matters of our humanity: bodily integrity, identity and individuality, lineage and kinship, freedom and self-command, eros and aspiration, and the relations and strivings of body and soul. With its capture by analytic philosophy, however, and its inevitable routinization and professionalization, the field has by and large come to content itself with analyzing moral arguments, reacting to new technological developments and taking on emerging issues of public policy, all performed with a naive faith that the evils we fear can all be avoided by compassion, regulation and a respect for autonomy. Bioethics has made some major contributions in the protection of human subjects and in other areas where personal freedom is threatened; but its practitioners, with few exceptions, have turned the big human questions into pretty thin gruel.

One reason for this is that the piecemeal formation of public policy tends to grind down large questions of morals into small questions of procedure. Many of the country's leading bioethicists have served on national commissions or state task forces and advisory boards, where, understandably, they have found utilitarianism to be the only ethical vocabulary acceptable to all participants in discussing issues of law, regulation and public policy. As many of these commissions have been either officially under the aegis of NIH or the Health and Human Services Department, or otherwise dominated by powerful voices for scientific progress, the ethicists have for the most part been content, after some "values clarification" and wringing of hands, to pronounce their blessings upon the inevitable. Indeed, it is the bioethicists, not the scientists, who are now the most articulate defenders of human cloning: the two witnesses testifying before the National Bioethics Advisory Commission in favor of cloning human beings were bioethicists, eager to rebut what they regard as the irrational concerns of those of us in opposition. One wonders whether this commission, constituted like the previous commissions, can tear itself sufficiently free from the accommodationist pattern of rubber-stamping all technical innovation, in the mistaken belief that all other goods must bow down before the gods of better health and scientific advance.

If it is to do so, the commission must first persuade itself, as we all should persuade ourselves, not to be complacent about what is at issue here. Human cloning, though it is in some respects continuous with previous reproductive technologies, also represents something radically new, in itself and in its easily foreseeable consequences. The stakes are very high indeed. I exaggerate, but in the direction of the truth, when I insist that we are faced with having to decide nothing less than whether human procreation is going to remain human, whether children are going to be made rather than begotten, whether it is a good thing, humanly speaking, to say yes in principle to the road which leads (at best) to the dehumanized rationality of *Brave New World*. This is not business as usual, to be fretted about for a while but finally to be given our seal of approval. We must rise to the occasion and make our judgments as if the future of our humanity hangs in the balance. For so it does.

The State of the Art

If we should not underestimate the significance of human cloning, neither should we exaggerate its imminence or misunderstand just what is involved. The procedure is conceptually simple. The nucleus of a mature but unfertilized egg is removed and replaced with a nucleus obtained from a specialized cell of an adult (or fetal) organism (in Dolly's case, the donor nucleus came from mammary gland epithelium). Since almost all the hereditary material of a cell is contained within its nucleus, the renucleated egg and the individual into which this egg develops are genetically identical to the organism that was the source of the transferred nucleus. An unlimited number of genetically identical individuals—clones—could be produced by nuclear transfer. In principle, any person, male or female, newborn or adult, could be cloned, and in any quantity. With laboratory cultivation and storage of tissues, cells outliving their sources make it possible even to clone the dead.

The technical stumbling block, overcome by Wilmut and his colleagues, was to find a means of reprogramming the state of the DNA in the donor cells, reversing its differentiated expression and restoring its full totipotency, so that it could again direct the entire process of producing a mature organism. Now that this problem has been solved, we should expect a rush to develop cloning for other animals, especially livestock, in order to propagate in perpetuity the champion meat or milk producers. Though exactly how soon someone will succeed in cloning a human being is anybody's guess, Wilmut's technique, almost certainly applicable to humans, makes attempting the feat an imminent possibility.

Yet some cautions are in order and some possible misconceptions need correcting. For a start, cloning is not xeroxing. As has been reassuringly reiterated, the clone of Mel Gibson, though his genetic double, would enter the world hairless, toothless and peeing in his diapers, just like any other human infant. Moreover, the success rate, at least at first, will probably not be very high: the British transferred 277 adult nuclei into enucleated sheep eggs, and implanted twenty-nine clonal embryos, but they achieved the birth of only one live lamb clone. For this reason, among others, it is unlikely that, at least for now, the practice would be very popular, and there is no immediate worry of mass-scale production of multicopies. The need of repeated surgery to obtain eggs and, more crucially, of numerous borrowed wombs for implantation will surely limit use, as will the expense; besides, almost everyone who is able will doubtless prefer nature's sexier way of conceiving.

Still, for the tens of thousands of people already sustaining over 200 assisted-reproduction clinics in the United States and already availing themselves of in vitro fertilization, intracytoplasmic sperm injection and other techniques of assisted reproduction, cloning would be an option with virtually no added fuss (especially when the success rate improves). Should commercial interests develop in "nucleus-banking," as they have in sperm-banking; should famous athletes or other celebrities decide to market their DNA the way they now market their autographs and just about everything else; should techniques of embryo and germline genetic testing and manipulation arrive as anticipated, increasing the use of laboratory assistance in order to obtain "better" babies—should all this come to pass, then cloning, if it is permitted, could become more than a marginal practice simply on the basis of free reproductive choice, even without any social encouragement to upgrade the gene pool or to replicate superior types. Moreover, if laboratory research on human cloning proceeds, even without any intention to produce cloned humans, the existence of cloned human embryos in the laboratory, created to begin with only for research purposes, would surely pave the way for later baby-making implantations.

In anticipation of human cloning, apologists and proponents have already made clear possible uses of the perfected technology, ranging from the sentimental and compassionate to the grandiose. They include: providing a child for an infertile couple; "replacing" a beloved spouse or child who is dying or has died; avoiding the risk of genetic disease; permitting reproduction for homosexual men and lesbians who want nothing sexual to do with the opposite sex; securing a genetically identical source of organs or tissues perfectly suitable for transplantation; getting a child with a genotype of one's own choosing, not excluding oneself; replicating individuals of great genius, talent or beauty—having a child who really could "be like Mike"; and creating large sets of genetically identical humans suitable for research on, for instance, the question of nature versus nurture, or for special missions in peace and war (not excluding espionage), in which using identical humans would be an advantage. Most people who envision the cloning of human beings, of course, want none of these scenarios. That they cannot say why is not surprising. What is surprising, and welcome, is that, in our cynical age, they are saying anything at all.

The Wisdom of Repugnance

"Offensive." "Grotesque." "Revolting." "Repugnant." "Repulsive." These are the words most commonly heard regarding the prospect of human cloning. Such reactions come both from the man or woman in the street and from the intellectuals, from believers and atheists, from humanists and scientists. Even Dolly's creator has said he "would find it offensive" to clone a human being.

People are repelled by many aspects of human cloning. They recoil from the prospect of mass production of human beings, with large clones of look-alikes, compromised in their individuality; the idea of father—son or mother—daughter twins; the bizarre prospects of a woman giving birth to and rearing a genetic copy of herself, her spouse or even her deceased father or mother; the grotesqueness of conceiving a child as an exact replacement for another who has died; the utilitarian creation of embryonic genetic duplicates of oneself, to be frozen away or created when necessary, in case of need for homologous tissues or organs for transplantation; the narcissism of those who would clone themselves and the arrogance of others who think they know who deserves to be cloned or which genotype any child-to-be should be thrilled to receive; the Frankensteinian hubris to create human life and increasingly to control its destiny; man playing God. Almost no one finds any of the suggested reasons for human cloning compelling; almost everyone anticipates its possible misuses and abuses. Moreover, many people feel oppressed by the sense that there is probably nothing we can do to prevent it from happening. This makes the prospect all the more revolting.

Revulsion is not an argument; and some of yesterday's repugnances are today calmly accepted—though, one must add, not always for the better. In crucial cases, however, repugnance is the emotional expression of deep wisdom, beyond reason's power fully to articulate it. Can anyone really give an argument fully adequate to the horror which is father-daughter incest (even with consent), or having sex with animals, or mutilating a corpse, or eating human flesh, or even just (just!) raping or murdering another human being? Would anybody's failure to give full rational justification for his or her revulsion at these practices make that revulsion ethically suspect? Not at all. On the contrary, we are suspicious of those who think that they can rationalize away our horror, say, by trying to explain the enormity of incest with arguments only about the genetic risks of inbreeding.

The repugnance at human cloning belongs in this category. We are repelled by the prospect of cloning human beings not because of the strangeness or novelty of the undertaking, but because we intuit and feel, immediately and without argument, the violation of things that we rightfully hold dear. Repugnance, here as elsewhere, revolts against the excesses of human willfulness, warning us not to transgress what is unspeakably profound. Indeed, in this age in which everything is held to be permissible so long as it is freely done, in which our given human nature no longer commands respect, in which our bodies are regarded as mere instruments of our autonomous rational wills, repugnance may be the only voice left that speaks up to defend the central core of our humanity. Shallow are the souls that have forgotten how to shudder.

The goods protected by repugnance are generally overlooked by our customary ways of approaching all new biomedical technologies. The way we evaluate cloning ethically will in fact be shaped by how we characterize it descriptively, by the context into which we place it, and by the perspective from which we view it. The first task for ethics is proper description. And here is where our failure begins.

Typically, cloning is discussed in one or more of three familiar contexts, which one might call the technological, the liberal and the meliorist. Under the first, cloning will be seen as an extension of existing techniques for assisting reproduction and determining the genetic makeup of children. Like them, cloning is to be regarded as a neutral technique, with no inherent meaning or goodness, but subject to multiple uses, some good, some bad. The morality of cloning thus depends absolutely on the goodness or badness of the motives and intentions of the cloners: as one bioethicist defender of cloning puts it, "the ethics must be judged [only] by the way the parents nurture and rear their resulting child and whether they bestow the same love and affection on a child brought into existence by a technique of assisted reproduction as they would on a child born in the usual way."

The liberal (or libertarian or liberationist) perspective sets cloning in the context of rights, freedoms and personal empowerment. Cloning is just a new option for exercising an individual's right to reproduce or to have the kind of child that he or she wants. Alternatively, cloning enhances our liberation (especially women's liberation) from the confines of nature, the vagaries of chance, or the necessity for sexual mating. Indeed, it liberates women from the need for men altogether, for the process requires only eggs, nuclei and (for the time being) uteri—plus, of course, a healthy dose of our (allegedly "masculine") manipulative science that likes to do all these things to mother nature and nature's mothers. For those who hold this outlook, the only moral restraints on cloning are adequately informed consent and the avoidance of bodily harm. If no one is cloned without her consent, and if the clonant is not physically damaged, then the liberal conditions for licit, hence moral, conduct are met. Worries that go beyond violating the will or maiming the body are dismissed as "symbolic"—which is to say, unreal.

The meliorist perspective embraces valetudinarians and also eugenicists. The latter were formerly more vocal in these discussions, but they are now generally happy to see their goals advanced under the less threatening banners of freedom and technological growth. These people see in cloning a new prospect for improving human beings—minimally, by ensuring the perpetuation of healthy individuals by avoiding the risks of genetic disease inherent in the lottery of sex, and maximally, by producing "optimum babies," preserving outstanding genetic material, and (with the help of soon-to-come techniques for precise genetic engineering) enhancing inborn human capacities on many fronts. Here the morality of cloning as a means is justified solely by the excellence of the end, that is, by the outstanding traits or individuals cloned—beauty, or brawn, or brains.

These three approaches, all quintessentially American and all perfectly fine in their places, are sorely wanting as approaches to human procreation. It is, to say the least, grossly distorting to view the wondrous mysteries of birth, renewal and individuality, and the deep meaning of parent—child relations, largely through the lens of our reductive science and its potent technologies. Similarly, considering reproduction (and the intimate relations of family life!) primarily under the political-legal, adversarial, and individualistic notion of rights can only undermine the private yet fundamentally social, cooperative and duty-laden character of childbearing, child rearing and their bond to the covenant of marriage. Seeking to escape entirely from nature (in order to satisfy a natural desire or a natural right to reproduce!) is self-contradictory in theory and self-alienating in practice. For we are erotic beings only because we are embodied beings, and not merely intellects and wills unfortunately imprisoned in our bodies. And, though health and fitness are clearly great goods, there is something deeply disquieting in looking on our prospective children as artful products perfectible by genetic engineering, increasingly held to our willfully imposed designs, specifications and margins of tolerable error.

The technical, liberal and meliorist approaches all ignore the deeper anthropological, social and, indeed, ontological meanings of bringing forth new life. To this more fitting and profound point of view, cloning shows itself to be a major alteration, indeed, a major violation, of our given nature as embodied, gendered and engendering beings-and of the social relations built on this natural ground. Once this perspective is recognized, the ethical judgment on cloning can no longer be reduced to a matter of motives and intentions, rights and freedoms, benefits and harms, or even means and ends. It must be regarded primarily as a matter of meaning: Is cloning a fulfillment of human begetting and belonging? Or is cloning rather, as I contend, their pollution and perversion? To pollution and perversion, the fitting response can only be horror and revulsion; and conversely, generalized horror and revulsion are prima facie evidence of foulness and violation. The burden of moral argument must fall entirely on those who want to declare the widespread repugnances of humankind to be mere timidity or superstition.

Yet repugnance need not stand naked before the bar of reason. The wisdom of our horror at human cloning can be partially articulated, even if this is finally one of those instances about which the heart has its reasons that reason cannot entirely know.

The Profundity of Sex

To see cloning in its proper context, we must begin not, as I did before, with laboratory technique, but with the anthropology—natural and social—of sexual reproduction.

Sexual reproduction—by which I mean the generation of new life from (exactly) two complementary elements, one female, one male, (usually) through coitus—is established (if that is the right term) not by human decision, culture or tradition, but by nature; it is the natural way of all mammalian reproduction. By nature, each child has two complementary biological progenitors. Each child thus stems from and unites exactly two lineages. In natural generation, moreover, the precise genetic constitution of the resulting offspring is determined by a combination of nature and chance, not by human design: each human child shares the common natural human species genotype, each child is genetically (equally) kin to each (both) parent(s), yet each child is also genetically unique.

These biological truths about our origins foretell deep truths about our identity and about our human condition altogether. Every one of us is at once equally human, equally enmeshed in a particular familial nexus of origin, and equally individuated in our trajectory from birth to death—and, if all goes well, equally capable (despite our mortality) of participating, with a complementary other, in the very same renewal of such human possibility through procreation. Though less momentous than our common humanity, our genetic individuality is not humanly trivial. It shows itself forth in our distinctive appearance through which we are everywhere recognized; it is revealed in our "signature" marks of fingerprints and our self-recognizing immune system; it symbolizes and foreshadows exactly the unique, never-to-be-repeated character of each human life.

Human societies virtually everywhere have structured child-rearing responsibilities and systems of identity and relationship on the bases of these deep natural facts of begetting. The mysterious yet ubiquitous "love of one's own" is everywhere culturally exploited, to make sure that children are not just produced but well cared for and to create for everyone clear ties of meaning, belonging and obligation. But it is wrong to treat such naturally rooted social practices as mere cultural constructs (like left- or right-driving, or like burying or cremating the dead) that we can alter with little human cost. What would kinship be without its clear natural grounding? And what would identity be without kinship? We must resist those who have begun to refer to sexual reproduction as the "traditional method of reproduction," who would have us regard as merely traditional, and by implication arbitrary, what is in truth not only natural but most certainly profound.

Asexual reproduction, which produces "single-parent" offspring, is a radical departure from the natural human way, confounding all normal understandings of father, mother, sibling, grandparent, etc., and all moral relations tied thereto. It becomes even more of a radical departure when the resulting offspring is a clone derived not from an embryo, but from a mature adult to whom the clone would be an identical twin; and when the process occurs not by natural accident (as in natural twinning), but by deliberate human design and manipulation; and when the child's (or children's) genetic constitution is pre-selected by the parent(s) (or scientists). Accordingly, as we will see, cloning is vulnerable to three kinds of concerns and objections, related to these three points: cloning threatens confusion of identity and individuality, even in small-scale cloning; cloning represents a giant step (though not the first one) toward transforming procreation into manufacture, that is, toward the increasing depersonalization of the process of generation and, increasingly, toward the "production" of human children as artifacts, products of human will and design (what others have called the problem of "commodification" of new life); and cloning—like other forms of eugenic engineering of the next generation—represents a form of despotism of the cloners over the cloned, and thus (even in benevolent cases) represents a blatant violation of the inner meaning of parent—child relations, of what it means to have a child, of what it means to say "yes" to our own demise and "replacement." Before turning to these specific ethical objections, let me test my claim of the profundity of the natural way by taking up a challenge recently posed by a friend. What if the given natural human way of reproduction were asexual, and we now had to deal with a new technological innovation—artificially induced sexual dimorphism and the fusing of complementary gametes—whose inventors argued that sexual reproduction promised all sorts of advantages, including hybrid vigor and the creation of greatly increased individuality? Would one then be forced to defend natural asexuality because it was natural? Could one claim that it carried deep human meaning?

The response to this challenge broaches the ontological meaning of sexual reproduction. For it is impossible, I submit, for there to have been human life—or even higher forms of animal life—in the absence of sexuality and sexual reproduction. We find asexual reproduction only in the lowest forms of life: bacteria, algae, fungi, some lower invertebrates. Sexuality brings with it a new and enriched relationship to the world. Only sexual animals can seek and find complementary others with whom to pursue a goal that transcends their own existence. For a sexual being, the world is no longer an indifferent and largely homogeneous otherness, in part edible, in part dangerous. It also contains some very special and related and complementary beings, of the same kind but of opposite sex, toward whom one reaches out with special interest and intensity. In higher birds and mammals, the outward gaze keeps a lookout not only for food and predators, but also for prospective mates; the beholding of the many-splendored world is suffused with desire for union, the animal antecedent of human eros and the germ of sociality. Not by accident is the human animal both the sexiest animal—whose females do not go into heat but are receptive throughout the estrous cycle and whose males must therefore have greater sexual appetite and energy in order to reproduce successfully—and also the most aspiring, the most social, the most open and the most intelligent animal.

The soul-elevating power of sexuality is, at bottom, rooted in its strange connection to mortality, which it simultaneously accepts and tries to overcome. Asexual reproduction may be seen as a continuation of the activity of self-preservation. When one organism buds or divides to become two, the original being is (doubly) preserved, and nothing dies. Sexuality, by contrast, means perishability and serves replacement; of the two that come together to generate one soon will die. Sexual desire, in human beings as in animals, thus serves an end that is partly hidden from, and finally at odds with, the self-serving individual. Whether we know it or not, when we are sexually active we are voting with our genitalia for our own demise. The salmon swimming upstream to spawn and die tell the universal story: sex is bound up with death, to which it holds a partial answer in procreation.

The salmon and the other animals evince this truth blindly. Only the human being can understand what it means. As we learn so powerfully from the story of the Garden of Eden, our humanization is coincident with sexual self-consciousness, with the recognition of our sexual nakedness and all that it implies: shame at our needy incompleteness, unruly self-division and finitude; awe before the eternal; hope in the self-transcending possibilities of children and a relationship to the divine. In the sexually self-conscious animal, sexual desire can become eros, lust can become love. Sexual desire humanly regarded is thus sublimated into erotic longing for wholeness, completion and immortality, which drives us knowingly into the embrace and its generative fruit— as well as into all the higher human possibilities of deed, speech and song.

Through children, a good common to both husband and wife, male and female achieve some genuine unification (beyond the mere sexual "union," which fails to do so). The two become one through sharing generous (not needy) love for this third being as good. Flesh of their flesh, the child is the parents' own commingled being externalized, and given a separate and persisting existence. Unification is enhanced also by their commingled work of rearing. Providing an opening to the future beyond the grave, carrying not only our seed but also our names, our ways and our hopes that they will surpass us in goodness and happiness, children are a testament to the possibility of transcendence. Gender duality and sexual desire, which first draws our love upward and outside of ourselves, finally provide for the partial over-coming of the confinement and limitation of perishable embodiment altogether.

Human procreation, in sum, is not simply an activity of our rational wills. It is a more complete activity precisely because it engages us bodily, erotically and spiritually, as well as rationally. There is wisdom in the mystery of nature that has joined the pleasure of sex, the inarticulate longing for union, the communication of the loving embrace and the deep-seated and only partly articulate desire for children in the very activity by which we continue the chain of human existence and participate in the renewal of human possibility. Whether or not we know it, the severing of procreation from sex, love and intimacy is inherently dehumanizing, no matter how good the product.

We are now ready for the more specific objections to cloning.

The Perversities of Cloning

First, an important if formal objection: any attempt to clone a human being would constitute an unethical experiment upon the resulting child-to-be. As the animal experiments (frog and sheep) indicate, there are grave risks of mishaps and deformities. Moreover, because of what cloning means, one cannot presume a future cloned child's consent to be a clone, even a healthy one. Thus, ethically speaking, we cannot even get to know whether or not human cloning is feasible.

I understand, of course, the philosophical difficulty of trying to compare a life with defects against nonexistence. Several bioethicists, proud of their philosophical cleverness, use this conundrum to embarrass claims that one can injure a child in its conception, precisely because it is only thanks to that complained-of conception that the child is alive to complain. But common sense tells us that we have no reason to fear such philosophisms. For we surely know that people can harm and even maim children in the very act of conceiving them, say, by paternal transmission of the aids virus, maternal transmission of heroin dependence or, arguably, even by bringing them into being as bastards or with no capacity or willingness to look after them properly. And we believe that to do this intentionally, or even negligently, is inexcusable and clearly unethical.

The objection about the impossibility of presuming consent may even go beyond the obvious and sufficient point that a clonant, were he subsequently to be asked, could rightly resent having been made a clone. At issue are not just benefits and harms, but doubts about the very independence needed to give proper (even retroactive) consent, that is, not just the capacity to choose but the disposition and ability to choose freely and well. It is not at all clear to what extent a clone will truly be a moral agent. For, as we shall see, in the very fact of cloning, and of rearing him as a clone, his makers subvert the cloned child's independence, beginning with that aspect that comes from knowing that one was an unbidden surprise, a gift, to the world, rather than the designed result of someone's artful project.

Cloning creates serious issues of identity and individuality. The cloned person may experience concerns about his distinctive identity not only because he will be in genotype and appearance identical to another human being, but, in this case, because he may also be twin to the person who is his "father" or "mother"—if one can still call them that. What would be the psychic burdens of being the "child" or "parent" of your twin? The cloned individual, moreover, will be saddled with a genotype that has already lived. He will not be fully a surprise to the world.

People are likely always to compare his performances in life with that of his alter ego. True, his nurture and his circumstance in life will be different; genotype is not exactly destiny. Still, one must also expect parental and other efforts to shape this new life after the original—or at least to view the child with the original version always firmly in mind. Why else did they clone from the star basketball player, mathematician and beauty queen—or even dear old dad—in the first place?

Since the birth of Dolly, there has been a fair amount of doublespeak on this matter of genetic identity. Experts have rushed in to reassure the public that the clone would in no way be the same person, or have any confusions about his or her identity: as previously noted, they are pleased to point out that the clone of Mel Gibson would not be Mel Gibson. Fair enough. But one is short-changing the truth by emphasizing the additional importance of the intrauterine environment, rearing and social setting: genotype obviously matters plenty. That, after all, is the only reason to clone, whether human beings or sheep. The odds that clones of Wilt Chamberlain will play in the NBA are, I submit, infinitely greater than they are for clones of Robert Reich.

Curiously, this conclusion is supported, inadvertently, by the one ethical sticking point insisted on by friends of cloning: no cloning without the donor's consent. Though an orthodox liberal objection, it is in fact quite puzzling when it comes from people (such as Ruth Macklin) who also insist that genotype is not identity or individuality, and who deny that a child could reasonably complain about being made a genetic copy. If the clone of Mel Gibson would not be Mel Gibson, why should Mel Gibson have grounds to object that someone had been made his clone? We already allow researchers to use blood and tissue samples for research purposes of no benefit to their sources: my falling hair, my expectorations, my urine and even my biopsied tissues are "not me" and not mine. Courts have held that the profit gained from uses to which scientists put my discarded tissues do not legally belong to me. Why, then, no cloning without consent—including, I assume, no cloning from the body of someone who just died? What harm is done the donor, if genotype is "not me"? Truth to tell, the only powerful justification for objecting is that genotype really does have something to do with identity, and everybody knows it. If not, on what basis could Michael Jordan object that someone cloned "him," say, from cells taken from a "lost" scraped-off piece of his skin? The insistence on donor consent unwittingly reveals the problem of identity in all cloning.

Genetic distinctiveness not only symbolizes the uniqueness of each human life and the independence of its parents that each human child rightfully attains. It can also be an important support for living a worthy and dignified life. Such arguments apply with great force to any large-scale replication of human individuals. But they are sufficient, in my view, to rebut even the first attempts to clone a human being. One must never forget that these are human beings upon whom our eugenic or merely playful fantasies are to be enacted.

Troubled psychic identity (distinctiveness), based on all-too-evident genetic identity (sameness), will be made much worse by the utter confusion of social identity and kinship ties. For, as already noted, cloning radically confounds lineage and social relations, for "offspring" as for "parents." As bioethicist James Nelson has pointed out, a female child cloned from her "mother" might develop a desire for a relationship to her "father," and might under-

standably seek out the father of her "mother," who is after all also her biological twin sister. Would "grandpa,"
who thought his paternal duties were concluded, be
pleased to discover that the clonant looked to him for
paternal attention and support?

Social identity and social ties of relationship and responsibility are widely connected to, and supported by,
biological kinship. Social taboos on incest (and adultery)
everywhere serve to keep clear who is related to whom
(and especially which child belongs to which parents),
as well as to avoid confounding the social identity of parent and child (or brother and sister) with the social identity of lovers, spouses and co-parents. True, social identity is altered by adoption (but as a matter of the best
interest of already living children: we do not deliberately
produce children for adoption). True, artificial insemination and in vitro fertilization with donor sperm, or
whole embryo donation, are in some way forms of "prenatal adoption"—a not altogether unproblematic practice.
Even here, though, there is in each case (as in all sexual
reproduction) a known male source of sperm and a
known single female source of egg—a genetic father and
a genetic mother—should anyone care to know (as
adopted children often do) who is genetically related to
whom.

In the case of cloning, however, there is but one "parent." The usually sad situation of the "single-parent child"
is here deliberately planned, and with a vengeance. In
the case of self-cloning, the "offspring" is, in addition,
one's twin; and so the dreaded result of incest—to be
parent to one's sibling—is here brought about deliberately, albeit without any act of coitus. Moreover, all other
relationships will be confounded. What will father, grandfather, aunt, cousin, sister mean? Who will bear what
ties and what burdens? What sort of social identity will

someone have with one whole side—"father's" or "mother's"—necessarily excluded? It is no answer to say that our society, with its high incidence of divorce, re-marriage, adoption, extramarital childbearing and the rest, already confounds lineage and confuses kinship and responsibility for children (and everyone else), unless one also wants to argue that this is, for children, a prefer-able state of affairs.

Human cloning would also represent a giant step to-ward turning begetting into making, procreation into manufacture (literally, something "handmade"), a pro-cess already begun with in vitro fertilization and genetic testing of embryos. With cloning, not only is the process in hand, but the total genetic blueprint of the cloned in-dividual is selected and determined by the human arti-sans. To be sure, subsequent development will take place according to natural processes; and the resulting chil-dren will still be recognizably human. But we here would be taking a major step into making man himself simply another one of the man-made things. Human nature becomes merely the last part of nature to succumb to the technological project, which turns all of nature into raw material at human disposal, to be homogenized by our rationalized technique according to the subjective prejudices of the day. How does begetting differ from making? In natural procreation, human beings come to-gether, complementarily male and female, to give exist-ence to another being who is formed, exactly as we were, by what we are: living, hence perishable, hence aspiringly erotic, human beings. In clonal reproduction, by contrast, and in the more advanced forms of manufacture to which it leads, we give existence to a being not by what we are but by what we intend and design. As with any product of our making, no matter how excellent, the artificer stands above it, not as an equal but as a superior, transcending it by his will and creative prowess. Scientists who clone animals make it perfectly clear that they are engaged in instrumental making; the animals are, from the start, designed as means to serve rational human purposes. In human cloning, scientists and prospective "parents" would be adopting the same technocratic mentality to human children: human children would be their artifacts.

Such an arrangement is profoundly dehumanizing, no matter how good the product. Mass-scale cloning of the same individual makes the point vividly; but the violation of human equality, freedom, and dignity are present even in a single planned clone. And procreation dehumanized into manufacture is further degraded by commodification, a virtually inescapable result of allowing babymaking to proceed under the banner of commerce. Genetic and reproductive biotechnology companies are already growth industries, but they will go into commercial orbit once the Human Genome Project nears completion. Supply will create enormous demand. Even before the capacity for human cloning arrives, established companies will have invested in the harvesting of eggs from ovaries obtained at autopsy or through ovarian surgery, practiced embryonic genetic alteration, and initiated the stockpiling of prospective donor tissues. Through the rental of surrogate-womb services, and through the buying and selling of tissues and embryos, priced according to the merit of the donor, the commodification of nascent human life will be unstoppable.

Finally, and perhaps most important, the practice of human cloning by nuclear transfer—like other anticipated forms of genetic engineering of the next generation—would enshrine and aggravate a profound and mischievous misunderstanding of the meaning of having children and of the parent—child relationship. When a couple now chooses to procreate, the partners are saying yes to the emergence of new life in its novelty, saying yes not only to having a child but also, tacitly, to having whatever child this child turns out to be. In accepting our finitude and opening ourselves to our replacement, we are tacitly confessing the limits of our control. In this ubiquitous way of nature, embracing the future by procreating means precisely that we are relinquishing our grip, in the very activity of taking up our own share in what we hope will be the immortality of human life and the human species. This means that our children are not our children: they are not our property, not our possessions. Neither are they supposed to live our lives for us, or anyone else's life but their own. To be sure, we seek to guide them on their way, imparting to them not just life but nurturing, love, and a way of life; to be sure, they bear our hopes that they will live fine and flourishing lives, enabling us in small measure to transcend our own limitations. Still, their genetic distinctiveness and independence are the natural foreshadowing of the deep truth that they have their own and never-before-enacted life to live. They are sprung from a past, but they take an uncharted course into the future.

Much harm is already done by parents who try to live vicariously through their children. Children are sometimes compelled to fulfill the broken dreams of unhappy parents; John Doe Jr. or the III is under the burden of having to live up to his forebear's name. Still, if most parents have hopes for their children, cloning parents will have expectations. In cloning, such overbearing parents take at the start a decisive step that contradicts the entire meaning of the open and forward-looking nature of parent—child relations. The child is given a genotype that has already lived, with full expectation that this blueprint of a past life ought to be controlling of the life that is to come. Cloning is inherently despotic, for it seeks to make one's children (or someone else's children) after one's own image (or an image of one's choosing) and their future according to one's will. In some cases, the despotism may be mild and benevolent. In other cases, it will be mischievous and downright tyrannical. But despotism—the control of another through one's will—it inevitably will be.

Meeting Some Objections

The defenders of cloning, of course, are not wittingly friends of despotism. Indeed, they regard themselves mainly as friends of freedom: the freedom of individuals to reproduce, the freedom of scientists and inventors to discover and devise and to foster "progress" in genetic knowledge and technique. They want large-scale cloning only for animals, but they wish to preserve cloning as a human option for exercising our "right to reproduce"—our right to have children, and children with "desirable genes." As law professor John Robertson points out, under our "right to reproduce" we already practice early forms of unnatural, artificial and extramarital reproduction, and we already practice early forms of eugenic choice. For this reason, he argues, cloning is no big deal.

We have here a perfect example of the logic of the slippery slope, and the slippery way in which it already works in this area. Only a few years ago, slippery slope arguments were used to oppose artificial insemination and in vitro fertilization using unrelated sperm donors. Principles used to justify these practices, it was said, will be used to justify more artificial and more eugenic practices, including cloning. Not so, the defenders retorted, since we can make the necessary distinctions. And now, without even a gesture at making the necessary distinctions, the continuity of practice is held by itself to be justificatory.

The principle of reproductive freedom as currently enunciated by the proponents of cloning logically embraces the ethical acceptability of sliding down the entire rest of the slope—to producing children ectogenetically from sperm to term (should it become feasible) and to producing children whose entire genetic makeup will be the product of parental eugenic planning and choice. If reproductive freedom means the right to have a child of one's own choosing, by whatever means, it knows and accepts no limits.

But, far from being legitimated by a "right to reproduce," the emergence of techniques of assisted reproduction and genetic engineering should compel us to reconsider the meaning and limits of such a putative right. In truth, a "right to reproduce" has always been a peculiar and problematic notion. Rights generally belong to individuals, but this is a right which (before cloning) no one can exercise alone. Does the right then inhere only in couples? Only in married couples? Is it a (woman's) right to carry or deliver or a right (of one or more parents) to nurture and rear? Is it a right to have your own biological child? Is it a right only to attempt reproduction, or a right also to succeed? Is it a right to acquire the baby of one's choice?

The assertion of a negative "right to reproduce" certainly makes sense when it claims protection against state interference with procreative liberty, say, through a program of compulsory sterilization. But surely it cannot be the basis of a tort claim against nature, to be made good by technology, should free efforts at natural procreation fail.

Some insist that the right to reproduce embraces also the right against state interference with the free use of all technological means to obtain a child. Yet such a position cannot be sustained: for reasons having to do with the means employed, any community may rightfully prohibit surrogate pregnancy, or polygamy, or the sale of babies to infertile couples, without violating anyone's basic human "right to reproduce." When the exercise of a previously innocuous freedom now involves or impinges on troublesome practices that the original freedom never was intended to reach, the general presumption of liberty needs to be reconsidered.

We do indeed already practice negative eugenic selection, through genetic screening and prenatal diagnosis. Yet our practices are governed by a norm of health. We seek to prevent the birth of children who suffer from known (serious) genetic diseases. When and if gene therapy becomes possible, such diseases could then be treated, in utero or even before implantation—I have no ethical objection in principle to such a practice (though I have some practical worries), precisely because it serves the medical goal of healing existing individuals. But therapy, to be therapy, implies not only an existing "patient." It also implies a norm of health. In this respect, even germline gene "therapy," though practiced not on a human being but on egg and sperm, is less radical than cloning, which is in no way therapeutic. But once one blurs the distinction between health promotion and genetic enhancement, between so-called negative and positive eugenics, one opens the door to all future eugenic designs. "To make sure that a child will be healthy and have good chances in life": this is Robertson's principle, and owing to its latter clause it is an utterly elastic principle, with no boundaries. Being over eight feet tall will likely produce some very good chances in life, and so will having the looks of Marilyn Monroe, and so will a genius-level intelligence.

Proponents want us to believe that there are legitimate uses of cloning that can be distinguished from illegitimate uses, but by their own principles no such limits can be found. (Nor could any such limits be enforced in practice.) Reproductive freedom, as they understand it, is governed solely by the subjective wishes of the parents-to-be (plus the avoidance of bodily harm to the child). The sentimentally appealing case of the childless married couple is, on these grounds, indistinguishable from the case of an individual (married or not) who would like to clone someone famous or talented, living or dead. Further, the principle here endorsed justifies not only cloning but, indeed, all future artificial attempts to create (manufacture) "perfect" babies.

A concrete example will show how, in practice no less than in principle, the so-called innocent case will merge with, or even turn into, the more troubling ones. In practice, the eager parents-to-be will necessarily be subject to the tyranny of expertise. Consider an infertile married couple, she lacking eggs or he lacking sperm, that wants a child of their (genetic) own, and propose to clone either husband or wife. The scientist-physician (who is also co-owner of the cloning company) points out the likely difficulties—a cloned child is not really their (genetic) child, but the child of only one of them; this imbalance may produce strains on the marriage; the child might suffer identity confusion; there is a risk of perpetuating the cause of sterility; and so on—and he also points out the advantages of choosing a donor nucleus. Far better than a child of their own would be a child of their own choosing. Touting his own expertise in selecting healthy and talented donors, the doctor presents the couple with his latest catalog containing the pictures, the health records and the accomplishments of his stable of cloning donors, samples of whose tissues are in his deep freeze. Why not, dearly beloved, a more perfect baby?

The "perfect baby," of course, is the project not of the infertility doctors, but of the eugenic scientists and their supporters. For them, the paramount right is not the so-called right to reproduce but what biologist Bentley Glass called, a quarter of a century ago, "the right of every child to be born with a sound physical and mental constitution, based on a sound genotype...the inalienable right to a sound heritage." But to secure this right, and to achieve the requisite quality control over new human life, human conception and gestation will need to be brought fully into the bright light of the laboratory, beneath which it can be fertilized, nourished, pruned, weeded, watched, inspected, prodded, pinched, cajoled, injected, tested, rated, graded, approved, stamped, wrapped, sealed and delivered. There is no other way to produce the perfect baby.

Yet we are urged by proponents of cloning to forget about the science fiction scenarios of laboratory manufacture and multiple-copied clones, and to focus only on the homely cases of infertile couples exercising their reproductive rights. But why, if the single cases are so innocent, should multiplying their performance be so off-putting? (Similarly, why do others object to people making money off this practice, if the practice itself is perfectly acceptable?) When we follow the sound ethical principle of universalizing our choice—"would it be right if everyone cloned a Wilt Chamberlain (with his consent, of course)? Would it be right if everyone decided to practice asexual reproduction?"—we discover what is wrong with these seemingly innocent cases. The so-called science fiction cases make vivid the meaning of what looks to us, mistakenly, to be benign.

Though I recognize certain continuities between cloning and, say, in vitro fertilization, I believe that cloning differs in essential and important ways. Yet those who disagree should be reminded that the "continuity" argument cuts both ways. Sometimes we establish bad precedents, and discover that they were bad only when we follow their inexorable logic to places we never meant to go. Can the defenders of cloning show us today how, on their principles, we will be able to see producing babies ("perfect babies") entirely in the laboratory or exercising full control over their genotypes (including so-called enhancement) as ethically different, in any essential way, from present forms of assisted reproduction? Or are they willing to admit, despite their attachment to the principle of continuity, that the complete obliteration of "mother" or "father," the complete depersonalization of procreation, the complete manufacture of human beings and the complete genetic control of one generation over the next would be ethically problematic and essentially different from current forms of assisted reproduction? If so, where and how will they draw the line, and why? I draw it at cloning, for all the reasons given.

Ban the Cloning of Humans

What, then, should we do? We should declare that human cloning is unethical in itself and dangerous in its likely consequences. In so doing, we shall have the backing of the overwhelming majority of our fellow Americans, and of the human race, and (I believe) of most practicing scientists. Next, we should do all that we can to prevent the cloning of human beings. We should do this by means of an international legal ban if possible, and by a unilateral national ban, at a minimum. Scientists may secretly undertake to violate such a law, but they will be deterred by not being able to stand up proudly to claim the credit for their technological bravado and success. Such a ban on clonal babymaking, moreover, will not harm the progress of basic genetic science and technology. On the contrary, it will reassure the public that scientists are happy to proceed without violating the deep ethical norms and intuitions of the human community.

This still leaves the vexed question about laboratory research using early embryonic human clones, specially created only for such research purposes, with no intention to implant them into a uterus. There is no question that such research holds great promise for gaining fundamental knowledge about normal (and abnormal) differentiation, and for developing tissue lines for transplantation that might be used, say, in treating leukemia or in repairing brain or spinal cord injuries-to mention just a few of the conceivable benefits. Still, unrestricted clonal embryo research will surely make the production of living human clones much more likely. Once the genies put the cloned embryos into the bottles, who can strictly control where they go (especially in the absence of legal prohibitions against implanting them to produce a child)?

I appreciate the potentially great gains in scientific knowledge and medical treatment available from embryo research, especially with cloned embryos. At the same time, I have serious reservations about creating human embryos for the sole purpose of experimentation. There is something deeply repugnant and fundamentally transgressive about such a utilitarian treatment of prospective human life. This total, shameless exploitation is worse, in my opinion, than the "mere" destruction of nascent life. But I see no added objections, as a matter of principle, to creating and using cloned early embryos for research purposes, beyond the objections that I might raise to doing so with embryos produced sexually.

And yet, as a matter of policy and prudence, any opponent of the manufacture of cloned humans must, I think, in the end oppose also the creating of cloned human embryos. Frozen embryonic clones (belonging to whom?) can be shuttled around without detection. Commercial ventures in human cloning will be developed without adequate oversight. In order to build a fence around the law, prudence dictates that one oppose—for this reason alone—all production of cloned human embryos, even for research purposes. We should allow all cloning research on animals to go forward, but the only safe trench that we can dig across the slippery slope, I suspect, is to insist on the inviolable distinction between animal and human cloning.

Some readers, and certainly most scientists, will not accept such prudent restraints, since they desire the benefits of research. They will prefer, even in fear and trembling, to allow human embryo cloning research to go forward.

Very well. Let us test them. If the scientists want to be taken seriously on ethical grounds, they must at the very least agree that embryonic research may proceed if and only if it is preceded by an absolute and effective ban on all attempts to implant into a uterus a cloned human embryo (cloned from an adult) to produce a living child. Absolutely no permission for the former without the latter.

The National Bioethics Advisory Commission's recommendations regarding this matter should be watched with the greatest care. Yielding to the wishes of the scientists, the commission will almost surely recommend that cloning human embryos for research be permitted. To allay public concern, it will likely also call for a temporary moratorium—not a legislative ban—on implanting cloned embryos to make a child, at least until such time as cloning techniques will have been perfected and rendered "safe" (precisely through the permitted research with cloned embryos). But the call for a moratorium rather than a legal ban would be a moral and a practical failure. Morally, this ethics commission would (at best) be waffling on the main ethical question, by refusing to declare the production of human clones unethical (or ethical). Practically, a moratorium on implantation cannot provide even the minimum protection needed to prevent the production of cloned humans.

Opponents of cloning need therefore to be vigilant. Indeed, no one should be willing even to consider a recommendation to allow the embryo research to proceed unless it is accompanied by a call for prohibiting implantation and until steps are taken to make such a prohibition effective.

Technically, the National Bioethics Advisory Commission can advise the president only on federal policy, especially federal funding policy. But given the seriousness of the matter at hand, and the grave public concern that goes beyond federal funding, the commission should take a broader view. (If it doesn't, Congress surely will.) Given that most assisted reproduction occurs in the private sector, it would be cowardly and insufficient for the commission to say, simply, "no federal funding" for such practices. It would be disingenuous to argue that we should allow federal funding so that we would then be able to regulate the practice; the private sector will not be bound by such regulations. Far better, for virtually everyone concerned, would be to distinguish between research on embryos and baby-making, and to call for a complete national and international ban (effected by legislation and treaty) of the latter, while allowing the former to proceed (at least in private laboratories).

The proposal for such a legislative ban is without American precedent, at least in technological matters, though the British and others have banned cloning of human beings, and we ourselves ban incest, polygamy and other forms of "reproductive freedom." Needless to say, working out the details of such a ban, especially a global one, would be tricky, what with the need to develop appropriate sanctions for violators. Perhaps such a ban will prove ineffective; perhaps it will eventually be shown to have been a mistake. But it would at least place the burden of practical proof where it belongs: on the proponents of this horror, requiring them to show very clearly what great social or medical good can be had only by the cloning of human beings.

We Americans have lived by, and prospered under, a rosy optimism about scientific and technological progress. The technological imperative—if it can be done, it must be done—has probably served us well, though we should admit that there is no accurate method for weighing benefits and harms. Even when, as in the cases of environmental pollution, urban decay or the lingering deaths that are the unintended by-products of medical success, we recognize the unwelcome outcomes of technological advance, we remain confident in our ability to fix all the "bad" consequences—usually by means of still newer and better technologies. How successful we can continue to be in such post hoc repairing is at least an open question. But there is very good reason for shifting the paradigm around, at least regarding those technological interventions into the human body and mind that will surely effect fundamental (and likely irreversible) changes in human nature, basic human relationships, and what it means to be a human being. Here we surely should not be willing to risk everything in the naive hope that, should things go wrong, we can later set them right.

The president's call for a moratorium on human cloning has given us an important opportunity. In a truly unprecedented way, we can strike a blow for the human control of the technological project, for wisdom, prudence and human dignity. The prospect of human cloning, so repulsive to contemplate, is the occasion for deciding whether we shall be slaves of unregulated progress, and ultimately its artifacts, or whether we shall remain free human beings who guide our technique toward the enhancement of human dignity. If we are to seize the occasion, we must, as the late Paul Ramsey wrote, raise the ethical questions with a serious and not a frivolous conscience. A man of frivolous conscience announces that there are ethical quandaries ahead that we must urgently consider before the future catches up with us. By this he often means that we need to devise a new ethics that will provide the rationalization for doing in the future what men are bound to do because of new actions and interventions science will have made possible. In contrast a man of serious conscience means to say in raising urgent ethical questions that there may be some things that men should never do. The good things that men do can be made complete only by the things they refuse to do.

Ronald Bailey

What Exactly Is Wrong With Cloning People?

By now everyone knows that Scottish biotechnologists have cloned a sheep. The researchers say that in principle it should be possible to clone humans. That prospect has apparently frightened a lot of people, and quite a few of them are calling for regulators to ban cloning since we cannot predict what the consequences of it will be.

President Clinton rushed to ban federal funding of human cloning research and asked privately funded researchers to stop such research at least until the National Bioethics Advisory Commission issues a report on the ethical implications of human cloning. The commission, composed of scientists, lawyers, and ethicists, was appointed last year to advise the federal government on the ethical questions posed by biotechnology research and new medical therapies. Its report is now due in May. But Sen. Christopher Bond (R-Mo.) isn't waiting around for the commission's recommendations; he's already made up his mind. Bond introduced a bill to ban the federal funding of human cloning or human cloning research. "I want to send a clear signal," said the senator, "that this is something we cannot and should not tolerate. This type of research on humans is morally reprehensible." Carl Feldbaum, president of the Biotechnology Industry Organization, hurriedly said that human cloning should be immediately banned. Perennial Luddite Jeremy Rifkin grandly pronounced that cloning "throws every convention, every historical tradition, up for grabs." At the putative opposite end of the political spectrum, conservative columnist George Will chimed in: "What if the great given—a human being is a product of the union of a man and woman—is no longer a given?"

In addition to these pundits and politicians, a whole raft of bioethicists declared that they, too, oppose human cloning. Daniel Callahan of the Hastings Center said flat out: "The message must be simple and decisive: The human species doesn't need cloning." George Annas of Boston University agreed: "Most people who have thought about this believe it is not a reasonable use and should not be allowed... This is not a case of scientific freedom vs. the regulators." Given all of the brouhaha, you'd think it was crystal clear why cloning humans is unethical. But what exactly is wrong with it? Which ethical principle does cloning violate? Stealing? Lying? Coveting? Murdering? What? Most of the arguments against cloning amount to little more than a reformulation of the old familiar refrain of Luddites everywhere: "If God had meant for man to fly, he would have given us wings. And if God had meant for man to clone, he would have given us spores." Ethical reasoning requires more than that.

What would a clone be? Well, he or she would be a complete human being who happens to share the same genes with another person. Today, we call such people identical twins. To my knowledge no one has argued that twins are immoral. Of course, cloned twins would not be the same age. But it is hard to see why this age difference might present an ethical problem—or give clones a different moral status. "You should treat all clones like you would treat all monozygous [identical] twins or triplets," concludes Dr. H. Tristam Engelhardt, a professor of medicine at Baylor and a philosopher at Rice University. "That's it." It would be unethical to treat a human clone as anything other than a human being. If this principle is observed, he argues, all the other "ethical" problems for a secular society essentially disappear. John Fletcher, a professor of biomedical ethics in the medical school at the University of Virginia, agrees: "I don't believe that there is any intrinsic reason why cloning should not be done."

Let's take a look at a few of the scenarios that opponents of human cloning have sketched out. Some argue that clones would undermine the uniqueness of each human being. "Can individuality, identity and dignity be severed from genetic distinctiveness, and from belief in a person's open future?", asks George Will. Will and others have apparently fallen under the sway of what Fletcher calls "genetic essentialism." Fletcher says polls indicate that some 30 percent to 40 percent of Americans are genetic essentialists, who believe that genes almost completely determine who a person is. But a person who is a clone would live in a very different world from that of his genetic predecessor. With greatly divergent experiences, their brains would be wired differently. After all, even twins who grow up together are separate people—distinct individuals with different personalities and certainly no lack of Will's "individuality, identity and dignity." In addition, a clone that grew from one person's

DNA inserted in another person's host egg would pick up "maternal factors" from the proteins in that egg, altering its development. Physiological differences between the womb of the original and host mothers could also affect the clone's development. In no sense, therefore, would or could a clone be a "carbon copy" of his or her predecessor.

What about a rich jerk who is so narcissistic that he wants to clone himself so that he can give all his wealth to himself? First, he will fail. His clone is simply not the same person that he is. The clone may be a jerk too, but he will be his own individual jerk. Nor is Jerk Sr.'s action unprecedented. Today, rich people, and regular people too, make an effort to pass along some wealth to their children when they die. People will their estates to their children not only because they are connected by bonds of love but also because they have genetic ties. The principle is no different for clones.

Senator Bond and others worry about a gory scenario in which clones would be created to provide spare parts, such as organs that would not be rejected by the predecessor's immune system. "The creation of a human being should not be for spare parts or as a replacement," says Bond. I agree. The simple response to this scenario is: Clones are people. You must treat them like people. We don't forcibly take organs from one twin in and give them to the other. Why would we do that in the case of clones?

The technology of cloning may well allow biotechnologists to develop animals that will grow human-compatible organs for transplant. Cloning is likely to be first used to create animals that produce valuable therapeutic hormones, enzymes, and proteins.

But what about cloning exceptional human beings? George Will put it this way: "Suppose a cloned Michael

Jordan, age 8, preferred violin to basketball? Is it imaginable? If so, would it be tolerable to the cloner?" Yes, it is imaginable, and the cloner would just have to put up with violin recitals. Kids are not commercial property— slavery was abolished some time ago. We all know about Little League fathers and stage mothers who push their kids, but given the stubborn nature of individuals, those parents rarely manage to make kids stick forever to something they hate. A ban on cloning wouldn't abolish pushy parents.

One putatively scientific argument against cloning has been raised. As a National Public Radio commentator who opposes cloning quipped, "Diversity isn't just politically correct, it's good science." Sexual reproduction seems to have evolved for the purpose of staying ahead of ever-mutating pathogens in a continuing arms race. Novel combinations of genes created through sexual reproduction help immune systems devise defenses against rapidly evolving germs, viruses, and parasites. The argument against cloning says that if enough human beings were cloned, pathogens would likely adapt and begin to get the upper hand, causing widespread disease. The analogy often cited is what happens when a lot of farmers all adopt the same corn hybrid. If the hybrid is highly susceptible to a particular bug, then the crop fails.

That warning may have some validity for cloned livestock, which may well have to live in environments protected from infectious disease. But it is unlikely that there will be millions of clones of one person. Genomic diversity would still be the rule for humanity. There might be more identical twins, triplets, etc., but unless there are millions of clones of one person, raging epidemics sweeping through hordes of human beings with identical genomes seem very unlikely. But even if someday millions of clones of one person existed, who is to say that novel technologies wouldn't by then be able to control human pathogens? After all, it wasn't genetic diversity that caused typhoid, typhus, polio, or measles to all but disappear in the United States. It was modern sanitation and modern medicine.

There's no reason to think that a law against cloning would make much difference anyway. "It's such a simple technology, it won't be ban-able," says Engelhardt. "That's why God made offshore islands, so that anybody who wants to do it can have it done." Cloning would simply go underground and be practiced without legal oversight. This means that people who turned to cloning would not have recourse to the law to enforce contracts, ensure proper standards, and hold practitioners liable for malpractice.

Who is likely to be making the decisions about whether human cloning should be banned? When President Clinton appointed the National Bioethics Advisory Commission last year, his stated hope was that such a commission could come up with some sort of societal consensus about what we should do with cloning. The problem with achieving and imposing such a consensus is that Americans live in a large number of disparate moral communities. "If you call up the Pope in Rome, do you think he'll hesitate?" asks Engelhardt. "He'll say, 'No, that's not the way that Christians reproduce.' And if you live Christianity of a Roman Catholic sort, that'll be a good enough answer. And if you're fully secular, it won't be a relevant answer at all. And if you're in-between, you'll feel kind of generally guilty."

Engelhardt questions the efficacy of such commissions: "Understand why all such commissions are frauds. Imagine a commission that really represented our political and moral diversity. It would have as its members Jesse Jackson, Jesse Helms, Mother Teresa, Bella Abzug, Phyllis

Schafly. And they would all talk together, and they would never agree on anything... Presidents and Congresses rig—manufacture fraudulently—a consensus by choosing people to serve on such commissions who already more or less agree... Commissions are created to manufacture the fraudulent view that we have a consensus."

Unlike Engelhardt, Fletcher believes that the National Bioethics Advisory Commission can be useful, but he acknowledges that "all of the commissions in the past have made recommendations that have had their effects in federal regulations. So they are a source eventually of regulations." The bioethics field is littered with ill-advised bans, starting in the mid-1970s with the two-year moratorium on recombining DNA and including the law against selling organs and blood and Clinton's recent prohibition on using human embryos in federally funded medical research.

As history shows, many bioethicists succumb to the thrill of exercising power by saying no. Simply leaving people free to make their own mistakes will get a bioethicist no perks, no conferences, and no power. Bioethicists aren't the ones suffering, the ones dying, and the ones who are infertile, so they do not bear the consequences of their bans. There certainly is a role for bioethicists as advisers, explaining to individuals what the ramifications of their decisions might be. But bioethicists should have no ability to stop individuals from making their own decisions, once they feel that they have enough information.

Ultimately, biotechnology is no different from any other technology—humans must be allowed to experiment with it in order to find its best uses and, yes, to make and learn from mistakes in using it. Trying to decide in advance how a technology should be used is futile. The smartest commission ever assembled simply doesn't have the creativity of millions of human beings trying to live the best lives that they can by trying out and developing new technologies.

So why is the impulse to ban cloning so strong? "We haven't gotten over the nostalgia for the Inquisition," concludes Engelhardt. "We are people who are post-modernist with a nostalgia for the Middle Ages. We still want the state to have the power of the Inquisition to enforce good public morals on everyone, whether they want it or not."

Susan M. Wolf

Ban Cloning?
Why NBAC Is Wrong

In its report on cloning, NBAC recommended a ban of unprecedented scope.[1] Based on commission consensus that human cloning would currently be unsafe, NBAC called for congressional prohibition throughout the public and private sectors of all somatic cell nuclear transfer with the intent of creating a child. President Clinton promptly responded by proposing legislation to enact such a ban for five years.

NBAC was wrong to urge a ban. Cloning undoubtedly warrants regulation. But the ban proposed will not yield the sort of regulation required. Instead, it will reduce cloning to a political football in Congress, raise serious constitutional problems, and chill important research. NBAC defends its ban as a limited one, prohibiting somatic cell nuclear transfer (not all forms of cloning), when used to create a child (not in research), and for three to five years (not indefinitely). A congressional ban, however, is likely to be far broader.

NBAC erred by taking cloning out of context. Like any technology, cloning needs to be safe before used. But that counsels regulation, not a ban, which merely slows development of safe procedures. And cloning demands we deal with issues beyond safety on which NBAC achieved no consensus, issues bound up in the ethics of human experimentation and reproductive technologies. A better approach would extend human subjects protection into the private sphere and regulate reproductive technologies effectively, with a central advisory body for novel issues such as cloning. By failing to tackle private research and reproductive technologies, NBAC avoided the real job and instead proposed an isolated and misguided response to cloning.

The Regulatory Challenge

Human cloning clearly requires regulation. Indeed, some regulation already applies. President Clinton has barred all federal funds for cloning, covering both research and clinical application.[2] Earlier prohibitions on the use of federal money to create human embryos for research purposes would also impede cloning research with federal funds.[3] And federal regulations protecting human subjects would seem to block cloning in research covered by those regulations because cloning remains unsafe, at least for now.[4] This leaves two regulatory gaps that properly troubled NBAC: private sector research outside federal oversight and private clinical activity, especially infertility programs using reproductive technologies.

But by responding to these worries with a congressional ban, NBAC missed the target. Protecting human subjects in private research and regulating reproductive technologies are both long overdue. A ban on cloning just suppresses one technology, while these two systemic problems guarantee the development of other technologies in need of regulation. Some would argue that somatic cell cloning deserves to be singled out as the most threatening possibility. But that assumes a conclusion we have not had time to reach, that Dolly-style cloning raises radically more difficult problems than, for example, cloning by embryo splitting (which can also lead to a delayed twin, with cryopreservation).[5]

NBAC admits that protecting human subjects in private research offers advantages over a ban on cloning (pp. 99–100). Yet the commission balks. It first complains that extending human subjects protections requires legislation and thus delay. But Senator John Glenn (D., OH) has already proposed legislation[6] and enacting a congressional ban involves delay as well. The commission further complains that human subjects legislation would rely on decentralized institutional review boards (IRBs). But others have suggested creating a national IRB for novel questions,[7] and NBAC ought to be considering this among other improvements in human subjects protection anyway. Moreover, IRBs are actually part of a larger mechanism providing centralized federal agency review when needed. The commission's final objection is that human subjects legislation would not reach beyond research activity to clinical use, as in infertility clinics. But this merely counsels supplemental regulation of those clinics.

NBAC's report, in fact, suffers from minimal consideration of infertility, programs and reproductive technologies.[8] The commission acknowledges that the federal statute requiring fertility crime reporting would seem to require reporting of cloning (p. 88).[9] But it ignores the broader issues plaguing reproductive technologies: the inadequacy of federal and state regulation, state-to-state inconsistencies, and conflicts of interest inherent in industry self-regulation. The report overlooks the burgeoning literature on those problems and, indeed, reflects little input from infertility programs.[10]

Instead of developing a legal response to cloning that addresses the core problems of private research and underregulated reproductive technologies, NBAC simply called for a ban of cloning itself. That skirts the central problems, while adding new ones.

The Error in a Ban

No other bioethics controversy has been addressed by a ban as broad as the one NBAC advocates and the president now proposes. Its prohibition reaches all public and private institutions, whether or not federal money is involved or FDA approval is required. Limits on the use of federal money are common, but federal prohibitions on medical and scientific work in the private sector are not.

Moreover, the ban threatens substantial damage. The president's bill prohibits "somatic cell nuclear transfer with the intent of introducing the product of that transfer into a woman's womb or in any other way creating a human being," and would impose significant fines. Though NBAC insists it does not want to tamper with research in the private sphere, merely babymaking, this ban cannot avoid the former. The policing necessary to enforce the ban will require intruding into labs and monitoring the 'intent' of scientists. Research will thus be chilled. It will be chilled further by the vagueness of a prohibition that is meant to ban baby-making, but seems to reach intent to 'transfer,' even if a researcher knows no child will result, plus the intent to create a human being in if any unspecified "other way."

Beyond the ban's breadth and potential damage, NBAC

and the president have placed this weapon in the wrong hands. The ban is to be imposed by Congress itself, not a regulatory body poised to respond to developments in the technology. That turns cloning into a political football. Past congressional brawls over the related areas of embryo research and abortion predict the same for cloning. This means that although the president and NBAC would ban private-sector application not research, Congress is likely to ban research too, as one of the pending federal bills seems to propose.[11] And though the president and commission would ban only somatic cell nuclear transfer, Congress may well include other technologies such as embryo splitting (which, after all, is another form of cloning and may also produce a delayed twin). Two of the three federal bills pending appear to do exactly that.[12] But embryo splitting may allow a woman undergoing in vitro fertilization to avoid repeated exposure to drugs inducing superovulation, which may reduce her risk of ovarian cancer later in life. Finally, though NBAC and the president would limit the ban to five years, there is little reason to expect Congress to develop the political bravery to lift the ban at that point.

The ban proposed thus raises serious constitutional questions. The ban's prohibition of somatic cell nuclear transfer with the wrong intent and its unavoidable chilling effect on research may infringe freedom of scientific inquiry in violation of the First Amendment.[13] And the ban as proposed by the president may well be unconstitutionally vague in its statement of the prohibited intent.[14] The ban may also represent an unconstitutional infringement on the procreative liberty of infertile couples.[15] In any case, it may exceed the limits of federal power, especially since the regulation of health and clinical practice has traditionally fallen to the states.[16]

Beyond the constitutional questions, a ban at this point

is bad policy. NBAC's advocacy of this ban contradicts its call for careful study and debate in our pluralistic society. With only ninety days to report on cloning, NBAC admits more analysis is needed. Yet by calling now for a ban that is likely to sweep more broadly and last much longer than NBAC wants, the commission has in effect already yielded to those who claim cloning is wrong in all cases and for the indefinite future. This ends the important deliberation, embraces one absolutist moral perspective, and writes it into law.[17]

NBAC defends the ban as a safety measure preventing harm to potential children. But that reasoning does not justify this result. Indeed, the ban may well cause harm. A ban that inevitably chills research will prevent the development of a cloning technology that is physically safe for the children it produces. Some may protest that even physically safe cloning may threaten psychological harms. But that claim is purely speculative and can ground regulation and research, but not a ban; cloning may in fact save children from psychological difficulties involved in having an anonymous genetic parent through donor egg or sperm.

Moreover, a ban may cause harm to infertile couples, especially if it hardens into an indefinite prohibition. After all, cloning offers potential benefit in infertility cases. NBAC points to a couple each carrying a recessive gene for a serious disorder. Cloning would allow them to avoid conceiving an embryo with the disorder and facing selective abortion. In another case, a woman might carry a dominant gene for a disorder. Cloning would permit her to avoid genetic contribution from an egg donor and thus would keep the genetic parenting between the woman and her partner, something of value to many couples. Other cases would include a couple entirely lacking gametes.

All of these potential uses for cloning are controversial and might ultimately be rejected. But for NBAC to ban cloning because it currently is unsafe, with no agreement on the future benefits and harms if it becomes safe, is ill-advised. Stalling development of reproductive technologies may trap us in halfway measures, such as donors' genetic involvement, that may cause more harm than cloning.

A federal ban on cloning thus misses the big picture. Cloning is only one of many reproductive technologies that should be safe before application, be it intracytoplasmic sperm injection, cytoplasm transfer, or beyond. The task is to devise a regulatory approach that addresses safety while permitting research and progress in a sphere of immense importance to couples. Cloning should spur us to that delicate balancing act. Simply lowering the boom on cloning does the opposite.

A Better Model

There is a better way. Certainly we need improved regulation of assisted reproduction and human subjects experimentation in the private sphere.[18] But we have to combine that regulation with an advisory body providing oversight for cloning and other novel reproductive and genetic technologies.

The commission, president, and Congress should consider a model we have used before: agency regulation guided by an advisory body able to respond to improvements in the technology over time and more removed than Congress from partisan politics. Though NBAC's report compared policy options, strangely this was not among them.[19]

The Recombinant DNA Advisory Committee (RAC) is one example of such a body. RAC was formed over twenty years ago as an NIH advisory panel. When concern later erupted over human gene therapy, RAC (with its Working Group on Human Gene Therapy) showed how an advisory committee could hold the line, by refusing to consider germ-line gene therapy protocols for approval. It used not a legislative ban, but the committee's declared moratorium, continually subject to debate and reconsideration.

RAC's very accomplishments have fed criticism. As some forms of gene therapy became better understood (in part thanks to RAC), the committee's review began to seem an obstacle to scientific progress. The director of NIH restructured RAC earlier this year.[20] Now a smaller RAC will advise on ethical issues, surrendering authority to approve protocols to the FDA. Though RAC's authority has been reduced, this is a success story. A mechanism appropriate at the introduction of a controversial technology may require revamping later. What we use now to govern cloning must have the flexibility to evolve.

RAC is merely one example. And it is narrower than what we need for cloning: RAC's jurisdiction has been confined   to protocols requiring NIH approval. On cloning, as I have argued, we need to extend human subjects protections to private research and regulate reproductive technologies, with an advisory body for novel issues such as cloning.[21]

Certainly the details of the model can be debated. Indeed, rather than create a new advisory body, using a reinvigorated RAC, another preexisting entity, or NBAC itself (if its mission were restructured) might be considered. And some may argue we need two bodies, one for human subjects and the other for reproductive technologies. But surrendering cloning to a congressional ban, as NBAC suggests, attempts a delicate operation with far too blunt an instrument. It is slim consolation that under the president's proposal, NBAC will be continuing discussion on the sidelines.

NBAC might respond that it favored a limited ban to head off worse proposals in Congress. But a national bioethics commission should call for what is right, not merely what is expedient. Congressional bills in the panicked days after the announcement of Dolly should not drive the national bioethics agenda.

A congressional ban may seem simple and safe. Yet the issues posed by cloning are not simple. We have to balance the promise of research and the potential benefits against the need for regulation and caution. We have to do better than NBAC's ban.

References

[1] National Bioethics Advisory Commission, *Cloning Human Beings: Report and Recommendations of the National Bioethics Advisory Commission* (Rockville MD, June 1997).

[2] The White House, Office Of Communications, Directive on Cloning, 4 March 1997, 1997 Westlaw 91957 (White House).

[3] See "Statement by the President on NIH Recommendation Regarding Human Embryo Research," *U.S. Newswire* (2 December 1994); Omnibus Consolidated Appropriations Act, 1997, Pub. L. No. 104–208, §512, 110 Stat. 3009, 831.

[4] 45 C.F.R. Part 46 (1996). These regulations cover only research that is federally funded, at institutions offering assurances that all research will be subject to the regulations, or on drugs and devices needing FDA approval.

[5] NBAC's report leaves unclear the proper policy approach to embryo splitting. Chairman Shapiro's transmittal letter states, "We do not revisit...cloning...by embryo splitting." However, a report footnote ambiguously "observes that...any other technique to create a child genetically identical to an existing...individual would raise many if not all, of the same non-safety-related ethical concerns raised by...somatic cell nuclear transfer" (p. iii, n. 1). One would think that "any other technique" could include embryo splitting with

cryopreservation to produce a delayed genetic twin. However, the report claims that the capacity to produce a delayed genetic twin is a prospect "unique" to Dolly-style cloning, i.e., somatic cell nuclear transfer (pp. 3, 64). This leaves NBAC's approach to embryo splitting in confusion.

[6] S. 193, 105th Cong. (1997).

[7] See Carol Levine and Arthur L. Caplan, "Beyond Localism: A Proposal for a National Research Review Board," *IRB* 8, no. 2 (1986): 7–9; Alexander Morgan Capron, "An Egg Takes Flight: The Once and Future Life of the National Bioethics Advisory Commission," *Kennedy Institute of Ethics Journal* 7 (1997): 63–80, at 69.

[8] NBAC might respond that its mandated areas of study are human subjects research and genetic information, not reproductive technologies. But one cannot do justice to cloning without considering its most likely use in treating infertility. And a national commission should bring to cloning the necessary bioethics analysis, not just bureaucratically designated topic areas.

[9] See 42 U.S.C.A. §§263a-1 et seq.

[10] NBAC asserts, for example, that most reproductive technologies aside from in vitro techniques for fertilization involve no micromanipulation as substantial as somatic cell transfer (p. 32), without even analyzing techniques such as assisted hatching and cytoplasm transfer. The report also makes the startling suggestion that childlessness condemns one to immaturity: "Without reproduction one remains a child... With reproduction...one becomes a parent, taking on responsibilities for another that necessarily require abandoning some of the personal freedoms enjoyed before" (p. 77). An infertile adult does not automatically remain a "child" and may take on numerous responsibilities requiring self-sacrifice. Surely, these remarks would not have survived serious engagement with clinicians in infertility programs. NBAC's witness list includes none. Cf. Gina Kolata, "Ethics Panel Recommends a Ban on Human Cloning," *New York Times,* 8 June 1997, at 22 (quoting an NBAC member remarking that no IVF physicians addressed the commission).

[11] See H.B. 923: "It shall be unlawful...to use a human somatic cell for the process of producing a human clone." This seems to prohibit making even an embryo clone for research.

[12] See H.B. 922, S. 368.

[13] See generally Ira H. Carmen, *Cloning and the Constitution: An Inquiry into Governmental Policymaking and Genetic Experimentation* (Madison 1985); Richard Delgado and David R. Millen, "God, Galileo, and Government: Toward Constitutional Protection for Scientific Inquiry," *Washington Law Review* 53 (1978): 349–404.

[14] Cf. Lifchez v. Hartigan, 735 F. Supp. 1381 (N.D. Ill.), *aff'd without opinion,* 914 F.2d 260 (7th Cir. 1990), *cert. denied sub nom.* Scholberg v. Lifchez, 498 U.S. 1069 (1991) (striking down a statute on fetal experimentation as unconstitutionally vague).

[15] The shape of this argument is suggested by John A. Robertson in *Children of Choice: Freedom and the New Reproductive Technologies* (Princeton 1994), though he questions whether cloning is so different from other forms of reproduction as to fall outside of constitutional protection for procreative liberty (pp. 169–70). On constitutional protection for reproductive technologies, see also *Lifchez,* above.

[16] For the limits of federal power based on the Constitution's commerce clause, see, for example, U.S. v. Lopez, 514 U.S. 549 (1995).

[17] See also Alexander Morgan Capron, "Inside the Beltway Again: A Sheep of a Different Feather," *Kennedy Institute of Ethics Journal* 7 (1997): 171–79, at 176 ("[I]t would be a mistake to say everything we believe would be wrong to do should be a wrong to do. This is particularly true of cloning.").

[18] See also George J. Annas, "Regulatory Models for Human Embryo Cloning: The Free Market, Professional Guidelines, and Government Restrictions," *Kennedy Institute of Ethics Journal* 4 (1994): 235–49, 245–46.

[19] NBAC did mention RAC (p. 97), but in its discussion of voluntary moratoria (and even though RAC's moratorium on germline gene therapy proposals has been binding on researchers seeking federal funds, not voluntary).

[20] National Institutes of Health, "Notice of Action under the NIH Guidelines for Research Involving DNA Molecules," 62 Fed. Reg. 4782 (31 January 1997).

[21] Unlike a ban on cloning, my suggested approach is likely to survive constitutional scrutiny. Research is routinely disseminated interstate with substantial commercial effects. And the terrible history of research scandals would seem to justify extending protection to subjects in private research as a matter of civil and human rights. Moreover, there is little reason to

suspect infringement on researchers' freedom of inquiry from application of our current protective framework. Augmenting regulation of reproductive technologies, if carefully done to respect the constitutional need for a compelling justification to restrict access to procreative technologies, would seem defensible given extensive interstate commerce in reproductive services.

Sherwin B. Nuland

The Uncertain Art: Narcissus Looks into the Laboratory

Among the many ancient Greek medical writings that scholars of an earlier generation credited to Hippocrates, there is a particularly interesting essay that deals with the education of a physician. "Law"'s brief length of only five paragraphs, and certain of its trenchant observations, caused one translator to call it a "quaint little piece" and voice regret that "it has strangely been neglected by scholars." His concern was no doubt based on the fact that this particular gem contains more good sense per line than any of the approximately sixty treatises once thought to have been written by the Father of Medicine himself.

Some of the statements in "Law" are more aphoristic than the vast majority of those in *The Aphorisms* and exceed them in universality. And as for being timcless— well, try this one, about time itself: "It is time which imparts strength to all things and brings them to maturity." I found myself thinking about just this statement only a few days ago, while reading a newspaper account of yet another triumph in the world of molecular biology, this one being page-one-headlined by the exuberant *New York Times*: "In Big Advance in Cloning, Biologists Create 50 Mice."

Imagine that—the biologist as creator! Or, perhaps before too long, as Creator.

Not only did the researchers "churn out clones of adult mice," announced the *Times,* but they even went so far as to make clones of clones. One authority at Princeton University (to whom the article refers as a "mouse geneticist") "described the speed at which the cloning had progressed as breathtaking." He went further: " 'Absolutely,' he said, 'we're going to have cloning of humans.' " According to the mouse expert, even the safeguards of strict scientific protocol and the delay required to perfect the technique in monkeys would not prevent in vitro fertilization clinics from being able to add human cloning to their bag of tricks within five to ten years.

It's not enough that we are plunging pell-mell toward cloning one another. Even the genetic enhancement of laboratory-crafted people is now being talked about. This would mean quite a bit more than the current therapeutic aims of introducing genes into patients to fight or ward off disease or of cloning for the purposes of tissue and organ transplantation. Changes are now being considered that would improve the very germplasm, the permanent heredity, of these "created" clones. Traits thus made inherent would be potentially transferable to every succeeding generation. This goes beyond fantasizing about Bionic Man to conjuring up the dream of Designer Man.

The velocity of our head-over-heels rush to clinical fulfillment comes into perspective when we recall that only a bit more than a year and a half has passed since the newborn Dolly first made those appealing sheep's eyes at the television cameras. At that time, no serious scientist believed that an attempt at reproducing the feat in humans was possible within a decade. And now we are being told that a decade is the outer limit within which the process may be not only accomplished but even made available to the public just for the asking (and the paying).

Meanwhile, other researchers are less concerned with crafting an improved version of the present generation for transmission into the next than with playing around with a project that has been dear to mankind's heart ever since our species first made its appearance in dim prehistory. For these scientists, it is not sufficient to clone our bettered selves into interminable generations; they are experimenting with techniques that might have the potential to make some members of our generation themselves interminable. Their goal is the lengthening of life beyond any span that clinical and public health advances (which have already added some thirty-five years to our life expectancy during this century) might anticipate. What they are talking about now is an increase not only in expectancy, but in the very life span granted by nature and evolution to our species and every other.

Noting that a structure found at the end of the DNA molecule, called a telomere, decreases in size each time a cell divides, these researchers have been working with a gene that codes for the enzyme telomerase. Telomerase has the ability to maintain or even increase the length of the telomere. In the laboratory, such manipulation has resulted in a marked rise in the number of times a cell can divide before dying. As recently as two years ago, responsible molecular biologists scoffed at the idea that this work could extend the normal life span, but no longer. Telomerase is now a hot research topic.

There is something just a bit scary about the way researchers describe what they see in their experiments. They say the cells are rejuvenated, a word reminiscent of the age-old searchings for a source of renewed vigor that culminated earlier in this century in the "magical" effects of monkey gland extracts and other such nostrums for perpetuating youth.

Not only would some of the current rush to fruition have been deemed absurdly futuristic only a few years ago, but the often overheated media have flavored their reports of it with the promise of imminent wondrous applications to human happiness. Earlier this year, the selfsame *New York Times* reported telomerase's extension of cellular reproductive lines with a detailed story, in the lead paragraph of which was posed a tantalizing question: "If cells can be made to live indefinitely, can people be made immortal?" The large headline over the article read, "Longevity's New Lease on Life." Can anyone be blamed for believing that this fantasy is close to becoming reality?

The media are not without reason for enthusiasm. Daring statements are being made by otherwise cautious scientists about the implications of their work. As one after another of nature's hitherto closely guarded secrets is revealed by their relentless ingenuity, researchers have begun to allow themselves to think the previously unthinkable.

Some of their rumination, like that of the mouse geneticist, is public. As in his case, it generally takes the form of pithy quotes delivered over telephone lines in response to questing science writers, who then rush them into print for immediate consumption by a public eager to believe that a New Jerusalem of health and longevity is at hand. Perhaps egged on by a recently acquired prophetic image, many biomedical scientists have abandoned the restraint that has long characterized their breed. To the usual unbounded zeal for the next research step has been added a less usual unbounded zeal for the immediacy of clinical use. Because of a few awe-inspiring discoveries, many ordinary citizens have changed their opinion about how far we dare to look ahead and how fast we dare to go. Caught up in the infectious excitement of biomedical science and its commentators, we seem to have forgotten about the leavening effect of time's passage, and the maturity it can bring.

Our society has become very much like an overstimulated child. Perhaps such an analogy can be taken even further. The byproducts of biomedicine's brilliance have rubbed off on all of us, even those without the training or background to grasp fully the factual basis of the advances. The kind of child our society resembles just now is one whose intelligence far exceeds his maturity. Every teacher and every parent knows what a formula for disaster that can be. Among some of the scientists themselves, the brilliance-to-maturity ratio may be strikingly higher than among the general population, and not only because they tend to be smarter than the rest of us.

This might be the time to do just what wise teachers do when faced with such a situation in the classroom: a child whose intellectual attainments far outstrip his ability to deal with the consequences of being so smart, a child who is likely, therefore, to make mistakes in using his genius that will ultimately harm himself and others. What a wise teacher does with such a child is not to promote him to the next grade when the school year ends. The child stays where he is until his social abilities catch up to his brainpower. Years ago, it was the custom to push such brilliant kids forward rapidly through the grades, but the price—in psychological illness and even breakdowns—proved to be very high. Too many of these bright youngsters never fulfilled the promise of their intellectual gifts because they were not given the time to mature. Had they been kept back, they would have been allowed to grow up enough to comprehend what might happen as a result of their genius.

What I am suggesting here is a brake on the application of technologies whose consequences we can at present only begin to contemplate. For the first time in the annals of scientific research, we are faced with discoveries whose implications to society go far beyond the community of researchers, physicians, and those patients who would be directly involved. We may have reached the point where we can no longer afford to permit the scientists alone to determine how far to carry the applications of their work. Some might even suggest that the *direction* of research, too, should be influenced by open discussion in our society. Though most of us would be reluctant to take such a position, the borderline between the basic science laboratory and the laboratory for product development has become so obscured that even such a radical proposition might one day need to be entertained.

But regardless of the stance taken in such matters, one obvious truth must be acknowledged: when an entire society is to be affected, an entire informed society should participate in the decisions. The society should slow down and give itself time to think, time to confer, time to mature.

The federal government has shown signs of understanding the present dilemma. In 1995, President Clinton formed the National Bioethics Advisory Commission to deal with the kinds of issues raised by the new branches of research. In what may prove to be its most significant decision thus far, this panel—composed of representatives from the fields of medicine, nursing, religion, law, ethics, industry, education, and health advocacy—did in effect decide to keep the child back a grade by supporting the president's planned five-year moratorium on the use of federal funds to attempt human cloning. In its ninety days of deliberation, during which the commission heard testimony from a cross section of informed societal interests, it came down on the side of banning application, while supporting the need for continuing research. Implicit in its recommendations are two guiding and interrelated notions: first, although we have knowledge aplenty, there would be no benefit—even if it were practically possible—in ceasing to pursue even more knowledge; second, knowledge without wisdom is a clear and present danger. The members of the commission did not have to add the lesson of "Law," that wisdom comes only with maturity and maturity comes only with time.

Law, if not "Law," may in fact soon enter the arena. Senators Feinstein of California and Kennedy of Massachusetts—from sea to shining sea—have introduced a bill, S.R. 1611, that for ten years would prohibit attempts to clone a human being, while not restricting other kinds of cloning research, such as that on cells and tissues. The term of the proposed legislation is perhaps longer than even some moderate observers might wish, but events may permit it to be shortened. On the other hand, the term may need an extension once the manifold issues raised by the new science come more clearly into view.

If for no other reason, our society should at least pause briefly to think about its motivations for plunging forward without due consideration of the range of possible consequences or of the immediate financial cost of the research in a time of limited resources. The great advances in the real health of humanity in the past hundred years have occurred more as the result of such preventive measures as immunization, personal cleanliness, water purification, and other public health efforts than from any application—except perhaps antibiotics—of the technologies of cure to individual patients. These preventive measures—and not surgery, pharmacology, molecular biology, or the therapies given in hospitals—are the primary reason for our vastly improved life expectancy. It is health, after all, that should concern us. And it should concern us far more than the mere desire to perpetuate ourselves.

Prevention and early diagnosis are more direct routes to health and a good quality of life than any stratagem yet devised, or likely to be devised, in our lifetimes. As long as resources are finite, as they will always be, we would do well not to abandon the wisdom that has stood us in such good stead in the past. The magnificences served up daily by the molecular biologists may exhilarate us, but our real goal should not be the satisfaction of the egocentricity within each of us. To this end, we need to review not only our headlong dash into the arms of the researchers but our priorities as well.

The search for wisdom is always fraught with dangers, but those inherent in the present situation arise from the very fabric of human character. After all, who among us has not occasionally, or more than occasionally, cherished the notion that we might live forever, or that we might stay young far beyond our years, or that we might even continue to exist in some descendant who is, at least genetically, our duplicate? For some, these are more than just notions—they are a prevailing philosophy of life, even an obsession. Maybe this is why, when practical applications are only the glib predictions of overzealous researchers, keen votaries have uncritically hailed the future of genetic studies.

The prevailing mood of our time is self-absorption, and its natural extension, narcissism. Manifestations are everywhere apparent: the youth culture; the huge market in cosmetic surgery; the entire cult of "personal fulfillment"; the so-called human potential movement; the outsize emphasis on the individual as opposed to the cultural group and even the family; the popularity of new drugs to grow new hair or build new erections; and, finally, the very situation I am addressing here—the possibility that research in genetics will put us on the road toward eternal life. In pursuing vanity, far too many of us have simply lost hold of our senses. There has never been a period in human history during which the creed of self-indulgence has found so many apostles.

If there exists a single characteristic that unifies all self-absorption and vanity, it surely must be foolishness. Knowing lots of things does not make us any less foolish. Mere information is only the beginning of knowledge, and even knowledge does not of itself lead to maturity, nor does it guarantee good judgment. We need to grow up a lot more as a society before we are ready to play with the new toys being so efficiently made for us by the precocious scientists. Growing up takes time and reflection. T. S. Eliot reminds us that we have paid a high price for the compulsion to accelerate the engines of our existence:

Where is the Life we have lost in living?
Where is the wisdom we have lost in knowledge?
Where is the knowledge we have lost in information?

Philip Kitcher

Human Cloning

"Researchers Astounded" is not the typical phraseology of a headline on the front page of the *New York Times* (February 23, 1997). Lamb number 6LL3, better known as Dolly, took the world by surprise, sparking debate about the proper uses of biotechnology and inspiring predictable public fantasies (and predictable jokes). Recognizing that what is possible today with sheep will probably be feasible with human beings tomorrow, commentators speculated about the legitimacy of cloning Pavarotti or Einstein, about the chances that a demented dictator might produce an army of supersoldiers, and about the future of basketball in a world where the Boston Larry Birds play against the Chicago Michael Jordans. Polls showed that Mother Teresa was the most popular choice for person-to-be-cloned, although a film star (Michelle Pfeiffer) was not far behind, and Bill Clinton and Hillary Clinton obtained some support.

Mary Shelley may have a lot to answer for. The Frankenstein story, typically in one of its film versions, colors popular reception of news about cloning, fomenting a potent brew of associations—we assume that human lives can be created to order, that it can be done instantly, that we can achieve exact replicas, and, of course, that it is all going to turn out disastrously. Reality is much more sobering, and it is a good idea to preface debates about the morality of human cloning with a clear understanding of the scientific facts.

Over two decades ago, a developmental biologist, John Gurdon, reported the possibility of cloning amphibians. Gurdon and his coworkers were able to remove the nucleus from a frog egg and replace it with the nucleus from an embryonic tadpole. The animals survived and developed to adulthood, becoming frogs that had the same complement of genes within the nucleus as the tadpole embryo. Further efforts to use nuclei from adult donors were unsuccessful. When the nucleus from a frog egg was replaced with that from a cell taken from an adult frog, the embryo died at a relatively early stage of development. Moreover, nobody was able to perform Gurdon's original trick on mammals. Would-be cloners who tried to insert nuclei from mouse embryos into mouse eggs consistently ended up with dead fetal mice. So, despite initial hopes and fears, it appeared that the route to cloning adult human beings was doubly blocked: only transfer of embryonic DNA seemed to work, and even that failed in mammals.

Biologists had an explanation for the failure to produce normal development after inserting nuclei from adult cells. Although adult cells contain all the genes, they are also *differentiated,* set to perform particular functions, and this comes about because some genes are expressed in them, while others are "turned off." Regulation of genes is a matter of the attachment of proteins to the DNA so that some regions are accessible for transcription and others are not. So it was assumed that chromosomes in adult cells would have a complex coating of proteins on the DNA and this would prevent the transcription of genes that need to be activated in early development. In consequence, transferring nuclei from adult cells always produced inviable embryos. The "high-tech" solution to the problem—the "obvious" solution from the viewpoint of molecular genetics—is to use the arsenal of molecular techniques to strip away the protein coating, restore the DNA to its (presumed) original condition, and only then transfer the nucleus to the recipient egg. To date, nobody has managed to make this approach work.

The breakthrough came not from one of the major centers in which the genetic revolution is whirling on, but from the far less glamorous world of animal husbandry and agricultural research. In 1996, a team of workers at the Roslin Institute near Edinburgh, led by Dr. Ian Wilmut, announced that they had succeeded in producing two live sheep, Megan and Morag, by transplanting nuclei from embryonic sheep cells. One barrier had been breached: Wilmut and his colleagues had shown that just what Gurdon had done in frogs could be achieved in sheep. Yet it seemed that the major problem, that of tricking an egg into normal development when equipped with an *adult* cell nucleus, still remained. In retrospect, we can recognize that not quite enough attention was given to Wilmut's first announcement, for Megan and Morag testified to a new technique of nuclear transference.

Wilmut conjectured that the failures of normal development resulted from the fact that the cell that supplied the nucleus and the egg that received it were at different stages of the cell cycle. Using well-known techniques from cell biology, he "starved" both cells, so that both were in an inactive phase at the time of transfer. In a series of experiments, he discovered that inserting nuclei from adult cells (from the udder of a pregnant ewe) under this regime gave rise to a number of embryos, which could be implanted in ewes. Although there was a high rate of miscarriage, one of the pregnancies went to term. So, after beginning with 277 successfully transferred nuclei, Wilmut obtained one healthy lamb—the celebrated Dolly.

Wilmut's achievement raises three important questions: Will it be possible to perform the same operations on human cells? Will cloners be able to reduce the high rate of failure? What exactly is the relationship between a clone obtained in this way and previously existing animals? Answers to the first two of these are necessarily tentative, since predicting even the immediate trajectory of biological research is always vulnerable to unforeseen contingencies. (In the weeks after Gurdon's success, it seemed that cloning all kinds of animals was just around the corner; from the middle 1980s to 1996, it appeared that cloning adult mammals was a science-fiction fantasy.) However, unless there is some quite unanticipated snag, we can expect that Wilmut's technique will *eventually* work just as well on human cells as it does in sheep, and that failure rates in sheep (or in other mammals) will quickly be reduced. .

Assuming that Wilmut's diagnosis of the problems of mammalian cloning is roughly correct, then the crucial step involves preparing the cells for nuclear transfer by making them quiescent. Of course, learning how to "starve" human cells so that they are ready may involve some experimental tinkering. Probably there would be a fair bit of trial-and-error work before the techniques became sufficiently precise to allow for cmbryos to develop to the stage at which they can be implanted with a very high rate of success, and to overcome any potential difficulties with implantation or with the resultant pregnancy.

Many of the problems that prospective human cloners would face are likely to be analogues of obstacles to the various forms of assisted reproduction—and it is perfectly possible that the successes of past human reproductive technology would smooth the way for cloning.

On the third question we can be more confident. Dolly has the same nuclear genetic material as the adult pregnant ewe, from whose udder cell the inserted nucleus originally came. A different female supplied the egg into which the nucleus was inserted, and Dolly thus has the same mitochondrial DNA as this ewe; indeed, her early development was shaped by the interaction between the DNA in the nucleus and the contents of the cytoplasm, the contributions of different adult females. Yet a third sheep, the ewe into which the embryonic Dolly was implanted, played a role in Dolly's nascent life, providing her with a uterine environment. In an obvious sense, Dolly has three mothers—nucleus mother, egg mother, and womb mother—and no father (unless, of course, we give Dr. Wilmut that honor for his guiding role).

Now imagine Polly, a human counterpart of Dolly. Will Polly be a replica of any existing human being? Certainly she will not be the same person as any of the mothers— even the nuclear mother. Personal identity, as philosophers since John Locke have recognized, depends on continuity of memory and other psychological attitudes. There is no hope of ensuring personal survival by arranging for cloning through supplying a cell nucleus. Megalomaniacs with intimations of immortality need not apply.

Yet you might think that Polly might be very similar to her nuclear mother, perhaps extremely similar if we arranged for the nuclear mother to be the same person as the egg mother, and for that person's mother to be the womb mother. That combination of "parents" would seem to turn Polly into a close approximation of her nuclear mother's identical twin. An approximation, perhaps, but nobody knows how close. Polly and her nuclear mother differ in three ways in which identical twins are typically the same. They develop from eggs with different cytoplasmic constitutions, they are not carried to term in a common uterine environment, and their environments after birth are likely to be quite different.

Interestingly, during the next few years, Wilmut's technique will allow us to remedy our ignorance about the relative importance of various causes of phenotypic traits by performing experiments on nonhuman mammals. It will be possible to develop organisms with the same nuclear genes within recipient eggs with varied cytoplasms. By exploring the results, biologists will be able to discover the extent to which constituents of the egg outside the nucleus play a role in shaping the phenotype. They will also be able to explore the ways in which the uterine environment makes a difference. Perhaps they will find that variation in cytoplasm and difference in womb have little effect, in which case Polly will be a better approximation to an identical twin of her nuclear mother. More probably, I believe, they will expose some aspects of the phenotype that are influenced by the character of the cytoplasm or by the state of the womb, thus identifying ways in which Polly would fall short of perfect twinhood.

Even before these experiments are done, we know of some important differences between Polly and her nuclear mother. Unlike most identical twins, they will grow up in environments that are quite dissimilar, if only because the gap in their ages will correspond to changes in dietary fashions, educational trends, adolescent culture, and so forth. When these sources of variation are combined with the more uncertain judgments about effects of cytoplasmic factors and the prenatal environment, we can conclude that human clones will be less alike than identical twins, and quite possibly very much less alike.

Those beguiled by genetalk move quickly from the idea that clones are genetically identical (which is, to a first approximation, correct) to the view that clones will be replicas of one another. Identical twins reared together are obviously similar in many respects, but they are by no means interchangeable people. It is pertinent to recall the statistics about sexual orientation: 50 percent of male (identical) twins who are gay have a co-twin who is not. Minute differences in shared environments can obviously play a large role. How much more dissimilarity can we anticipate given the much more dramatic variations that I have indicated?

There will never be another you. If you hoped to fashion a son or daughter exactly in your own image, you would be doomed to disappointment. Nonetheless, you might hope to use cloning technology to have a child of a particular kind—just as the obvious agricultural applications focus on single features of domestic animals, like their capacity for producing milk. Some human characteristics are under tight genetic control, and if we wanted to ensure that our children carried genetic diseases like Huntington's and Tay-Sachs, then, of course, we could do so, although the idea is so monstrous that it only surfaces in order to be dismissed. Perhaps there are other features that are relatively insusceptible to niceties of the environment, aspects of body morphology, for example. An obvious example is eye color.

Imagine a couple determined to do what they can to produce a Hollywood star. Fascinated by the color of Elizabeth Taylor's eyes, they obtain a sample of tissue from the actress and clone a young Liz. For reasons already discussed, it is probable that Elizabeth II would be different from Elizabeth I, but we might think that she would have that distinctive eye color. Supposing that to be so, should we conclude that the couple will realize their dream? Probably not. Waiving issues about intelligence, poise and acting ability, and supposing that the movie moguls of the future respond only to physical attractiveness, the eyes may not have it. Apparently tiny incidents in early development may modify the shape of the orbits, producing a combination of features in which the eye color no longer has its bewitching effect. At best, the confused couple can only hope to raise the probability that their daughter will capture the hearts of millions.

Physical attractiveness, the real target of the couple's plan, turns on more than eye color, and that is the general way of things. The traits we value most are produced by a complex interaction between genotypes and environments, and by fixing the genotype, we can only increase our chances of achieving the results we want. Demented dictators bent on invading their neighbors can do no more than add to the likelihood of generating the "master race." Before we startle ourselves with the imagined sound of jackboots marching across the frontier, we should remember that there is no shortcut to the process of rearing children and training them in whatever ways are appropriate to our ends. Indeed, when we appreciate that point, we can see that if the dictators are slightly less demented, they will do what military recruiters have always done, namely select on grounds of physical fitness, ease of indoctrination, courage and such traits, and then invest extensively in military academies. Cloning adds very little to the chances of success.

Similar points apply to the fantasies of cloning Einstein, Mother Teresa, or Yo-Yo Ma. The chances of generating true distinction in any area of complex human activity, whether it be scientific accomplishment, dedication to the well-being of others, or artistic expression, are infinitesimal. *Perhaps* cloning would allow us to raise the probability from infinitesimal to very, very tiny. A program designed to use cloning to transform human life by having a higher number of outstanding individuals would, at most, give a minute number of "successes" at the cost of vastly more "failures." Those who worry that Dolly is one survivor among 277 attempts should find this scenario far more disturbing.

Garish popular fantasies dissolve when confronted with the facts about the biotechnology of cloning, suggesting that only rich recluses, hermetically sealed in ignorance, should be tempted by the projects that fascinate and horrify us most. Yet there are other more mundane ventures that have a closer connection with reality. Parents who demand less than truly outstanding performance, but still have a preferred dimension on which they want their children to excel, might turn to cloning in hopes of raising their chances. Had my wife and I been seriously concerned to bring into the world sons who would have dominated the basketball court or been mainstays of the defensive line, then we would have been ill-advised to proceed in the old-fashioned method of reproduction. At a combined weight of less than 275 pounds and a combined height of just over eleven feet, we would have done far better to transfer a nucleus from some strapping star of the NBA or the NFL. Perhaps, by doing so, we would significantly have raised the chances of having a son on the high-school basketball or football team. Success, even at that rather modest goal, would not have been guaranteed, since there are all kinds of ways in which the boy's development might have gone differently (think of accidents, competing interests, dislike of competitive sports, and so forth). Nor would cloning necessarily have been the best way for us to proceed: Maybe we could have employed the results of genetic testing to produce, by *in vitro* fertilization, a fertilized egg having alleles at crucial loci that predispose to a large, muscular body; maybe we could have used artificial insemination, or have adopted a son. Nevertheless, cloning would surely have raised the probabilities of our obtaining the child we wanted.

Just that final phrase indicates the moral squalor of the story. As I have imagined it, we have a plan for the life to come laid down in advance; we are determined to do what we can to make it come out a certain way—and, presumably, if it does not come out that way, it will count as a failure. Throughout the discussion of utopian eugenics, I insisted that prenatal decisions should be guided by reflection on the quality of the nascent life, and I understood that in terms of creating the conditions under which a child could form a central set of desires, a conception of what his or her life means that had a decent chance of being satisfied. In the present scenario, there is a crass failure to recognize the child as an independent being, one who should form his own sense of who he is and what his life means. The contours of the life are imposed from without.

Parents have been tempted to do similar things before. James Mill had a plan for his son's life, leading him to begin young John Stuart's instruction in Greek at age three and his Latin at age eight. John Stuart Mill's *Autobiography* is a quietly moving testament to the cramping effect of his felt need to live out the life his eminent father had designed for him. In early adulthood, Mill *fils* suffered a nervous breakdown, from which he recovered, going on to a career of great intellectual distinction. Although John Stuart partially fulfilled his father's aspirations for him, one of the most striking features of his philosophical work is his passionate defense of human freedom. The central point about what was wrong with this father's attitude toward a son has never been better expressed than in the splendid prose of *On Liberty*: "Mankind are greater gainers by suffering each other to live as seems good to themselves than by compelling each to live as seems good to the rest."

If cloning human beings is undertaken in the hope of generating a particular kind of person, a person whose standards of what matters in life are imposed from without, then it is morally repugnant, not because it involves biological tinkering but because it is continuous with other ways of interfering with human autonomy that we ought to resist. Human cloning would provide new ways of committing old moral errors. To discover whether or not there are morally permissible cases of cloning, we need to see if this objectionable feature can be removed, if there are situations in which the intention of the prospective parents is properly focused on the quality of human lives but in which cloning represents the only option for them. Three scenarios come immediately to mind.

The case of the dying child. Imagine a couple whose only son is slowly dying. If the child were provided with a kidney transplant within the next ten years, he would recover and be able to lead a normal life. Unfortunately, neither parent is able to supply a compatible organ, and it is known that individuals with kidneys that could be successfully transplanted are extremely rare. However, if a brother were produced by cloning, then it would be possible to use one of his kidneys to save the life of the elder son. Supposing that the technology of cloning human beings has become sufficiently reliable to give the couple a very high probability of successfully producing a son with the same complement of nuclear genes, is it permissible for them to do so?

The case of the grieving widow. A woman's much-loved husband has been killed in a car crash. As the result of the same crash, the couple's only daughter lies in a coma, with irreversible brain damage, and she will surely die in a matter of months. The widow is no longer able to bear children. Should she be allowed to have the nuclear DNA from one of her daughter's cells inserted in an egg supplied by another woman, and to have a clone of her child produced through surrogate motherhood?

The case of the loving lesbians. A lesbian couple, devoted to one another for many years, wish to produce a child. Because they would like the child to be biologically connected to each of them, they request that a cell nucleus from one of them be inserted in an egg from the other, and that the embryo be implanted in the woman who donated the egg. (Here, one of the women would be nuclear mother and the other would be both egg mother and womb mother.) Should their request be accepted?

In all of these instances, unlike the ones considered earlier, there is no blatant attempt to impose the plan of a new life, to interfere with a child's own conception of what is valuable. Yet there are lingering concerns that need to be addressed. The first scenario, and to a lesser extent the second, arouses suspicion that children are being subordinated to special adult purposes and projects. Turning from John Stuart Mill to one of the other great influences on contemporary moral theory, Immanuel Kant, we can formulate the worry as a different question about respecting the autonomy of the child: Can these cases be reconciled with the injunction "to treat humanity whether in your own person or in that of another, always as an end and never as a means only"?

It is quite possible that the parents in the case of the dying child would have intentions that flout that principle. They have no desire for another child. They are desperate to save the son they have, and if they could only find an appropriate organ to transplant, they would be delighted to do that; for them the younger brother would simply be a cache of resources, something to be used in saving the really important life. Presumably, if the brother were born and the transplant did not succeed, they would regard that as a failure. Yet the parental attitudes do not have to be so stark and callous (and, in the instances in which parents have actually contemplated bearing a child to save an older sibling, it is quite clear that they are much more complex). Suppose we imagine that the parents plan to have another child in any case, that they are committed to loving and cherishing the child for his or her own sake. What can be the harm in planning that child's birth so as to allow their firstborn to live?

The moral quality of what is done plainly depends on the parental attitudes, specifically on whether or not they have the proper concern for the younger boy's well-being, independently of his being able to save his elder brother. Ironically, their love for him may be manifested most clearly if the project goes awry and the first child dies. Although that love might equally be present in cases where the elder son survives, reflective parents will probably always wonder whether it is untinged by the desire to find some means of saving the first-born—and, of course, the younger boy is likely to entertain worries of a similar nature. He would by no means be the first child to feel himself a second-class substitute, in this case either a helpmeet or a possible replacement for someone loved in his own right.

Similarly, the grieving widow might be motivated solely by desire to forge some link with the happy past, so that the child produced by cloning would be valuable because she was genetically close to the dead (having the same nuclear DNA as her sister, DNA that derives from the widow and her dead husband). If so, another person is being treated as a means to understandable, but morbid, ends. On the other hand, perhaps the widow is primarily moved by the desire for another child, and the prospect of cloning simply reflects the common attitude of many (though not all) parents who prize biological connection to their offspring. However, as in the case of the dying child, the participants, if they are at all reflective, are bound to wonder about the mixture of attitudes surrounding the production of a life so intimately connected to the past.

The case of the loving lesbians is the purest of the three, for here we seem to have a precise analogue of the situation in which heterosexual couples find themselves. Cloning would enable the devoted pair to have a child biologically related to both of them. There is no question of imposing some particular plan on the nascent life, even the minimal one of hoping to save another child or to serve as a reminder of the dead, but simply the wish to have a child who is their own, the expression of their mutual love. If human cloning is ever defensible, it will be in contexts like this.

During past decades, medicine has allowed many couples to overcome reproductive problems and to have biological children. The development of techniques of assisted reproduction responds to the sense that couples who have problems with infertility have been deprived of something that it is quite reasonable for people to value, and that various kinds of manipulations with human cells are legitimate responses to their frustrations. Yet serious issues remain. How close an approximation to the normal circumstances of reproduction and the normal genetic connections should we strive to achieve? How should the benefits of restoring reproduction be weighed against possible risks of the techniques? Both kinds of questions arise with respect to our scenarios.

Lesbian couples already have an option to produce a child who will be biologically related to both. If an egg from one of them is fertilized with sperm (supplied, say, by a male relative of the other) and the resultant embryo is implanted in the womb of the woman who did not give the egg, then both have a biological connection to the child (one is egg mother, the other womb mother). That method of reproduction might even seem preferable, diminishing any sense of burden that the child might feel because of special biological closeness to one of the mothers and allowing for the possibility of having children of either sex. The grieving widow might turn to existing techniques of assisted reproduction and rear a child conceived from artificial insemination of one of her daughter's eggs. In either case, cloning would create a closer biological connection —but should that extra degree of relationship be assigned particularly high value?

My discussion of all three scenarios also depends on assuming that human cloning works smoothly, that there are no worrisome risks that the pregnancy will go awry, producing a child whose development is seriously disrupted. Dolly, remember, was one success out of 277 tries, and we can suppose that early ventures in human cloning would have an appreciable rate of failure. We cannot know yet whether the development of technology for cloning human beings would simply involve the death of early embryos, or whether, along the way, researchers would generate malformed fetuses and, from time to time, children with problems undetectable before birth. During the next few years, we shall certainly come to know much more about the biological processes involved in cloning mammals, and the information we acquire may make it possible to undertake human cloning with confidence that any breakdowns will occur early in development (before there is a person with rights). Meanwhile, we can hope that the continuing transformation of our genetic knowledge will provide improved methods of transplantation, and thus bring relief to parents whose children die for lack of compatible organs.

Should human cloning be banned? Until we have much more extensive and detailed knowledge of how cloning can be achieved (and what the potential problems are) in a variety of mammalian species, there is no warrant for trying to perform Wilmut's clever trick on ourselves. I have suggested that there are some few circumstances in which human cloning might be morally permissible, but, in at least two of these, there are genuine concerns about attitudes to the nascent life, while, in the third, alternative techniques, already available, offer almost as good a response to the underlying predicament. Perhaps, when cloning techniques have become routine in non-human mammalian biology, we may acknowledge human cloning as appropriate relief for the parents of dying children, for grieving widows, and for loving lesbians. For now, however, we do best to try to help them in other ways.

Dolly, we are told, like the scientist who helped her into existence, is learning to live with the television cameras. Media fascination with cloning plainly reached the White House, provoking President Clinton first to refer the issue to his newly formed Bioethics Advisory Committee, later to ban federal funding of applications of cloning technology to human beings. The February 27, 1997, issue of *Nature* featuring Dolly offered a less-than-positive assessment of the presidential reaction: "At a time when the science policy world is replete with technology foresight exercises, for a U.S. president and other politicians only now to be requesting guidance about what appears in today's *Nature* is shaming."

At the first stages of the Human Genome Project, James Watson argued for the assignment of funds to study the "ethical, legal, and social implications" of the purely scientific research. Watson explicitly drew the analogy with the original development of nuclear technology, recommending that, this time, scientific and social change might go hand in hand. Almost a decade later, the mapping and sequencing are advancing faster than most people had anticipated—and the affluent nations remain almost where they were in terms of supplying the social backdrop that will put the genetic knowledge to proper use. That is not for lack of numerous expert studies that outline the potential problems and that propose ways of overcoming them. Much has been written. Little has been done. In the United States we still lack the most basic means of averting genetic discrimination, to wit universal health coverage, but Britain and even the continental European nations are little better placed to cope with what is coming.

The belated response to cloning is of a piece with a general failure to translate clear moral directives into regulations and policies. Dolly is a highly visible symbol, but behind her is a broad array of moral issues that citizens of affluent societies seem to prefer to leave in the shadows. However strongly we feel about the plight of loving lesbians, grieving widows, or even couples whose children are dying, deciding the legitimate employment of human cloning in dealing with their troubles is not our most urgent problem. Those who think that working out the proper limits of human cloning is the big issue are suffering from moral myopia.

General moral principles provide us with an obligation to improve the quality of human lives, where we have the opportunity to do so, and developments in biotechnology provide opportunities and challenges. If we took the principles seriously, we would be led to demand serious investment in programs to improve the lives of the young, the disabled, and the socially disadvantaged. That is not quite what is going on in the "civilized" world. Making demands for social investment seems quixotic, especially at a time when, in America, funds for poor children and disabled people who are out of work are being slashed, and when, in other affluent countries, there is serious questioning of the responsibilities of societies to their citizens. Yet the application of patronizing adjectives does nothing to undermine the legitimacy of the demands. What is truly shameful is not that the response to possibilities of cloning came so late, nor that it has been confused, but the common reluctance of all the affluent nations to think through the implications of time-honored moral principles and to design a coherent use of the new genetic information and technology for human well-being.

Richard Lewontin

The Confusion over Cloning

There is nothing like sex or violence for capturing the immediate attention of the state. Only a day after Franklin Roosevelt was told in October 1939 that both German and American scientists could probably make an atom bomb, a small group met at the President's direction to talk about the problem and within ten days a committee was undertaking a full-scale investigation of the possibility. Just a day after the public announcement on February 23, 1997, that a sheep, genetically identical to another sheep, had been produced by cloning, Bill Clinton formally requested that the National Bioethics Advisory Commission "undertake a thorough review of the legal and ethical issues associated with the use of this technology..."

The President had announced his intention to create an advisory group on bioethics eighteen months before, on the day that he received the disturbing report of the cavalier way in which ionizing radiation had been administered experimentally to unsuspecting subjects.[1] The commission was finally formed, after a ten-month delay, with Harold Shapiro, President of Princeton, as chair, and a membership consisting largely of academics from the fields of philosophy, medicine, public health, and law, a representation from government and private foundations, and the chief business officer of a pharmaceutical company. In his letter to the commission the President referred to "serious ethical questions, particularly with respect to the possible use of this technology to clone human embryos" and asked for a report within ninety days. The commission missed its deadline by only two weeks.

In order not to allow a Democratic administration sole credit for grappling with the preeminent ethical issue of the day, the Senate held a day-long inquiry on March 12, a mere three weeks after the announcement of Dolly. Lacking a body responsible for any moral issues outside the hanky-panky of its own membership, the Senate assigned the work to the Subcommittee on Public Health and Safety of the Committee on Labor and Human Resources, perhaps on the grounds that cloning is a form of the production of human resources. The testimony before the subcommittee was concerned not with issues of the health and safety of labor but with the same ethical and moral concerns that preoccupied the bioethics commission. The witnesses representing the biotechnology industry were especially careful to assure the senators that they would not dream of making whole babies and were interested in cloning solely as a laboratory method for producing cells and tissues that could be used in transplantation therapies.

It seems pretty obvious why, just after the Germans' instant success in Poland, Roosevelt was in a hurry. The problem, as he said to Alexander Sachs, who first informed him about the possibility of the Bomb, was to "see that the Nazis don't blow us up." The origin of Mr. Clinton's sense of urgency is not so clear. After all, it is not as if human genetic clones don't appear every day of the week, about thirty a day in the United States alone, given that there are about four million births a year with a frequency of identical twins of roughly 1 in 400.[2] So it cannot be the mere existence of *Doppelgänger* that creates urgent problems (although I will argue that parents of twins are often guilty of a kind of psychic child abuse). And why ask the commission on bioethics rather than a technical committee of the National Institutes of Health or the National Research Council? Questions of individual autonomy and responsibility for one's own actions, of the degree to which the state ought to interpose itself in matters of personal decision, are all central to the struggle over smoking, yet the bioethics commission has not been asked to look into the bioethics of tobacco, a matter that would certainly be included in its original purpose.

The answer is that the possibility of human cloning has produced a nearly universal anxiety over the consequences of hubris. The testimony before the bioethics commission speaks over and over of the consequences of "playing God." We have no responsibility for the chance birth of genetically identical individuals, but their deliberate manufacture puts us in the Creation business, which, like extravagant sex, is both seductive and frightening. Even Jehovah botched the job despite the considerable knowledge of biology that He must have possessed, and we have suffered the catastrophic consequences ever since. According to Haggadic legend, the Celestial Cloner put a great deal of thought into technique. In deciding on which of Adam's organs to use for Eve, He had the problem of finding tissue that was what the biologist calls "totipotent," that is, not already committed in development to a particular function. So He cloned Eve

> not from the head, lest she carry her head high in arro-
> gant pride, not from the eye, lest she be wanton-eyed,
> not from the ear lest she be an eavesdropper, not from
> the neck lest she be insolent, not from the mouth lest
> she be a tattler, not from the heart lest she be inclined to
> envy, not from the hand lest she be a meddler, not from
> the foot lest she be a gadabout

but from the rib, a "chaste portion of the body." In spite of all the care and knowledge, something went wrong, and we have been earning a living by the sweat of our brows ever since. Even in the unbeliever, who has no fear of sacrilege, the myth of the uncontrollable power of creation has a resonance that gives us all pause. It is impossible to understand the incoherent and unpersuasive document produced by the National Bioethics Advisory Commission except as an attempt to rationalize a deep cultural prejudice, but it is also impossible to understand it without taking account of the pervasive error that confuses the genetic state of an organism with its total physical and psychic nature as a human being.

After an introductory chapter, placing the issue of cloning in a general historical and social perspective, the commission begins with an exposition of the technical details of cloning and with speculations on the reproductive, medical, and commercial applications that are likely to be found for the technique. Some of these applications involve the clonal reproduction of genetically engineered laboratory animals for research or the wholesale propagation of commercially desirable livestock; but these raised no ethical issues for the commission, which, wisely, avoided questions of animal rights.

Specifically human ethical questions are raised by two possible applications of cloning. First, there are circumstances in which parents may want to use techniques of assisted reproduction to produce children with a known genetic makeup for reasons of sentiment or vanity or to serve practical ends. Second, there is the possibility of producing embryos of known genetic constitution whose cells and tissues will be useful for therapeutic purposes. Putting aside, for consideration in a separate chapter, religious claims that human cloning violates various scriptural and doctrinal prescriptions about the correct relation between God and man, men and women, husbands and wives, parents and children, or sex and reproduction, the commission then lists four ethical issues to be considered: individuality and autonomy, family integrity, treating children as objects, and safety.

The most striking confusion in the report is in the discussion of individuality and autonomy. Both the commission report and witnesses before the Senate subcommittee were at pains to point out that identical genes do not make identical people. The fallacy of genetic determinism is to suppose that the genes "make" the organism. It is a basic principle of developmental biology that organisms undergo a continuous development from conception to death, a development that is the unique consequence of the interaction of the genes in their cells, the temporal sequence of environments through which the organisms pass, and random cellular processes that determine the life, death, and transformations of cells. As a result, even the fingerprints of identical twins are not identical. Their temperaments, mental processes, abilities, life choices, disease histories, and deaths certainly differ despite the determined efforts of many parents to enforce as great a similarity as possible.

Frequently twins are given names with the same initial letter, dressed identically with identical hair arrangements, and given the same books, toys, and training. There are twin conventions at which prizes are offered for the most similar pairs. While identical genes do indeed contribute to a similarity between them, it is the pathological compulsion of their parents to create an inhuman identity between them that is most threatening to the individuality of genetically identical individuals.

But even the most extreme efforts to turn genetic clones into human clones fail. As a child I could not go to the movies or look at a picture magazine without being confronted by the genetically identical Dionne quintuplets, identically dressed and coifed, on display in "Quintland" by Dr. Dafoe and the Province of Ontario for the amusement of tourists. This enforced homogenization continued through their adolescence, when they were returned to their parents' custody. Yet each of their unhappy adulthoods was unhappy in its own way, and they seemed no more alike in career or health than we might expect from five girls of the same age brought up in a rural working-class French Canadian family. Three married and had families. Two trained as nurses, two went to college. Three were attracted to a religious vocation, but only one made it a career. One died in a convent at age twenty, suffering from epilepsy, one at age thirty-six, and three remain alive at sixty-three. So much for the doppelgänger phenomenon. The notion of "cloning Einstein" is a biological absurdity.

The Bioethics Advisory Commission is well aware of the error of genetic determinism, and the report devotes several pages to a sensible and nuanced discussion of the difference between genetic and personal identity. Yet it continues to insist on the question of whether cloning violates an individual human being's "unique qualitative identity."

And even if it is a mistake to believe such crude genetic determinism according to which one's genes determine one's fate, what is important for oneself is whether one *thinks* one's future is open and undetermined, and so still to be largely determined by one's own choices. [emphasis added]

Moreover, the problem of self-perception may be worse for a person cloned from an adult than it is for identical twins, because the already fully formed and defined adult presents an irresistible persistent model for the developing child. Certainly for the general public the belief is widely expressed that a unique problem of identity is raised by cloning that is not already present for twins. The question posed by the commission, then, is not whether genetic identity per se destroys individuality, but whether the erroneous state of public understanding of biology will undermine an individual's own sense of uniqueness and autonomy.

Of course it will, but surely the commission has chosen the wrong target of concern. If the widespread genomania propagated by the press and by vulgarizers of science produces a false understanding of the dominance that genes have over our lives, then the appropriate response of the state is not to ban cloning but to engage in a serious educational campaign to correct the misunderstanding. It is not Dr. Wilmut and Dolly who are a threat to our sense of uniqueness and autonomy, but popularizers like Richard Dawkins who describes us as "gigantic lumbering robots" under the control of our genes that have "created us, body and mind."

Much of the motivation for cloning imagined by the commission rests on the same mistaken synecdoche that substitutes "gene" for "person." In one scenario a self-infatuated parent wants to reproduce his perfection or a single woman wants to exclude any other contribution to her offspring. In another, morally more appealing story a family suffers an accident that kills the father and leaves an only child on the point of death. The mother, wishing to have a child who is the biological offspring of her dead husband, uses cells from the dying infant to clone a baby. Or what about the sterile man whose entire family has been exterminated in Auschwitz and who wishes to prevent the extinction of his genetic patrimony?

Creating variants of these scenarios is a philosopher's parlor game. All such stories appeal to the same impetus that drives adopted children to search for their "real," i.e., biological, parents in order to discover their own "real" identity. They are modern continuations of an earlier preoccupation with blood as the carrier of an individual's essence and as the mark of legitimacy. It is not the possibility of producing a human being with a copy of someone else's genes that has created the difficulty or that adds a unique element to it. It is the fetishism of "blood" which, once accepted, generates an immense array of apparent moral and ethical problems. Were it not for the belief in blood as essence, much of the motivation for the cloning of humans would disappear.

The cultural pressure to preserve a biological continuity as the form of immortality and family identity is certainly not a human universal. For the Romans, as for the Japanese, the preservation of family interest was the preeminent value, and adoption was a satisfactory substitute for reproduction. Indeed, in Rome the foster child (*alumnus*) was the object of special affection by virtue of having been adopted, i.e. acquired by an act of choice.

The second ethical problem cited by the commission, family integrity, is neither unique to cloning nor does it appear in its most extreme form under those circumstances. The contradictory meanings of "parenthood" were already made manifest by adoption and the old-fashioned form of reproductive technology, artificial insemination from anonymous semen donors. Newer technology like *in vitro* fertilization and implantation of embryos into surrogate mothers has already raised issues to which the possibility of cloning adds nothing. A witness before the Senate subcommittee suggested that the "replication of a human by cloning would radically alter the definition of a human being by producing the world's first human with a single genetic parent."[3] Putting aside the possible priority of the case documented in Matthew 1:23, there is a confusion here. A child by cloning has a full double set of chromosomes like anyone else, half of which were derived from a mother and half from a father. It happens that these chromosomes were passed through another individual, the cloning donor, on their way to the child. That donor is certainly not the child's "parent" in any biological sense, but simply an earlier offspring of the original parents. Of course this sibling may claim parenthood over its delayed twin, but it is not obvious what juridical or ethical principle would impel a court or anyone else to recognize that claim.

There is one circumstance, considered by the commission, in which cloning is a biologically realistic solution to a human agony. Suppose that a child, dying of leukemia, could be saved by a bone marrow replacement. Such transplants are always risky because of immune incompatibilities between the recipient and the donor, and these incompatibilities are a direct consequence of genetic differences. The solution that presents itself is to use bone marrow from a second, genetically identical, child who has been produced by cloning from the first.[4] The risk to a bone marrow donor is not great, but suppose it were a kidney that was needed. There is, moreover, the possibility that the fetus itself is to be sacrificed in order to provide tissue for therapeutic purposes. This scenario presents in its starkest form the third ethical issue of concern to the commission, the objectification of human beings. In the words of the commission:

To objectify a person is to act towards the person without regard for his or her own desires or well-being, as a thing to be valued according to externally imposed standards, and to control the person rather than to engage her or him in a mutually respectful relationship.

We would all agree that it is morally repugnant to use human beings as mere instruments of our deliberate ends. Or would we? That's what I do when I call in the plumber. The very words "employment" and "employee" are descriptions of an objectified relationship in which human beings are "thing(s) to be valued according to externally imposed standards." None of us escapes the objectification of humans that arises in economic life. Why has no National Commission on Ethics been called into emergency action to discuss the conceptualization of human beings as "factory hands" or "human capital" or "operatives"? The report of the Bioethics Advisory Commission fails to explain how cloning would significantly increase the already immense number of children whose conception and upbringing were intended to make them instruments of their parents' frustrated ambitions, psychic fantasies, desires for immortality, or property calculations.

Nor is there a simple relation between those motivations and the resulting family relations. I myself was conceived out of my father's desire for a male heir, and my mother, not much interested in maternity, was greatly relieved when her first and only child filled the bill. Yet, in retrospect, I am glad they were my parents. To pronounce a ban on human cloning because sometimes it will be used for instrumental purposes misses both the complexity of human motivation and the unpredictability of developing personal relationships. Moreover, cloning does not stand out from other forms of reproductive technology in the degree to which it is an instrument of parental fulfillment. The problem of objectification permeates social relations. By loading all the weight of that sin on the head of one cloned lamb, we neatly avoid considering our own more general responsibility.

The serious ethical problems raised by the prospect of human cloning lie in the fourth domain considered by the bioethics commission, that of safety. Apparently, these problems arise because cloned embryos may not have a proper set of chromosomes. Normally, a sexually reproduced organism contains in all its cells two sets of chromosomes, one received from its mother through the egg and one from the father through the sperm. Each of these sets contains a complete set of the different kinds of genes necessary for normal development and adult function. Even though each set has a complete repertoire of genes, for reasons that are not well understood we must have two sets and only two sets to complete normal development. If one of the chromosomes should accidentally be present in only one copy or in three, development will be severely impaired.

Usually we have exactly two copies in our cells because in the formation of the egg and sperm that combined to produce us, a special form of cell division occurs that puts one and only one copy of each chromosome into each egg and each sperm. Occasionally, however, especially in people in their later reproductive years, this mechanism is faulty and a sperm or egg is produced in which one or another chromosome is absent or present more than once. An embryo conceived from such a faulty gamete will have a missing or extra chromosome. Down's syndrome, for example, results from an extra Chromosome 21, and Edward's syndrome, almost always lethal in the first few weeks of life, is produced by an extra Chromosome 18.

After an egg is fertilized in the usual course of events

by a sperm, cell division begins to produce an embryo, and the chromosomes, which were in a resting state in the original sperm and egg, are induced to replicate new copies by signals from the complex machinery of cell division. The division of the cells and the replication of more chromosome copies are in perfect synchrony so every new cell gets a complete exact set of chromosomes just like the fertilized egg. When clonal reproduction is performed, however, the events are quite different. The nucleus containing the egg's chromosomes are removed and the egg cell is fused with a cell containing a nucleus from the donor that already contains a full duplicate set of chromosomes. These chromosomes are not necessarily in the resting state and so they may divide out of synchrony with the embryonic cells. The result will be extra and missing chromosomes so that the embryo will be abnormal and will usually, but not necessarily, die.

The whole trick of successful cloning is to make sure that the chromosomes of the donor are in the right state. However, no one knows how to make sure. Dr. Wilmut and his colleagues know the trick in principle, but they produced only one successful Dolly out of 277 tries. The other 276 embryos died at various stages of development. It seems pretty obvious that the reason the Scottish laboratory did not announce the existence of Dolly until she was a full-grown adult sheep is that they were worried that her postnatal development would go awry. Of course, the technique will get better, but people are not sheep and there is no way to make cloning work reliably in people except to experiment on people. Sheep were chosen by the Scottish group because they had turned out in earlier work to be unusually favorable animals for growing fetuses cloned from embryonic cells. Cows had been tried but without success. Even if the methods could be made eventually to work as well in humans as in sheep,

how many human embryos are to be sacrificed, and at
what stage of their development?[5] Ninety percent of the
loss of the experimental sheep embryos was at the so-
called "morula" stage, hardly more than a ball of cells. Of
the twenty-nine embryos implanted in maternal uter-
uses, only one showed up as a fetus after fifty days *in
utero*, and that lamb was finally born as Dolly.

Suppose we have a high success rate of bringing cloned
human embryos to term. What kinds of developmental
abnormalities would be acceptable? Acceptable to whom?
Once again, the moral problems said to be raised by cloning are not unique to that technology. Every form of reproductive technology raises issues of lives worth living,
of the stage at which an embryo is thought of as human,
as having rights including the juridical right to state protection. Even that most benign and widespread prenatal
intervention, amniocentesis, has a non-negligible risk of
damaging the fetus. By concentrating on the acceptability of cloning, the commission again tried to finesse the
much wider issues.

They may have done so, however, at the peril of legiti-
mating questions about abortion and reproductive technology that the state has tried to avoid, questions raised from a
religious standpoint. Despite the secular basis of the American polity, religious forces have over and over played an
important role in influencing state policy. Churches and
religious institutions were leading actors in the abolitionist
movement and the Underground Railroad,[6] the modern civil
rights movement and the resistance to the war in Vietnam.
In these instances religious forces were part of, and in the
case of the civil rights movement leaders of, wider social
movements intervening on the side of the oppressed against
then-reigning state policy. They were both liberatory and
representative of a widespread sentiment that did not ultimately depend upon religious claims.

The present movements of religious forces to intervene

in issues of sex, family structure, reproductive behavior, and abortion are of a different character. They are perceived by many people, both secular and religious, not as liberatory but as restrictive, not as intervening on the side of the wretched of the earth but as themselves oppressive of the widespread desire for individual autonomy. They seem to threaten the stable accommodation between Church and State that has characterized American social history. The structure of the commission's report reflects this current tension in the formation of public policy. There are two separate chapters on the moral debate, one labeled "Ethical Considerations" and the other "Religious Perspectives." By giving a separate and identifiable voice to explicitly religious views the commission has legitimated religious conviction as a front on which the issues of sex, reproduction, the definition of the family, and the status of fertilized eggs and fetuses are to be fought.

The distinction made by the commission between "religious *perspectives*" and "ethical *considerations*" is precisely the distinction between theological hermeneutics—interpretation of sacred texts—and philosophical inquiry. The religious problem is to recognize God's truth. If a natural family were defined as one man, one woman, and such children as they have produced through loving procreation; if a human life, imbued by God with a soul, is definitively initiated at conception; if sex, love, and the begetting of children are by revelation morally inseparable; then the work of bioethics commissions becomes a great deal easier. Of course, the theologians who testified were not in agreement with each other on the relevant matters, in part because they depend on different sources of revelation and in part because the meaning of those sources is not unambiguous. So some theologians, including Roman Catholics, took human beings to be "stewards" of a fixed creation, gardeners tending what has already been planted. Others, notably Jewish and Islamic scholars, emphasized a "partnership" with God that includes improving on creation. One Islamic authority thought that there was a positive imperative to intervene in the works of nature, including early embryonic development, for the sake of health.

Some Protestant commentators saw humans as "co-creators" with God and so certainly not barred from improving on present nature. In the end, some religious scholars thought cloning was definitively to be prohibited, while others thought it could be justified under some circumstances. As far as one can tell, fundamentalist Protestants were not consulted, an omission that rather weakens the usefulness of the proceedings for setting public policy. The failure to engage directly the politically most active and powerful American religious constituency, while soliciting opinions from a much safer group of "religious scholars," can only be understood as a tactic of defense of an avowedly secular state against pressure for a yet greater role for religion. Perhaps the commission was already certain of what Pat Robertson would say.

The immense strength of a religious viewpoint is that it is capable of abolishing hard ethical problems if only we can correctly decipher the meaning of what has been revealed to us.[7] It is a question of having the correct "perspective." Philosophical "considerations" are quite another matter. The painful tensions and contradictions that seem to the secular moral philosopher to be unresolvable in principle, but that demand de facto resolution in public and private action, did not appear in the testimony of any of the theologians. While they disagreed with one another, they did not have to cope with internal contradictions in their own positions. That, of course, is a great attraction of the religious perspective. It is not only poetry that tempts us to a willing suspension of disbelief.

Notes

[1] Report of the specially created Advisory Committee on Human Radiation Experiments (October 3, 1995).

[2] In fact, identical twins are genetically *more* identical than a cloned organism is to its donor. All the biologically inherited information is not carried in the genes of a cell's nucleus. A very small number of genes, sixty out of a total of 100,000 or so, are carried by intracellular bodies, the mitochondria. These mitochondrial genes specify certain essential enzyme proteins, and defects in these genes can lead to a variety of disorders. The importance of this point for cloning is that the egg cell that has had its nucleus removed to make way for the genes of the donor cell has not had its mitochondria removed. The result of the cell fusion that will give rise to the cloned embryo is then a mixture of mitochondrial genes from the donor and the recipient. Thus, it is not, strictly speaking, a perfect genetic clone of the donor organism. Identical twins, however, *are* the result of the splitting of a fertilized egg and have the same mitochondria as well as the same nucleus.

[3] G.J. Annas, "Scientific discoveries and cloning: Challenges for public policy," testimony of March 12, 1997.

[4] There is always the possibility, of course, that gene mutations have predisposed the child to leukemia, in which case the transplant from a genetic clone only propagates the defect.

[5] It has recently been announced that a cow has been cloned successfully, but by an indirect method that, if applied in humans, raises the following ethical problem. The method involves cloning embryos from adult cells, but then breaking up the embryos to use cells for a round of cloning. In other words, the calf owes its life to many destroyed embryos.

[6] An example was the resistance to the Fugitive Slave Acts by the pious Presbyterians of Oberlin, Ohio, an excellent account of which may be found in Nat Brandt, *The Town that Started the Civil War* (Syracuse 1990).

[7] Once, impelled by a love of contradiction, I asked a friend learned in the Talmud whether meat from a cow into which a single pig gene had been genetically engineered would be kosher. His reply was that the problem would not arise for the laws of *kashruth* because to make any mixed animal was already a prohibited thing.

Leon Eisenberg

Would Cloned Humans Really Be Like Sheep?

The recent proof, by DNA-microsatellite analysis[1] and DNA-fingerprinting techniques,[2] that Dolly the sheep had indeed been cloned as Wilmut et al. claimed,[3] and the report by Wakayama et al.[4] of the successful cloning of more than 20 healthy female mice are likely to reactivate discussions of the ethics of cloning humans and to provoke more calls to ban experiments on mammalian cloning altogether. From the standpoint of biologic science, a ban on such laboratory experiments would be a severe setback to research in embryology.[5] From the standpoint of moral philosophy, the ethical debate has been so obscured by incorrect assumptions about the relation between a potential human clone and its adult progenitor that the scientific issues must be reexamined in order to clarify the relation between genotype and phenotype. There are powerful biologic objections to the use of cloning to alter the human species, objections that make speculations about the ethics of the process largely irrelevant.

Experiments in Cloning

A clone is the aggregate of the asexually produced progeny of an individual organism. Reproduction by cloning in horticulture involves the use of cuttings of a single plant to propagate desired botanical characteristics indefinitely. In microbiology, a colony of bacteria constitutes a clone if its members are the descendants of a single bacterium that has undergone repeated asexual fission. The myriad bacteria in the clone each have precisely the same genetic complement as that of the progenitor cell and are indistinguishable from one another.

Success in cloning mammals demonstrates unequivocally that at least some of the nuclei in fully differentiated mammalian cells contain the full complement of potentially active genetic material that is present in the zygote. What distinguishes differentiated cells is the sets of genes that are turned "off" or "on." The cloning experiments in animals suggest that similar techniques might make it possible to clone humans. Such cloning would involve transferring a human ovum to a test tube, removing its nucleus, replacing it with a somatic-cell nucleus from the donor of the ovum or another person, allowing the ovum with its new diploid nucleus to differentiate to the blastula stage, and then implanting it in a "host" uterus. The resultant person, on attaining maturity, would be an identical genetic twin of the adult nuclear donor. This hypothetical outcome, although remote, has given rise to speculation about the psychological, ethical, and social consequences of producing clones of human beings. The futuristic scenarios evoked by the prospect of human cloning contain implicit assumptions about the mechanisms of human development. Examination of these underlying premises highlights themes that can be traced back to Greek antiquity, themes that recur in contemporary debates about the sources of differences between groups with respect to such characteristics as intelligence and aggression.[6]

Theories of Development

The enigmas of human development have concerned philosophers and naturalists since people first began to wonder how plants and animals emerged from the products of fertilization.[7] Despite the fact that there is no resemblance between the physical appearance of the seed and the form of the adult organism, the plant or animal to which it gives rise is an approximate replica of its progenitors. The earliest Greek explanation was preformation—that is, the seed contains all adult structures in miniature. This ancient speculation, found in the Hippocratic corpus, was given poetic expression by Seneca:[8] "In the seed are enclosed all the parts of the body of the man that shall be formed. The infant that is born in his mother's womb has the roots of the beard and hair that he shall wear one day." The theory of preformation was so powerful that 1600 years later, when the microscope was invented, the first microscopists to examine a sperm were able to persuade themselves that they could see in its head a homunculus with all the features of a tiny but complete man. Improvements in the microscope and the establishment of embryology as an experimental science made the doctrine progressively more difficult to sustain in its original form. With better microscopical resolution, the expected structures could not be seen, and experimental manipulation of embryos produced abnormal "monsters" that' could not, by definition, have already been present in the seed.

The alternative view, that of epigenesis, was formulated by Aristotle. Having opened eggs at various stages of development, he observed that the individual organs did not all appear at the same time, as preformation theory demanded. He did not accept the argument that differences in the size of the organs could account for the failure to see them all at the same time. Others as well as Aristotle had noted that the heart is visible before the lungs, even though the lungs are ultimately much larger. Unlike his predecessors, Aristotle began with the observable data. He concluded that new parts were formed in succession and did not merely unfold from precursors already present: [9]

It is possible, then, that A should move B and B should move C, that, in fact, the case should be the same as with the automatic machines shown as curiosities. For the parts of such machines while at rest have a sort of potentiality of motion in them, and when any external force puts the first of them into motion, immediately the next is moved in actuality... In like manner also that from which the semen comes...sets up the movement in the embryo and makes the parts of it by having touched first something though not continuing to touch it... While there is something that makes the parts, this does not exist as a definite object, nor does it exist in the semen at the first as a complete part.

This is the first statement of the theory of epigenesis: successive stages of differentiation in the course of development give rise to new properties and new structures. The genetic code in the zygote determines the range of possible outcomes. Yet the genes that arc active in the zygote serve only to initiate a sequence, the outcome of which is dependent on the moment-to-moment interactions between the products of successive stages in development. For example, the potential for differentiating into pancreatic tissue is limited to cells in a particular zone of the embryo. But these cells will produce prozymogen, the histologic marker of pancreatic tissue, only if they are in contact with neighboring mesenchymal cells; if they are separated from mesenchyme, their evolution is arrested, despite their genetic potential.[10] At the same time, the entire process is dependent on the adequacy of the uterine environment, defects in which lead to anomalous development and miscarriage.

Outcomes of Human Cloning

The methodological barriers to successful human cloning are formidable. Nonetheless, even if the necessary virtuosity lies in a more distant future than science-fiction enthusiasts suggest, one can argue that a solution exists in principle and attempt to envisage the possible outcomes.

Restricting Genetic Diversity

One negative consequence of very wide scale cloning is that it would lead to a marked restriction in the diversity of the human gene pool. Such a limitation would endanger the ability of our species to survive major environmental changes. Genetic homogeneity is compatible only with adaptation to a very narrow ecological niche. Once that niche is perturbed (e.g., by the invasion of a new predator or a change in temperature or water supply), extinction may follow. For example, the "green revolution" in agriculture has led to the selective cultivation of grain seeds chosen for high yield under modern conditions of fertilization and pest control. Worldwide food production, as a result, is now highly vulnerable to new blights because of our reliance on a narrow range of genotypes.[11] Recognition of this threat has led to a call for the creation of seed banks containing representatives of "wild" species as protection against catastrophe from new blights or changed climatic conditions, to which the current high-yield grains prove particularly vulnerable.[12] Indeed, the loss of species (genetically distinct populations) is impoverishing global biodiversity as the result of shrinking habitats.[13]

Precisely the same threat would hold for humans, were we to replace sexual reproduction with cloning. The extraordinary biologic investment in sexual reproduction (as compared with asexual replication) provides a measure of its importance to the evolution of species. Courtship is expensive in its energy requirements, reproductive organs are elaborate, and there are extensive differences between male and female in secondary sexual characteristics. The benefit of sexual reproduction is the enhancement of diversity (by the crossover between homologous chromosomes during meiosis and by the combining of the haploid gametes of a male and a female). The new genetic combinations so produced enable the species to respond as a population to changing environmental conditions through the selective survival of adaptable genotypes.

Cloning Yesterday's People for Tomorrow's Problems

The choice of whom to clone could be made only on the basis of phenotypic characteristics manifested during the several decades when the persons being considered for cloning had come to maturity. Let us set aside the problem of assigning value to particular characteristics and assume that we agree on the traits to be valued, however unrealistic that assumption.

By definition, the genetic potential for these characteristics must have existed in the persons who now exhibit them. But the translation of that potential into the phenotype occurs in the particular environment in which development occurs. Even if we agree on the genotype we wish to preserve, we face a formidable barrier: we know so little of the environmental features necessary for the flowering of that genotype that we cannot specify in detail the environment we would have to provide, both before and after birth, to ensure a phenotypic outcome identical to the complex of traits we seek to perpetuate.

Let us make a further dubious assumption and suppose the day has arrived when we can specify the environment necessary for the flowering of the chosen phenotype. Nonetheless, the phenotype so admirably suited to the world in which it matured may not be adaptive to the world a generation hence. That is, the traits that lead a person to be creative or to exhibit leadership at one moment in history may not be appropriate at another. Not only is the environment not static, it is altered by our own extraordinary impact on our ecology. The proliferation of our species changes patterns of disease[14, 15]; our methods of disease control, by altering population ratios, affect the physical environment itself.[16] Social evolution demands new types of men and women. Cloning would condemn us always to plan the future on the basis of the past (since the successful phenotype cannot be identified sooner than adulthood).

The Connection between Genotype and Phenotype

For the student of biology, cloning is a powerful and instructive method with great potential for deepening our understanding of the mechanisms of differentiation during development. The potential of a given genotype can only be estimated from the varied manifestations of the phenotype over as wide a range of environments as are compatible with its survival. The wider the range of environments, the greater the diversity observed in the phenotypic manifestations of the one genotype. Human populations possess an extraordinary range of latent variability. Dissimilar genotypes can produce remarkably similar phenotypes under the wide range of conditions that characterize the environments of the inhabitable portions of the globe. The differences resulting from genotypic variability are manifested most clearly under extreme conditions, when severe stresses overwhelm the homeostatic mechanisms that ordinarily act as buffers against small perturbations.

Phenotypic identity requires identity between genotypes, which cloning can ensure, and identity between environmental interactions, which it cannot ensure. At the most trivial level, we can anticipate less similarity even in physical appearance between cell donor and cloned recipient than that which is observed between one-egg twins. Placental attachment and fetal-maternal circulation can vary substantially, even for uniovular twins housed in one uterus. Developmental circumstances will be more variable between donor and cloned recipient, who will have been carried by different women.

Postnatal Environmental Effects on the Human Brain

Let us force the argument one step further by assuming that the environmental conditions for the cloned infant have been identical to those of his or her progenitor, so that at birth the infant is a replica of the infant its "father" or "mother" was at birth. Under such circumstances (and within the limits of the precision of genetic specification), the immediate pattern of central nervous system connections and their responses to stimulation will be the same as those of the progenitor at birth.

However, even under these circumstances, the future is not predestined. The human species is notable for the proportion of brain development that occurs postnatally. Other primate brains increase in weight from birth to maturity by a factor of 2 to 2.5, but the human brain increases by a factor of 3.5 to 4.

There is a fourfold increase in the neocortex, with a marked elaboration of the receiving areas for the teloreceptors, a disproportionate expansion of the motor area for the hand in relation to the representation of other parts, a representation of tongue and larynx many times greater, and a great increase in the "association" areas. The elaboration of pathways and interconnections is highly dependent on the quantity, quality, and timing of intellectual and emotional stimulation. The very structure of the brain, as well as the function of the mind, emerges from the interaction between maturation and experience.[17]

Nature and nurture jointly mold the structure of the brain. The basic plan of the central nervous system is laid down in the human genome, but the detailed pattern of connections results from competition between axons for common target neurons. Consider the steps in the formation of alternating ocular layers in the lateral geniculate bodies. Early in embryogenesis, axons from both eyes enter each of the geniculate nuclei and intermingle. How does the separation of layers for each eye, essential for vision, come about? It results from periodic waves of spontaneous electrical activity in retinal ganglion cells, because immature cell membranes are unstable. If these electrical outbursts are abolished experimentally, the layers simply do not become separated.[18] Competition between the two eyes, driven by spontaneous retinal activity, determines eye-specific lateral geniculate connections.[19] Neither the genes governing the retina nor the genes governing the geniculate specify the alternating ocular layers; it is the interaction between retina and geniculate during embryogenesis that brings it about. Furthermore, the precise targeting of projections from lateral geniculate to occipital cortex is dependent on electrical activity in the geniculate. Abolishing these action potentials with an infusion of tetrodotoxin results in projections to cortical areas that are normally bypassed and a marked reduction in projections to visual cortex.[20]

Postnatal stimulation is required to form the ocular dominance columns in the occipital cortex.[21] Both eyes of the newborn must receive precisely focused stimulation from the visual environment during the early months of postnatal life in order to fine-tune the structure of the cortex. If focused vision in one eye of a kitten or an infant monkey is interfered with, the normal eye "captures" most neurons in the occipital cortex in the absence of competition from the deprived eye. The change becomes irreversible if occlusion is maintained throughout the sensitive period. Amblyopia in humans, characterized by incongruent visual images from the two eyes, results in permanent loss of effective vision from the unused eye if the defect is not corrected within the first five years of life.

Thus, which of the overabundant neurons live and which die is determined by the amount and consistency of the stimulation they receive. Interaction between organism and environment leads to patterned neuronal activity that determines which synapses will persist.[22] Experience molds the brain in a process that continues throughout life. Myelination in a key relay zone in the hippocampal formation continues to increase from childhood through at least the sixth decade of life.[23] And recent research has provided evidence that neurons in the dentate gyrus of the hippocampus continue to divide in the adult brain.[24]

Changes in the Brain with Use

Techniques of functional brain mapping reveal marked variations in cortical representation that depend on prior experience. Manipulation of sensory inputs leads to reorganization of the cortex in monkey[25] and humans.[26] The motor cortex in violinists displays a substantially larger representation of the fingers of the left hand (the one used to play the strings) than of the fingers of the right (or bowing) hand. Moreover, the area of the brain dedicated to finger representation is larger in musicians than in nonmusicians.[27] Sterr et al[28] compared finger representation in the somatosensory cortex in blind persons who used three fingers on each hand to read Braille with that in Braille readers using only one finger on one hand and in sighted readers. They found a substantial enlargement of hand representation in the Braille readers who used two hands, with topographic changes on the postcentral gyrus.

If enlargement of cortical areas accompanies increases in activity, shrinkage follows loss. Within days after mastectomy, the amputation of an arm or leg, or the correction of syndactyly, the cortical sensory map changes. Intact areas have an enlarged representation at the expense of areas from which innervation has been removed.[29, 30] What begins prenatally continues throughout life. Structure follows function.

Becoming Human

There is yet another level of complexity in the analysis of personality development. The human traits of interest to us are polygenic rather than monogenic; similar outcomes can result from the interaction between different genomes and different social environments. To produce another Wolfgang Amadeus Mozart, we would need not only Wolfgang's genome but his mother's uterus, his father's music lessons, his parents' friends and his own, the state of music in 18th-century Austria, Haydn's patronage, and on and on, in ever-widening circles. Without Mozart's set of genes, the rest would not suffice; there was, after all, only one Wolfgang Amadeus Mozart. But we have no right to the converse assumption: that his genome, cultivated in another world at another time, would result in the same musical genius. If a particular strain of wheat yields different harvests under different conditions of climate, soil, and cultivation, how can we assume that so much more complex a genome as that of a human being would yield its desired crop of operas, symphonies, and chamber music under different circumstances of nurture?

In sum, cloning would be a poor method indeed for improving on the human species. If widely adopted, it would have a devastating impact on the diversity of the human gene pool. Cloning would select for traits that have been successful in the past but that will not necessarily be adaptive to an unpredictable future. Whatever phenotypes might be produced would be extremely vulnerable to the uncontrollable vicissitudes of the environment.

Proposals for human cloning as a method for "improving" the species are biologic nonsense. To elevate the question to the level of an ethical issue is sheer casuistry. The problem lies not in the ethics of cloning a human but in the metaphysical cloud that surrounds this hypothetical cloned creature. Pseudobiology trivializes ethics and distracts our attention from real moral issues: the ways in which the genetic potential of humans born into impoverished environments today is stunted and thwarted. To improve our species, no biologic sleight of hand is needed. Had we the moral commitment to provide every child with what we desire for our own, what a flowering of humankind there would be.

References

[1] Ashworth D, Bishop M, Campbell K, et al. DNA microsatellite analysis of Dolly. Nature 1998;394:329.

[2] Signer EN, Dubrova YE, Jeffreys AJ, et al. DNA fingerprinting Dolly Nature 1998;394:329–30.

[3] Wilmut I, Schnicke AE, McWhir J, Kind AJ, Campbell KH. Viable off spring derived from fetal and adult mammalian cells. Nature 1997;385: 810–3. [Erratum, Nature 1997;386:200.]

[4] Wakayama T, Perry AC, Zuccotti M, Johnson KR, Yanagimachi R. Full-term development of mice from enucleated oocytes injected with cumulus cell nuclei. Nature 1998;394:369–74.

[5] Berg P, Singer M. Regulating human cloning. Science 1998;282:413.

[6] Eisenberg L. The human nature of human nature. Science 1972;176:123–8.

[7] Needham J. A history of embryology. New York: Abelard-Schuman, 1959.

[8] Idem, A history of embryology. New York: Abelard-Schuman, 1959:66.

[9] Idem, A history of embryology. New York: Abelard-Schuman, 1959:47–8.

[10] Grobstein C. Cytodifferentiation and its controls. Science 1964;143:643–50.

[11] Harlan JR. Our vanishing genetic resources. Science 1975;188:618–21.

[12] National Research Council. Genetic vulnerability of major crops. Washington, D.C.: National Academy of Sciences, 1972.

[13] Hughes JB, Daily GC, Ehrlich PR. Population diversity: its extent and extinction, Science 1997;278:689–92.

[14] Black FL. Infectious diseases in primitive societies. Science 1975;187:515–8.

[15] Idem, Why did they die? Science 1992;258:1739–40.

[16] Ormerod VTE. Ecological effect of control of African trypanosomiasis. Science 1976;191:815–21.

[17] Eisenberg L. The social construction of the human brain. Am J Psychiatry 1995;152:1563–75.

[18] Shatz CJ, Stryker MP. Prenatal tetrodotoxin infusion blocks segregation of retinogeniculate afferents. Science 1988;242:87–9.

[19] Penn AA, Riquelme PA, Feller MB, Shatz CJ. Competition in retinogeniculate patterning driven by spontaneous activity. Science 1998;279:2108–12.

[20] Catalano SM, Shatz CJ. Activity-dependent cortical target selection by thalamic axons. Science 1998;281:559–62.

[21] Wiesci TN. The postnatal development of the visual cortex and the influence of environment (the 1981 Nobel Prize lecture). Stockholm, Sweden: Nobel Foundation, 1982.

[22] Nelson CA, Bloom FE. Child development and neuroscience. Child Dev 1997;68:970–87

[23] Benes FM, Turtle M, Khan Y, Farol P. Myelination of a key relay zone in the hippocampal formation occurs in the human brain during childhood, adolescence, and adulthood. Arch Gen Psychiatry 1994;51:447–84.

[24] Eriksson PS, Perfileva E, Björk-Eriksson T, et al. Neurogenesis in the adult human hippocampus. Nat Med 1998;4:1313–7

[25] Wang X, Merzenich MM, Sameshima K, Jenkins WM. Remodeling of hand representation in adult cortex determined by timing of tactile stimulation. Nature 1995;378:71–5.

[26] Hamdy S, Bothwell JC, Aziz Q, Singh KD, Thompson DG. Long-term reorganization of human motor cortex driven by short-term sensory stimulation. Nat Neurosci 1998;1:64–8.

[27] Schlaug G, Janke L, Huang Y, Steinmetz H. In vivo evidence of structural brain asymmetry in musicians. Science 1995;267:699–701.

[28] Sterr A, Muller MM, Elbert T, Rockstroh B, Pantev C, Taub E. Perceptual correlates of changes in cortical representation of fingers in blind multifinger Braille readers. J Neurosci 1998;18:4417–23.

[29] Yang TT, Gallen CC, Ramachandran VS, Cobb S, Schwartz BL, Bloom FE. Noninvasive detection of cerebral plasticity in adult human somatosensory cortex. Neuroreport 1994;5:701–4.

[30] Mogilner A, Grossman JA, Ribary U, et al. Somatosensory cortical plasticity in adult humans revealed by magnetoencephalography. Proc Natl Acad Sci U S A 1993;90:3593–7.

Carson Strong

Cloning and Infertility

Although there are important moral arguments against cloning[1] human beings, it has been suggested that there might be exceptional cases in which cloning humans would be ethically permissible.[2-3] One type of supposed exceptional case involves infertile couples who want to have children by cloning. This paper explores whether cloning would be ethically permissible in infertility cases and the separate question of whether we should have a policy allowing cloning in such cases. One caveat should be stated at the beginning, however. After the cloning of a sheep in Scotland, scientists pointed out that using the same technique to clone humans would, at present, involve substantial risks of producing children with birth defects.[4-6] This concern over safety gives compelling support to the view that it would be wrong to attempt human cloning now. Thus, we do not reach the debate about exceptional cases unless the issue of safety can be set aside. I ask the reader to consider the possibility that in the future humans could be cloned without a significantly elevated risk of birth defects from the cloning process itself. The remainder of this paper assumes, for sake of argument, that cloning technology has advanced to that point. Given this assumption, would cloning in the infertility cases be ethically permissible, and should it be legally permitted?

An example of the type of case in question is a scenario in which the woman cannot produce ova and the man cannot produce sperm capable of fertilizing ova.[7] Like many couples, they wish to have a child genetically related to at least one of them. One approach would use sperm and ova donated by family members, but suppose that no family donors are available in this case. Let us assume, in other words, that cloning is the only way they could have a child genetically related to one of them. Imagine the couple asking their infertility doctor to help them have a child by cloning. This would involve replacing the nucleus of a donated ovum with that of a cell taken from either member of the couple. Suppose that an ovum donor is available who is willing to participate in this process. The infertile couple would decide whether to duplicate genetically the woman or the man. They could try to have a girl or a boy or possibly a child of each sex—fraternal twins. They could use cloning again to have subsequent children: perhaps one the opposite sex of a first child; or another the same sex; or twins again, among other possibilities.

Many would consider cloning ethically unjustifiable in such cases. Following the birth of Dolly the sheep clone, the response from ethicists, politicians, and journalists was overwhelmingly against cloning human beings.[8-12] In fact, few issues in bioethics seem to have reached the high level of consensus found in our society's opposition to human cloning. This opposition rests on a number of concerns, religious and secular. I will focus on the secular arguments, which include at least the following main ones. First, the persons produced would lack genetic uniqueness, and this might be psychologically harmful to them. Second, this reproductive method transforms babymaking into a process similar to manufacturing. Children would become products made according to specification; this would objectify children and adversely affect parental attitudes toward children and other aspects of parent-child relationships. Third, additional abuses might occur if this technology were obtained by totalitarian regimes or other unscrupulous persons.

My main thesis is that the ethics of cloning is not as clear-cut as many seem to think. Specifically, when the arguments against cloning are applied to infertility cases like the one described above, they are not as strong as they might initially appear. Such cases can reasonably move us away from the view that cloning humans is always wrong. Moreover, the arguments for legally prohibiting cloning in such cases are not strong enough to support such restrictions.

Whether cloning in the above case is ethically justifiable rests on the following question: Which is weightier, infertile couples' reproductive freedom to use cloning or the arguments against cloning humans? To address this question, we need to examine closely both the importance of the freedom of infertile couples to utilize cloning and the arguments against its use.

Freedom of Infertile Couples to Use Cloning

Let us begin by asking why the freedom of infertile couples to use cloning should be valued. Because a main reason to use cloning in the above case is to have children who are genetically related to at least one member of the couple, we need to ask whether reasons can be given to value the having of genetically related children. It is worth noting that studies[13-18] have identified a number of reasons people actually give for having genetically related offspring, some of which seem selfish and confused. For example, some people desire genetic children as a way to demonstrate their virility or femininity. The views on which these reasons seem to be based—that virility is central to the worth of a man, and that women must have babies to prove their femininity—are unwarranted. They stereotype sex-roles and overlook ways self-esteem can be enhanced other than by having genetic offspring. Another example involves desiring a genetic child in order to "save" a shaky marriage. This reason fails to address the sources of the marital problems, and the added stress of raising the child might make the marital relationship even more difficult. Some commentators seem to think that the desire for genetic offspring is always unreasonable, as in these examples.[19] Rather than make this assumption, we should consider whether there are defensible reasons that could be given for desiring genetic offspring.

I have explored this question elsewhere, focusing on a category of procreation commonly referred to as "having a child of one's own," sometimes stated simply as "having a child" or "having children.[20] Although these expressions can be interpreted in several ways, I use them to refer to begetting, by sexual intercourse, a child whom one rears or helps rear. This, of course, is the common type of procreation, in which parents raise children genetically their own. My strategy was to try to understand why having genetic offspring might be meaningful to people in this ordinary scenario, and then use this understanding to address assisted reproductive technologies. For the common type of procreation, I identified six reasons people might give for valuing the having of genetic offspring. Briefly, they are as follows: having a child involves participation in the creation of a person; it can be an affirmation of a couple's mutual love and acceptance of each other; it can contribute to sexual intimacy; it provides a link to future persons; it involves experiences of pregnancy and childbirth; and it leads to experiences associated with child rearing. However, the above infertility case differs in several ways from the ordinary type of procreation, including the fact that children would not be created by sexual intercourse. Because of these differences, not all the reasons that might be given in justifying the desire for genetic offspring in the common scenario would be strong reasons in the cloning situation. Nevertheless, I believe that at least the following two reasons would be significant.

Participation in the Creation of a Person

When one 'has a child of one's own,' as defined above, a normal outcome is the creation of an individual with self-consciousness. Philosophers have regarded the phenomenon of self-consciousness with wonder, noting that it raises perplexing questions: What is the relationship between body and mind? How can the physical matter of the brain give rise to consciousness? It is ironic that although we have difficulty giving satisfactory answers to these questions, we can create self-consciousness with relative ease. Each of us who begets or gestates a child who becomes self-conscious participates in the creation of a person. One might say that in having children we participate in the mystery of the creation of self-consciousness. For this reason, among others, some might regard creating a person as an important event, perhaps one with metaphysical or spiritual dimensions (p. 114).[21] Perhaps not all who have children think about procreation in these terms, but this is a reason that can be given to help justify the desire for genetic offspring.

Similarly, the infertile couple might reasonably value the use of cloning because it would enable them to participate in the creation of a person. The member of the couple whose chromosomes are used would participate by providing the genetic material for the new person. Regardless of whose chromosomes are used, if the woman is capable of gestating, she could participate by gestating and giving birth to the child.

It might be objected that the infertile couple could participate in the creation of a person by using donor gametes or preembryos, in the sense that they would authorize the steps taken in an attempt to create a person. Also, if the woman were the gestational mother and used donor gametes or preembryos, then she would participate biologically in the creation of the person. In reply, although these would constitute types of participation, a more direct involvement would occur if one member of the couple contributed genetically to the creation of the child. From the body of one of them would come the makeup of the new person. Cloning would be the only way that the man, in fact, could participate biologically in the creation of the person. This more direct involvement would increase the degree to which the couple participates in the creation of a person, and for some this greater participation might be especially meaningful.

Affirmation of Mutual Love

In the ordinary type of procreation, intentionally having children can be an affirmation of a couple's mutual love and acceptance of each other. It can be a deep expression of acceptance to say to another, in effect, "I want a child to come forth from your body and mine." In such a context there might be an anticipation that the bond between the couple will grow stronger because of common children to whom each has a biological relationship. To intentionally seek the strengthening of their personal bond in this manner can be a further affirmation of mutual love and acceptance.

In the infertility case in question, if cloning is used, then the child would not receive genes from both parents. Nevertheless, a similar affirmation of mutual love is possible if the woman is capable of being the gestational mother and the man's genes are used. In that situation, it remains true that the child comes forth from their two bodies. Assuming mutual love, the woman bears a child having the genes of the man who loves her and is loved by her. Alternatively, suppose that the woman's genes are used. The man then can become the social father of a child having the genes of the woman who loves him and is loved by him; to seek to become social parents in this manner can also be an affirmation of mutual acceptance.

It might be objected that having children by donor gametes or preembryos —or even adopting children—can also be an affirmation of mutual acceptance, for each member of the couple selects the other to be a social parent of their children. These types of affirmation could enrich the couple's relationship with each other. In response, although these would indeed be forms of affirmation, they can be viewed as different from the affirmation involved in trying to have genetically related children. Intentionally to create a child having the partner's genes might be regarded by some as a special type of affirmation, one that would enrich the couple's relationship in its own distinctive way. For some couples, this type of affirmation might have special significance.

In stating these two reasons, I do not mean to imply that one *ought* to desire genetic offspring, much less that one ought to desire cloning if necessary to have genetically related children. Rather, the point is that the desire for genetic offspring—and hence the desire for cloning in the situation being considered—could be supported by reasons that deserve consideration. Although not everyone in the infertile couple's situation would want to pursue cloning, some might. These reasons also help explain why *freedom* to use cloning to have biological children might be considered valuable; namely, because some couples might value either the opportunity to participate directly in the creation of a person or an affirmation of mutual love that can be associated with that endeavor, or both.

Arguments against Cloning

Let us turn to the considerations against cloning, beginning with the arguments based on lack of genetic uniqueness. What exactly are the adverse effects envisioned for persons who are genetically identical to others? Perhaps the most obvious concerns involve the possibility of being one of *many* genetically identical persons—perhaps one of hundreds of clones, or thousands, or even more. One argument is that the clones would be psychologically harmed, in that they would feel insignificant and have low self-esteem. If I know that I am one of many who physically are exact duplicates, then I might easily believe that there is little or nothing special about me. Apart from what the clones would feel, objections to multiple cloning can also be made from a deontological perspective; it would be an affront to their human dignity to be one of so many genetic replicas. There would also be a serious violation of personal autonomy if the clones were under the control of those who produced them.

Lack of genetic uniqueness can raise concerns even if there are not many clones. Imagine, for example, being the single clone of a person 30 years older. There might be a tendency for the older person's life to be regarded as a standard to be met or exceeded by the younger one. If the clone feels pressured to accept that standard, this might be a significant impediment to freedom in directing one's own life. In addition, knowing that one is a clone might be psychologically harmful in this situation too. For example, self-esteem could be diminished; perhaps the child would regard herself as nothing more than a copy of someone who has already traveled the path ahead.

Although these arguments initially appear persuasive, we need to consider the conclusions reached when we apply them to the infertility case. To begin, the arguments based on large cohorts of clones would not be relevant. The couple might create only one or two children using cloning; thus, their use of cloning can be distinguished from scenarios in which large numbers of clones are produced.

The argument that the parent's life might be regarded as a standard would be relevant, but a response can be given. For one thing, parents' lives often are held up as standards, even in the absence of cloning. This can be either good or bad for the child, depending on how it is handled; it has the potential to promote as well as inhibit development of the child's talents, abilities, and autonomy. Similarly, a clone's being given a role model or standard is not necessarily bad. It depends on how the standard is used and regarded by those directly involved. If it is used by parents in a loving and nurturing manner, it can help children develop their autonomy, rather than inhibit it.

It might be objected that when the child is genetically identical to the parent, there will be a tendency for the parent to be less forgiving when the child fails to meet expectations. If so, the parental standard might tend to thwart rather than promote the child's developing autonomy. In reply, it should be noted that this concern is rather speculative. We do not know the extent, if any, to which the child's being genetically identical would tend to promote a domineering attitude on the part of the parent. Moreover, there is a way to address this concern other than forbidding the infertile couple to use cloning; in particular, the couple could be counseled about the possible psychological dimensions of parenthood through cloning. Psychological counseling already is widely accepted in preparing infertile couples for various noncoital reproductive methods, such as donor insemination and surrogate motherhood. Similarly, it would be appropriate to offer psychological counseling if cloning is made available to infertile couples. The aims of such counseling could include raising awareness about, and thereby attempting to prevent or reduce problems associated with, a possible tendency of parents to be too demanding.

With regard to the claim that cloning even a single child would be psychologically harmful, it can be replied that such claims misuse the concept of 'harm.' Specifically, there is a serious problem with the claim that it would *harm* a child to bring her into being in circumstances where she would experience adverse psychological effects from being a clone. To explain this problem, we need to consider what it means to be harmed.

Harming versus Wronging

I shall draw upon Joel Feinberg's detailed and helpful discussions of what is involved in being harmed.[22-23] A key point is that persons are harmed only if they are caused to be worse off than they otherwise would have been. As Feinberg expresses it, one harms another only if the victim's personal interest is in a worse condition than it would have been had the perpetrator not acted as he did.[24] The claim that cloning harms the children who are brought into being, therefore, amounts to saying that the children are *worse off than they would have been if they had not been created.* Many readers will see problems with such an assertion. Some will say that it fails to make sense because it attempts to compare nonexistence with something that exists, and therefore it is neither true nor false. Others will maintain that it is *false.* Whether incoherent or false, it should be rejected. Because I have addressed the relative merits of these two criticisms elsewhere, I will not repeat that discussion, except to say that the better explanation of what is wrong with the statement seems to be that it is false.[25-26] To see its falsity, let us consider what a life would have to be like in order reasonably to say that it is worse for the person living it than nonexistence. I suggest that a life would have to be so filled with pain and suffering that these negative experiences greatly overshadow any pleasurable or other positive experiences the individual might have. If a neonate were born with a painful, debilitating, and fatal genetic disease, for example, we could reasonably make such a statement. However, the gap between such a neonate and a child cloned by an infertile couple is exceedingly great. Even if the cloned child experienced adverse psychological states associated with being a clone, that would not amount to a life filled with pain and suffering. Thus, the concept of harm is not appropriate for describing the cloned individual's condition.

I have applied the usual concept of harm to situations involving cloning. However, there is an objection that should be considered. It might be asserted that applying this concept of harm to this type of situation leads to implausible conclusions. Specifically, it seems to imply that it is ethically justifiable knowingly to create a child who will suffer disadvantages—even serious ones—as long as those disadvantages are not so severe that the life will be worse than nonexistence. To illustrate, consider a hypothetical situation in which a person with cystic fibrosis asks to be cloned, and a cure for cystic fibrosis is not yet available. Suppose that a physician knows about the cystic fibrosis but nevertheless provides the cloning, and the child later suffers the adverse effects of cystic fibrosis. It seems wrong for the physician to carry out the cloning in this example. According to the usual concept of harm, however, the child in this scenario is not harmed by being cloned, given that her life is better than nonexistence. If we cannot say that the child is harmed, then how can we account for our view that the cloning is unethical?

In reply, we can account for cloning being unethical in such a case without inventing a new concept of harm. Although the child is not harmed by being cloned, we can say that she is *wronged*. In particular, we can say that a certain right of the child is violated. It has been suggested that there is a type of birthright according to which people have a right to be born free of serious impediments to their well being.[27-30] It is important not to misunderstand this right; it is not a 'right to be born' but rather a right possessed by all persons who *are* born. Also, it is not what one might call a 'right against nature'; if a child is born with serious handicaps through the fault of no one, then the right in question is not violated. The right would only be violated if someone negligently or intentionally created a child with the requisite handicaps. I suggest that we can account for the wrongness of cloning in the cystic fibrosis example by positing such a birthright, a right that one's circumstances of birth be free of impediments that would seriously impair one's ability to develop in a healthy manner and to realize a normal potential. Negligently or intentionally creating a child who faces such severe impediments is a violation of that right, which I shall refer to as a right to a decent minimum opportunity for development. The handicaps imposed on the child with cystic fibrosis are not so severe that we could reasonably say that her life is worse than nonexistence, but they are severe enough to impair seriously her ability to develop.

An objection can be made against using the concept 'being wronged' to describe what is unethical about cloning in the cystic fibrosis example. Specifically, if the child were to claim that she was wronged by those who created her, it would commit her to the judgment that their duty had been to refrain from doing what they did; but if they had refrained, it would have led to her never being born, an even worse result from her point of view. Thus, it is argued, the child cannot reasonably claim that her creators should have acted otherwise, given that her life with cystic fibrosis is preferable to nonexistence. If she cannot make this claim, then she has no genuine grievance against them and cannot claim that they wronged her.[31-32]

However, this objection is mistaken. Perhaps we can see this more clearly by considering a similar type of situation. Instead of acts that cause a person to come into being, let us consider actions that cause an existing person to continue to live—that is, *life-saving* actions. Both types of acts have the result that a person exists who otherwise would not be in existence. Consider a patient who has suffered substantial bleeding because of a ruptured ulcer. Suppose that blood transfusions are necessary to save her life but she refuses transfusions on religious grounds and is considered mentally competent. Imagine that a physician provides transfusions despite her refusal, with the result that the patient's life is saved. Let us suppose, also, that the patient later states that she is better off having been kept alive. According to the objection in question, the patient cannot reasonably claim that the physician should have refrained from treating, given that her continued life is better than nonexistence. If she cannot make this claim, then she cannot claim that the physician wronged her.

But this conclusion is incorrect. Clearly, the patient can validly claim that she was wronged; her rights to informed consent and self-determination were violated. The benefits caused by the physician's act do not alter the fact that these rights were infringed. If a beneficial outcome removed all wrongness of the act, that would mean that paternalism, when successfully carried out, is ethically justifiable. This would be inconsistent with the view that competent patients have a right to refuse life-saving treatment. Similarly, the fact that the cloned child with cystic fibrosis has a life that is better than nonexistence does not mean that the child was not wronged. More generally, a child who is intentionally or negligently brought into being in circumstances where she lacks a decent minimum opportunity for development is wronged, even if her life is better than nonexistence, just as a competent patient who is forced to receive life-saving treatment is wronged, even though her subsequent life is preferable to nonexistence.[33]

Assuming there is a right to a decent minimum opportunity for development, the question arises concerning how serious the impediments must be in order for the right to be violated. No doubt, there is room for disagreement concerning this issue, and a sharp line probably cannot be drawn. Nevertheless, a basic concept can be stated: the impediments must be severe, not minor. As examples, I would suggest that creating a clone who has cystic fibrosis or Down's syndrome would violate the right in question, but creating a clone with, say, nearsightedness would not in itself constitute violation of the right.

Can we say, in the infertility case, that the cloned child would experience psychological problems of such magnitude that the right to a decent minimum opportunity for development would be violated? I suggest that the answer would depend largely on the approach taken by the parents in raising the child. Consider a hypothetical world in which the parents of cloned children always undermine their self-esteem. Then we might reasonably say that being a clone is associated with such serious impediments that the act of cloning violates the child's right to a decent minimum opportunity for development. Consider another hypothetical world in which many but not all parents of cloned children undermine their self-esteem. Then we might reasonably say that cloning puts a child at risk of experiencing obstacles severe enough to constitute a violation of the right in question. Depending on the level of risk involved, we might decide that cloning is wrong because the risk is unacceptably high. In yet another hypothetical world, the parents of cloned children are no more likely to undermine their self-esteem than the parents of other children. In that world it would not be reasonable to say that cloning in itself violates the right in question. If we were to allow infertile couples to use cloning, then which of these hypothetical worlds would the real world be most like? The fact is, we do not know. And this is the problem with the argument that cloned children would experience severe psychological obstacles to wellbeing; it is based on empirical assumptions concerning how cloned children would generally be treated by parents and others, and we lack evidence supporting those assumptions.

The Argument from Parent–Child Relationships

Let us consider the argument that children would be objectified and parent–child relationships generally would be adversely affected. This argument arises from reflection on what it would be like if there were a widespread practice of controlling the characteristics of our offspring. This practice might involve the insertion and deletion of genes in human preembryos, as well as cloning and other laboratory techniques not yet envisioned. In some cases, such manipulations might have a therapeutic goal; perhaps disease-causing genes would be replaced by normal ones. Objections to such therapeutic manipulations have been based mainly on concerns about whether they can be performed safely. But other forms of genetic control might have the much different goal of enhancing offspring nondisease characteristics, such as height, intelligence, and body build, and it is especially this type of control that raises concerns about undesirable changes in the attitudes and expectations of parents toward their children.[34-35] The specific concerns can be expressed by a number of questions: If a child failed to manifest the qualities she was designed to have, would the parents be less inclined to accept the child's weaknesses? Would children be regarded more as objects and less as persons? Would less tolerance for imperfection result in less compassion toward the handicapped? Would children who recognize their own shortcomings blame their parents for failing to design them better? Would such feelings sometimes disrupt family relationships? Would knowledge of being designed make a child feel more controlled by parents? Would this result, for example, in greater adolescent rebelliousness? These and other questions suggest a number of ways in which disharmony could enter into parent–child relationships.

However, a reply can be made. Although these are important concerns, their bearing on infertility cases is tangential. Because cloning does not involve inserting and deleting genes, concerns over whether these particular manipulations can be done safely are not directly applicable. Also, cloning in the infertility cases does not involve efforts to enhance the child's genetic makeup. Thus, the concerns expressed above that are specific to enhancement do not directly apply, either; these include the concern that modifying children in order to enhance their characteristics objectifies them. The claim that cloning in the infertility case objectifies the child is weakened by the fact that the purpose is not to design the child but to have a genetically related child, in the only way that is possible. In addition, the number of cases like the one being considered—those in which there is both male and female infertility and use of family donors has been ruled out—would be relatively small. Thus, it is difficult to argue that cloning restricted to such cases would result in widespread changes in parent–child relationships. For these reasons, the arguments in question do not succeed in showing that cloning in the infertility cases would be wrong.

The Argument Based on Abuses

The third argument is that abuses might occur if the technology of cloning is used by unscrupulous persons. A paradigm of such envisioned abuse is found in Aldous Huxley's *Brave New World,* in which multiple genetically identical persons are produced and conditioned to fill defined social roles.[36] Other variations of such abuse could be imagined, in which cloning plays a role in the systematic control of persons by determining their genetic makeup and upbringing.

In reply, it seems clear that we can distinguish such abuse from the infertility case in question; the couple's trying to have a child would not constitute such abuse or even remotely approach it. Perhaps it will be objected that permitting cloning in the infertility cases would facilitate development of the technology, thereby making it more likely that unscrupulous persons could use it. In reply, this objection assumes that human preembryos would not be created by cloning as part of research. In the future it might become useful to create such preembryos, not for the purpose of transferring them to a woman's uterus, but for studies in any of a number of scientific areas, perhaps including preembryo development, cell differentiation, immunologic properties of cells, or the creation of cell lines using stem cells. Some of these scientific areas—or others not mentioned here— might be considered important enough in the future to justify creating human preembryos by cloning for purposes of laboratory studies.[37] Thus, the technology of cloning humans might go forward, even if use of that technology to produce babies is proscribed.

Although the main arguments against cloning are not persuasive when applied to the infertility cases, at least two additional arguments can be presented that focus more directly on those cases. First, consider a son who is, as we might put it, genetically identical to his mother's husband. Some might be concerned by the somewhat oedipal nature of this situation. Would knowing that one's mother is sexually attracted to someone genetically identical to oneself cause special psychological problems for the child? Would the ill effects be great enough to make life worse than nonexistence? Would the right to a decent minimum opportunity for development be violated? Second, consider a father whose daughter is genetically identical to his wife. Would there tend to be a higher incidence of sexual abuse in this type of situation? These questions raise legitimate concerns, but because the answers are highly speculative at present, these concerns do not constitute definitive arguments against the particular use of cloning in question. However, they suggest possible topics for inclusion in preimplantation counseling, if such counseling is provided.

In summary, some main reasons have been identified supporting freedom to use cloning in the type of infertility case being considered. Also, each of the main arguments against cloning has been shown to involve substantial difficulties when applied to the infertility cases. It seems reasonable to conclude that the arguments against cloning are not compelling enough, either singly or collectively, to support the conclusion that cloning is wrong in such cases.

Cloning versus Collaborative Reproduction

It might be objected that it would be ethically preferable for the couple to have children who are not genetically related to them. Adoption would be a possibility, or donor gametes or preembryos could be used. If the woman is capable of gestating using donor gametes or preembryos, then at least she could be biologically related to the child. In reply, some infertile couples prefer not to adopt, even if that is the only way they can have children to raise. Moreover, if the couple tried to adopt, there would be a significant chance that their attempt would be unsuccessful because of the difficulties involved in adoption.

The claim that using donated gametes or preembryos would be ethically preferable to cloning overlooks the problems associated with third-party collaborative reproduction. Such arrangements raise a number of difficult issues because of the separation of genetic and social parenthood: What should the children be told about their origins? When and how should any informing take place? What if the child later wants to meet the genetic parents?

For example, when there is male-factor infertility, the man often prefers secrecy concerning his inability to beget. As a result, couples often choose not to reveal the fact of gamete donation to the child and others. This creates the problem of there being a significant deception at the center of the family relationship. Maintaining this deception can take its toll, including a substantial emotional burden on the couple. Also, such deception is at odds with the values of honesty and trust that should bind families together. On the other hand, children who are told the truth about their origins might develop strong desires to meet their genetic parents. If these wishes are frustrated, the result might be substantial emotional distress for the child. Thus, depending on how these various issues are handled, adverse psychological consequences are possible for the child and family. It would be reasonable for the couple to prefer not to encounter these problems, and cloning would provide a way to avoid them. The existence of these problems calls into question the claim that third-party collaborative reproduction would be less ethically problematic for the couple than cloning.

It might be objected that cloning would also raise difficult issues for the couple. For example, should the fact of cloning be revealed to the child, and if so, when and how? If the child is not told, then she will not suffer any psychological ill effects arising from knowledge of being a clone. But if such children were never told, then they would be deprived of important information about their background. Should family and friends be told about the cloning? Or should they be led to believe that the child simply "looks like" one of the parents?[38] There might be disagreements between husband and wife over whom, when, and how to tell. In reply, although these too are difficult issues, their existence seems to indicate that the two approaches to reproduction are at a standoff in this regard; both raise issues that carry the potential for interpersonal conflict within the family. Because of this parity, it is not obvious that third-party collaborative reproduction is ethically preferable to cloning.

I have been discussing a situation in which cloning is the only way for a couple to have a child genetically related to one of them. However, the arguments I have stated in support of cloning are applicable to other infertility cases in which the alternative is third-party collaboration. Suppose the woman cannot produce ova, but donor ova and the husband's sperm could be used. The couple might nevertheless prefer cloning in order to avoid the complications associated with third-party gamete donation discussed above.[39] Alternatively, suppose the man cannot produce sperm but the woman's ova could be used with donor insemination. A preference for cloning might be based, not solely on male ego, but also on a desire to avoid the problems associated with third-party reproduction. Moreover, the three main arguments against cloning do not fare better when applied to these types of infertility cases. Again, cloning does not harm the child, nor is it clear that the right to a decent minimum opportunity for development would be violated. The argument that parent–child relationships generally would be adversely affected continues to be unpersuasive because enhancement is not involved and, although we now are dealing with a larger class of infertile couples, the number still is relatively small compared to the general population. These scenarios also would be distinguishable from *Brave New World* abuses. Thus, the arguments against cloning do not constitute compelling reasons to override the freedom of infertile couples to use cloning in these cases either.

Cloning as a Bridge to Future Remedies for Infertility

Research in gene therapy is resulting in the discovery of ways to insert genes into human cells. This is increasing the plausibility of the view that in the future it might be possible to insert, and perhaps delete, a variety of chosen genes. Such modifications could be performed on cells prior to using them for cloning. By means of such techniques, a child created with cloning technology could have genes from both parents. Starting with a cell from one parent, one might change hair color, skin complexion, and eye color, using genes from the other parent. Perhaps genetic defects causing infertility and susceptibilities to other diseases would also be corrected. The child then would be genetically unique. Thus, the argument against cloning based on lack of genetic uniqueness would no longer be applicable. Prohibiting cloning in the future might prevent us from helping infertile couples in these ways.

Such modifications would not necessarily include changes that constitute 'enhancement,' such as higher intelligence, better body build, or greater height; the goal could be to make the child genetically different from either parent, rather than to produce a 'superior' child. In that event, objections to genetically enhancing our offspring would not be applicable. Moreover, this particular use of genetic technology—to help an infertile couple have a child—would also be distinguishable from *Brave New World* abuses.

This type of reproduction would not be cloning, strictly speaking. The term "cloning" in both scientific and lay usage implies the production of a genetically identical copy. In fact, we lack a common term to refer specifically to the type of reproduction being envisioned.

It might be objected that we could not ethically create children in this manner because developing the technology would involve experimenting on unconsenting subjects. It might be claimed, for example, that it would be unethical to try to alter genetically a child's hair color because some unintended adverse genetic modification might occur. It might be argued that altered hair color is not a significant enough benefit to justify the risks involved. In reply, it is conceivable that our technology might advance to the point where the risks involved in such an attempt would be low. Moreover, if being a clone exposes one to the risk of adverse psychological effects, as opponents of cloning maintain, then alterations that prevent one from being a clone might have benefits significant enough to outweigh the risks. Therefore, I do not believe we can reasonably claim that such genetic modifications could never ethically be done. If such modifications could be performed safely, this type of reproduction might be ethically *preferable* to reproduction using donor gametes or preembryos because the problems associated with third-party collaboration would be avoided.

Should Exceptional Cases Be Permitted?

I have argued that cloning humans could sometimes be ethically defensible in cases of infertility. It might be objected that cloning should not be permitted even in those cases in which it is ethically justifiable. One argument supporting this objection begins by claiming that a general prohibition of human cloning is warranted, based on the reasons against cloning discussed above. Legal restrictions are needed to prevent the creation of cohorts of multiple clones, as well as other clear abuses of cloning technology. Restrictions also are needed to prevent a widespread practice of cloning, thereby avoiding the feared ill effects on parent–child relationships. Moreover, it is claimed that practical problems involved in attempting to enforce a general policy against human cloning while permitting exceptions provide grounds for not allowing the exceptions.[40] In particular, it would be difficult for authorities to gather the evidence needed to distinguish allowable from nonallowable cases. For example, fertile couples might have children by cloning, yet claim that they are infertile. Prosecution could not reasonably proceed unless evidence ruling out infertility were obtained. Assuming that an infertility doctor assisted the couple in the cloning, often that doctor's testimony and records would be crucial evidence. However, such confidential records are protected in the absence of a court order, and establishing 'reasonable cause' for such court orders might be difficult in many cases. Moreover, the couple could refuse to release the records voluntarily, claiming (perhaps disingenuously) that the information is too personal and sensitive. The legal protection of medical records behind which such couples could hide is itself important and based on constitutional guarantees against unreasonable invasions of privacy. It can be argued that relaxing such protections in order to distinguish permitted from nonpermitted cloning would be too intrusive of reproductive privacy. Thus, if we permit cloning in the infertility cases, in effect we open the door for anyone to use cloning and get away with it.

In reply, it is possible to have widespread compliance with a law even though there are difficulties in detecting violations. If we were to make cloning except in infertility cases illegal not only for the couples using it but also for the physicians carrying it out, I believe that we would see widespread compliance. Most physicians will choose to avoid illegal activity, even if authorities would face difficulties in detecting violations. This tendency could be reinforced if the penalties for being convicted of the violation are high, even though the likelihood of detection is relatively low. Although a few cases of cloning might occur outside the allowed exceptions, it is doubtful that we would see the sort of widespread practice that the policy in question would attempt to prevent. Reproductive privacy can be protected while having a generally effective policy that prohibits cloning except in cases of infertility.

Another objection is that it would be inconsistent to permit cloning for infertile couples but not fertile ones. If reproductive freedom is important enough to permit infertile couples to use cloning, then why shouldn't all couples be allowed to use it, if that is their desire? According to this argument, if permitting the infertile to clone children commits us logically to allowing everyone to do so, then we should not allow the infertile to clone.

A reply to this objection can be based on the fundamental reasons we give in explaining why procreative freedom is worthy of protection. I identified six reasons that can be given in helping explain why freedom to have children is important. It is worth noting that the goals and values reflected in those six reasons can be achieved by fertile couples without resorting to cloning. By having a child through sexual intercourse, they can: participate in the creation of a person; affirm their mutual love through procreation; deepen their sexual intimacy; obtain a link to future persons; and have experiences associated with pregnancy, childbirth, and child rearing. Therefore, in prohibiting those who are fertile from using cloning, we do not deprive them of the ability to pursue what is valuable about having children. However, when we forbid the infertile to use cloning, we force them to choose either not to realize any of those valued goals or to pursue collaborative reproduction with its associated difficulties. This is the morally relevant difference, I would suggest, that can justify differing policies for fertile and infertile couples. In conclusion, there do not appear to be good reasons to disallow exceptions to cloning for infertile couples.

Notes

[1] In this paper, the term "cloning" refers to creating a child by

transferring the nucleus of a somatic cell into an enucleated egg cell. This method should be distinguished from blastomere separation, which involves the division of a preembryo when its cells are totipotent. Although both produce individuals with identical chromosomes, the two methods have different ethical implications. For example, cloning by nuclear transfer involves the possibility of creating numerous duplicates of the original individual, but in blastomere separation only a few copies can be produced, as explained in Cohen J, Tomkin G. The science, fiction, and reality of embryo cloning. *Kennedy Institute of Ethics Journal* 1994;4:193–203.

2 National Bioethics Advisory Commission. *Cloning Human Beings: Report and Recommendations of the National Bioethics Advisory Commission* (Rockville MD, 1997), 79–81; http://www.nih.gov/nbac/nbac.htm.

3 Winston R. The promise of cloning for human medicine: not a moral threat but an exciting challenge. *British Medical journal* 1997;314:913–4.

4 See note 2, National Bioethics Advisory Commission 1997:ii–iii,13, 23–4.

5 The researchers who produced Dolly used nuclei from three sources: late embryos, fetal cell cultures, and cell cultures derived from the mammary gland of an adult sheep. Of 277 preembryos created using mammary cells, only one developed into a live lamb. Sixty-two percent of fetuses from all three sources failed to survive until birth, compared to an estimated 6% fetal loss rate after natural mating. This high rate of fetal loss suggests an increased incidence of genetic anomalies. For data on the total number of preembryos and live births, see Wilmut I, Schnieke AE, McWhir J, Kind AJ, Campbell KHS. Viable offspring derived from fetal and adult mammalian cells. *Nature* 1997;385:810–3.

6 Stewart C. Nuclear transplantation: an udder way of making lambs. *Nature* 1997;385:769, 771.

7 This situation could result from various medical conditions: the woman's ovaries might have been surgically removed, or she might suffer from premature ovarian failure—the inability of ovaries to produce ova; the man could have testes that produce no sperm, or perhaps a small number of sperm are produced but attempts to perform intracytoplasmic sperm injection (ICSI) using donor ova have been unsuccessful, among other possibilities. For a discussion of the uses and limitations

of ICSI, see Silber SJ. What forms of male infertility are there left to cure? *Human Reproduction* 1995;10:503–4.

[8] Recer P. Clone fear may slow research. *AP Online* 1997; Mar 5:19:20EST.

[9] Nash JM. The age of cloning. *Time* 1997;Mar 10:60–61,64–5.

[10] Butler D, Wadman M. Calls for cloning ban sell science short. *Nature* 1997;386:8–9.

[11] Masood E. Cloning technique "reveals legal loophole." *Nature* 1997;Feb 27; http://www.nature.com.

[12] Harris J. Is cloning an attack on human dignity? *Nature* 1997;387:754.

[13] Pohlman E, assisted by Pohlman JM. *The Psychology of Birth Planning* (Cambridge MA, 1969), 48–81.

[14] Pohlman E. Motivations in wanting conceptions. In: Peck E, Senderowitz J, eds. *Pronatalism: The Myth of Mom and Apple Pie* (New York 1974), 159–90.

[15] Veevers JE. The social meanings of parenthood. *Psychiatry* 1973;36:291–310.

[16] Arnold F. *The Value of Children: A Cross-National Study* (Honolulu 1975).

[17] Laucks EC. *The Meaning of Children: Attitudes and Opinions of a Selected Group of U.S. University Graduates* (Boulder 1981).

[18] Gould RE. The wrong reasons to have children. In: Peck E, Senderowitz J, eds. *Pronatalism: The Myth of Mom and Apple Pie* (New York 1974), 193–8.

[19] Kahn A. Clone mammals...clone man? *Nature* 1997;386:119. Kahn states, "the debate has in the past perhaps paid insufficient attention to the current strong social trend towards a fanatical desire for individuals not simply to have children but to ensure that these children also carry their genes."

[20] Strong C. *Ethics in Reproductive and Perinatal Medicine: A New Framework* (New Haven 1997), 13–22.

[21] Ellin J. Sterilization, privacy, and the value of reproduction. In: Davis JW, Hoffmaster B, Shorter S, eds. *Contemporary Issues in Biomedical Ethics* (Clifton NJ, 1978), 109–25.

[22] Feinberg J. *Harm to Others* (New York 1984), 31–64.

[23] Feinberg J. Wrongful life and the counterfactual element in harming. *Social Philosophy and Policy* 1987;4:145–78.

[24] See note 23, Feinberg 1987:149. Feinberg's discussion is more extensive; this is only one of six conditions he identifies as necessary and sufficient for harming, pp. 150–53.

[25] See note 20, Strong 1997:90–92.

[26] Also see note 23, Feinberg 1987:158–9.

[27] Bayles MD. Harm to the unconceived. *Philosophy and Public Affairs* 1976;5:292–304.

[28] Also see note 22, Feinberg 1984:99.

[29] Steinbock B, McClamrock R. When is birth unfair to the child? *Hastings Center Report* 1994;24(6):15–21.

[30] Also see note 20, Strong 1997:92–5.

[31] This type of objection is put forward by Feinberg. See note 23, Feinberg 1987:168.

[32] A similar objection is stated by Brock DW. The non-identity problem and genetic harms—the case of wrongful handicaps. *Bioethics* 1995;9:269–75.

[33] For this response to the objection in question see note 20, Strong 1997:93–4.

[34] Botkin JR. Prenatal screening: professional standards and the limits of parental choice. *Obstetrics and Gynecology* 1990;75:875–80.

[35] Strong C. Tomorrow's prenatal genetic testing: should we test for 'minor' diseases? *Archives of Family Medicine* 1993;2:1187–93.

[36] The method of genetic duplication that Huxley described did not involve replacement of the nucleus of an egg cell. In his fictional account, the fertilized egg was described as "budding" when "Bokanovsky's Process" was applied to it; the result could be as many as "ninety-six identical twins."

[37] See note 3, Winston 1997.

[38] We can imagine friends saying, for example, "He's the spitting image of his father," but not realizing, because of the age difference, that they are genetically identical.

[39] Cloning in such a case would involve an ovum donor, but the chromosomes would be removed from the ovum. Although mitochondrial DNA in the ovum would be inherited by the child, the ovum donor would not be a "genetic mother" in the ordinary sense of that term. Thus, although there would be third-party collaboration, it would not involve the difficulties typically associated with third-party genetic parentage.

[40] This type of objection is suggested in *Cloning Human Beings.* See note 2, National Bioethics Advisory Commission 1997:81–2.

Timothy F. Murphy

Entitlement to Cloning: A Response to Strong

Carson Strong has argued that if human cloning were safe it should be available to some infertile couples as a matter of ethics and law.[1] He holds that cloning by somatic cell nuclear transfer (SCNT) should be available as a reproductive option for infertile couples who could not otherwise have a child genetically related to one member of the couple. In this analysis, Strong overlooks an important category of people to whom his argument might apply, couples he has not failed to consider elsewhere.[2] In this discussion, however, Strong refers exclusively to opposite sex couples facing obstacles such as surgically removed ovaries and the inability to produce sperm. In fact, however, there are many adult couples who, while fertile in and of themselves, are not fertile as couples. This group includes not only opposite sex couples but coupled same sex partners as well. I believe the defenses Strong offers regarding the use of SCNT by opposite sex infertile couples would extend to same sex couples for two reasons. First, some same sex couples might face the inability to have a genetically related child, and second, Strong's arguments ultimately ground a general defense of SCNT independent of the question of a couple's fertility.

Somatic Nuclear Transfer for All?

Strong holds that SCNT should be accessible to couples who have no other recourse to the conception of a genetically related child. He excludes from consideration opposite sex couples who could use assisted reproductive technologies (ARTs). In his view, SCNT is a kind of reproductive last resort.

Strong underestimates the power of the arguments he marshals in favor of his conclusions. I will stipulate that he cogently disposes of a number of the main arguments raised against SCNT, including: (a) threats to individual uniqueness, (b) necessary harms to children, (c) threats to parent–child relationships, (d) the availability of other ARTs, (e) the objectification of children, and (f) the potential for abuse by totalitarian regimes and other unscrupulous parties. In each instance, Strong has something interesting to say about why these issues do not constitute insuperable obstacles to the use of SCNT by infertile couples. It is, however, unclear why the arguments he offers would not also pertain to the use of SCNT by fertile couples. For example, a cloned child born to a fertile couple would be no more or less an individual than a cloned child born to an infertile couple. It is not obvious either that a cloned child would be any more "objectified" simply by virtue of being born to a fertile couple than to an infertile couple. The clones of fertile couples would not obviously be more susceptible to the abuses of authoritarian government than clones of infertile couples. And so on. If Strong's arguments are correct, it is unclear why they are convincing only for infertile couples who can have genetically related children no other way.

Same Sex Couples as Infertile Couples

How might these observations apply to same sex couples? There is no arguing that left to their own devices, same sex couples are infertile as a matter of biological course. That incapacity has, however, not deterred same sex partners from entering into pair-bonded relationships. The extent of same-sex coupled relationships is not well studied, though it is clear that these kinds of relationships exist in both historical precedent and contemporary culture.[3, 4] Moreover, same sex couples are not so reproductively impoverished that they do not have children, even if they must reach outside pair-bonded relationships for help.

Men and women are fertile or infertile independent of sexual orientation. Many same sex couples therefore have children by conception during prior opposite sex relationships, by adoption, by foster parenting, through surrogate mothers, or by the use of ARTs such as insemination or in vitro fertilization and embryo transfer (IVF/ET). Certainly, coupled women have one advantage over coupled men in that they can gestate a child if one of them is able and willing. (There are other ways for women to share maternity; for example, one donates the ovum for IVF while the other gestates the child following ET.[5]) Sometimes formidable obstacles in clinical practices and the law stand in the way of gay and lesbian access to adoption, foster parenting, and ARTs. Nevertheless, the barriers are sometimes permeable, and gay men and lesbians do find ways to use these mechanisms to have children. The point remains true nevertheless that as infer tile couples, same sex partners must necessarily reach outside their relationship for assistance in having children. I propose that we see this infertility as *situational infertility.* Something like this state obtains for opposite sex couples when they are unable to conceive as a couple even though each partner is apparently fertile. I believe that Strong's arguments offer prima facie reasons for extending moral and legal entitlement to SCNT to situationally infertile couples-same sex and otherwise.

First, Strong's view that SCNT should be available to infertile couples who cannot procreate (and maintain a genetic link to one parent) would apply without modification to a limited number of same sex couples. It would apply to same sex couples if both partners were incapable of producing gametes and if standard ARTs (such as intracytoplasmic sperm injection) failed consistently. Unless there were some harm or wrong to children or other damaging condition that proved a moral obstacle, it appears that Strong's defense of the use of SCNT would apply to same sex couples in these circumstances.

Second, if my analysis above is correct—that Strong ultimately offers a general defense of SCNT—same sex couples would as a matter of course have moral entitlement to SCNT whether or not they were infertile in the particular way just described. The most important limiting condition on access would, again, turn out to be damage to the child. Before I say something about the prospect of harm and damage, I want to point out that Strong mentions the matter of joining genetic materials from two persons into the nucleus of the cell to be used in SCNT, but he does not sketch out its implication for same sex couples. If the genetic complement of a single cell could be modified through gene insertion, it could be possible to use SCNT to procreate children genetically related to two males or to two females. For example, the relevant genes for one woman's (or man's) eye, hair texture, and other simple traits could be inserted into a nucleus that is otherwise a copy of her (or his) partner's genome. This cell would then be induced into embryogenesis and transferred into a uterus. The resultant child would thus share genetic heritage from both partners. This kind of intervention is speculative, of course, but the thought experiment does show ways in which both same sex partners could come to share genetic parentage of a child. If so, the prospect of using SCNT—as against other mechanisms of having a child—might appear more attractive to same sex couples than any other ART insofar as it offered the opportunity for a child genetically related to both parents. (SCNT clones would be, of course "twins" of the person whose somatic cell was used in the procedure. If there were shared genetic "parentage" involved in SCNT, however, then the resultant child would not be a clone properly speaking. The child would have traits of all contributors to the genome of the cell used in SCNT. In some instances this would be something like a "fraternal twin" of the genetic parents, however many of them there might be.)

Same Sex Couples and Their Children

None of the justifications Strong offers on behalf of SCNT appears limited to opposite sex couples. He identifies these justifications in terms of a couple's desire to participate in the creation of a person; the affirmation of mutual love between partners; deepening of sexual intimacy; obtaining a link to future persons; and having the experiences associated with pregnancy, childbirth, and child rearing. Nothing in any of these rationales is absent in principle from the rationale of same sex couples as they contemplate having children. The nature of individual motivations will vary from couple to couple, but there is no aspect of a homosexual orientation that disables these profoundly intimate reasons for wanting to have a child or to have a child of a certain kind.

The only apparent limitation on the use of SCNT by same sex couples would appear to be the possibility of harm to children born into those relationships. Because this is an entirely speculative matter at present, there are no actual outcomes to evaluate. Nevertheless, as one tries to piece together the likely effects of cloning, it does appear that objectionable outcomes may be avoidable. Dire outcomes for other ARTs have been predicted, and those woeful states have failed to materialize. IVF/ET has brought us no closer to the uniform castes of a brave new world than has unassisted conception. "Test-tube babies" appear no less wanted and loved than other babies. One might argue that a child would not be *harmed* by being born to same sex partners but is nevertheless *wronged.* This kind of hybrid philosophical and religious argument is offered by the Roman Catholic Church, which holds that a child has the right to be born of married, opposite sex spouses.[6] On this view a child could be *wronged* even if it suffered no psychological or other kind of harm as a result of being born to other kinds of parents. This argument is hard to credit if the nature of same sex relationships by itself is morally neutral or beneficial—which I will stipulate for the sake of the argument[7]—and if no harm worthy of the name befalls children born in and raised in those relationships. Indeed, there is no credible evidence that shows children of same sex couples to be generally worse off than children of opposite sex couples. On the contrary, what evidence there is describes the general well-being of such children.[8, 9] Unless there were demonstrable, predictable, and consistent damages to a child being born into same sex coupled relationships, the use of SCNT in those relationships should be defended as a matter of ethics and law. If children procreated in same sex relationships were predictably and consistently damaged by these relationships, then a prima facie barrier to SCNT would be in order. The available evidence does not support such a conclusion, and there is at present no reason to think that the use of SCNT would by itself effect a change in that state of affairs.

Same Sex Couples and SCNT

In 1997 a sheep now more famous than Mary's little lamb set off an avalanche of rhetoric that was almost seamless in its repudiation of human cloning. Since then more measured analysis has set aside the most extravagant worries about SCNT.[10-12] Even the hastily summoned National Bioethics Advisory Commission found it impossible to advance a philosophically cogent argument against SCNT per se. Carson Strong's analysis belongs to this second wave of analysis; he thinks there may be good, though limited, reasons to use SCNT. I have tried to show, however, that his arguments justify access to SCNT for more couples than he is prepared to admit.

I have tried to show that if we accept the arguments as given, Strong offers no reason why SCNT should be limited exclusively to infertile or to opposite sex couples. If my analysis is correct, SCNT should be added to the list of defensible procreative options as soon as it can be shown to be as safe as other mechanisms of conception and/or embryogenesis—for infertile *and* infertile couples, for opposite sex *and* same sex couples. I draw this conclusion in the full knowledge that same sex couples do face social and legal barriers to adoption, foster parentage, insemination facilities, and IVF/ ET.[13] In one celebrated instance, a court removed a child from her mother's custody because the woman was in a lesbian relationship.[14] I expect that the question of legal access to SCNT will be as politically difficult for same sex couples as access to other means of having children has proven. (I also believe that the relative importance of SCNT for gay men and lesbians is very much a live and unsettled question.[15] Nevertheless, I believe that this resistance is conceptually ill founded. Barring evidence that children born via SCNT to same sex couples are predictably and consistently harmed, or barring the emergence of a philosophically persuasive argument that children are *wronged* by being born to same sex parents, there do not appear to be convincing rationales barring the use of SCNT by same sex couples. The most important ethical questions at stake govern the practice rather than the principle of SCNT. Strong's arguments make clear that SCNT could be a defensible practice and that same sex *and* opposite sex couples should be entitled to use it. And not only after everything else has failed.

Notes

[1] Strong C. Cloning and infertility. *Cambridge Quarterly of Healthcare Ethics* 1998;7:279–93.

[2] Strong C. *Ethics in Reproductive and Perinatal Medicine* (New Haven 1997), 85–110.

[3] Bell AP, Weinberg MS. *Homosexualities: A Study of Diversity among Men and Women* (New York 1978).

[4] Laumann EO, Gagnon JH, Michael RT, Michaels S. *The Social Organization of Sexuality: Sexual Practices in the United States* (Chicago 1994).

[5] Murphy TF. Lesbian mothers and genetic choices. *Ethics and Behavior* 1993;3:211, 220–2.

[6] Congregation for the Doctrine of the Faith. Respect for human life in its origins and on the dignity of procreation: reply to

certain questions of the day. *New York Times* 1987; Mar. 11:A14–A17.

[7] Murphy TF. Homosex/ethics. In: Murphy TF, ed. *Gay Ethics: Controversies in Civil Rights and Sexual Science* (New York 1994), 9–25.

[8] Patterson CJ. Lesbian and gay families with children: public policy implications of social science research. *Journal of Social Issues* 1996;5:29–50.

[9] Patterson CJ. Children of lesbian and gay parents. In: Ollendick T, Prinz R, eds. *Advances in Clinical Child Psychology,* vol. 19. (New York 1997), 235–82.

[10] Pence GE. *Who's Afraid of Human Cloning?* (Totowa NJ, 1997).

[11] Pence GE, ed. *Flesh of My Flesh: The Ethics of Cloning Humans* (Totowa NJ, 1998).

[12] National Bioethics Advisory Commission. *Cloning Human Beings: Report and Recommendations of the National Bioethics Advisory Commission* (Washington DC: NBAC, 1997).

[13] Moskowitz EH. In the courts. *Hastings Center Report* 1996;26(4):47–8.

[14] Gover T. Fighting for our children. *Advocate* 1997;Nov. 26:22–30.

[15] Murphy TF. Our children, our selves: the meaning of cloning for gay people. See note 11, Pence 1998:141–9.

Glenn McGee and Ian Wilmut

A Model for Regulating Cloning

Regrettably, there may be individuals on earth who would find the prospect of participation in clinical trials of human reproduction through somatic cell nuclear transfer acceptable or even appealing.

Odd, imaginative, and unlikely examples have been proffered. In one, a woman whose husband is killed seeks to clone another of her already born young children to have another child with the husband.[1] In another a young couple, whose genes code for the lethal Tay-Sachs disease, requests nuclear transfer so that germ-line gene therapy can be conducted on the embryo to remove the condition. In still a third, the extremely rare woman with disease in the mitochondria of her cells might request cloning with donor egg in order to avoid passing on her lethal disorder through her own egg. These odd, hard cases miss the more general context within which any request for human cloning might originate.

Those who encounter fertility problems not easily re-

221

mediable by therapy to the reproductive organs can walk several paths. Each has risks and benefits for the individuals, couples, and families involved. Some choose to play supportive or parenting roles in their extended families, or marry into families with children. Some enroll in adoption programs. Others turn to clinical medicine, where a wide and expanding range of techniques is aimed at providing a pregnancy and eventually a child. It is the hope of those who choose this last set of options that the resultant children will share some or many hereditary traits with his or her parents.

For patients with some kinds of infertility affecting the gametes, the use of donated sperm or eggs can greatly improve the likelihood of successful fertilization and pregnancy. Choosing to utilize donated gametes or embryos carries benefits and hazards. The benefit is a child that shares some of its parents' genes and in many cases a fetus that can perhaps be carried by its eventual mother. However, there are important long-term risks associated with donor gametes. Even the best screening of donors cannot rule out the presence of hereditary risks for disease that are hidden in the donor's DNA, risks the donor may not know. The child may want or even need to know about the medical and social history of his or her "donor parent." The existence of an additional donor-parent may present long term problems for the child and family. This issue may be particularly acute when viewed against the backdrop of the goals of in vitro fertilization, namely to preserve a strong genetic link in the nuclear family.

Individuals and families may at some point present their gynecologists, urologists, and infertility specialists with requests for somatic cell nuclear transfer. The challenge of such requests must be set in broad international and interdisciplinary context. The international debate about safety in clinical cloning research is a significant first step toward debate among scientists, clinicians, clergy, and the public about the panoply of new discoveries in reproductive science and medicine. Significant questions are coming into focus: Who is best suited to ensure the safety of children born through new reproductive technologies, and how ought they to make decisions? What relationships should exist between parties who participate in new reproductive technologies and how ought such relationships to be consecrated? We argue that answers to these and other questions should be framed not by broad governmental paternalism in science and medicine, but instead on the model of progressive, regional social oversight aimed at protecting the long-term interests of children. We call this the adoption model, and in this essay describe and defend its application to human cloning law and ethics.

It is patent that human cloning should not proceed to the clinical research stage. A moratorium on clinical trials of human cloning is warranted on safety grounds, as there is no pathway from animal to pre-clinical to clinical human experimentation that would not involve significant risks to human children.[2] As we have noted elsewhere, it is doubtful even in the long term that an individual or couple will present a rationale for the use of human cloning technologies that is compelling when balanced against the risks.[3] In this essay a scientist and an ethicist argue that social restrictions on human cloning can best be justified and implemented on the model of law and policy about adoption.

Regulation and debate about human reproduction may be modeled on three different emphases. We will call these models the **reproductive freedom model,** the **pediatric model**, and the **adoption model.**

This century has seen the birth of an entirely new kind of jurisprudence about sexuality and reproduction. Fueled by scientific developments like birth control and *in vitro* fertilization, and against the backdrop of international civil rights reform, courts in the 20th century framed a new dimension of the freedom of expression: the right to choose one's progeny. The right to make one's own decisions about reproduction has several strata. A right against government interference in reproduction is most clearly codified in American case law about discontinuation of pregnancy. *Roe vs. Wade* and *Casey* carve out a right to reproductive privacy and link pregnancy to other central human expressions of flourishing.

Indeed the central tenet of reproductive freedom is the fairly obvious fact that the reproductive life is central to self-identity, flourishing, and free expression more generally, for individuals and for families. While marriage is highly regulated, as are numerous sexual practices, no license is required for childbearing.

Because families and individuals have such broad freedoms in making children, advocates of reproductive freedom have maintained that it would be inappropriate, even discriminatory, to apply special restrictions to those who are infertile. Why ought the infertile person to be forced to undergo special screening prior to pregnancy when individuals whose reproductive capacity is intact can initiate pregnancy in the most unorthodox ways imaginable without fear of social scrutiny?

The argument against state interference in reproduction is a negative freedom.[4] Arguments for positive freedoms in reproduction, for entitlement to reproductive services, proceed apace. The standard of care for treatment of infertility is not obvious. While the clinical dimensions and etiology of a patient's infertility may be apparent, if the patient's underlying pathology cannot be treated (e.g., the testes repaired), it becomes unclear what the "cure" will be. Is the patient who has two children through *in vitro* fertilization cured? Which techniques, with what ends, should augment or substitute for reproductive capacity? Any answer to these questions will be textured by subjective considerations such as patients' ability to pay for services, the allocation of government resources to infertility research and treatment, and the technological limits of existing treatments.

Those who advocate the primary role of reproductive freedom in the human cloning debate point to the importance of allowing individuals and families to think for themselves about having children.[5] If the state allows couples to have children in squalor or single parent families, how can it reasonably proscribe human cloning as either unsafe or irresponsible? Some American scholars go so far as to argue that U.S. restrictions on human cloning would violate the Americans with Disabilities Act, a law prohibiting discrimination against, in this case, the infertile.

On the opposite side of the human cloning fence are those who argue that human cloning would in some way harm children, and should be prevented in the interest of safety. The argument is made in the spirit of what we call the pediatric model, which emphasizes not the rights of procreators but the responsibility to care for those created.

In the 20th century, healthcare for very young and very vulnerable children has become such a high priority as to rate inclusion in public health policy around the world. To see the enormous changes in the meaning and status of children one need only turn to the copious literature on the creation of childhood as an institution, which takes place during this century. Where one hundred years ago children made up a significant segment of the workforce, and infant mortality was a staggering 30–40% in some nations, today many parents can expect that their children will have access to comprehensive medical and educational resources. The identification of children's needs begins early, and among the very best selling books in the world are guides to pregnancy and early childhood. Incredible amounts are spent on neonatal intensive care and high-risk obstetrical care, as the most vulnerable infants imaginable are kept alive even after extremely premature birth.

In ordinary terms, far from the tertiary care hospital, the pediatric metaphor is felt in public practice and policy about pregnancy and childhood. Parents in many nations come to know their child not as a child but as a fetus, with interests even early on in pregnancy. This can be mundane—an unnecessary ultrasound examination recorded on videotape to allow a mom to show the entire family her 8-week fetus. The presence of the fetus as an organism with interests has also presented extraordinary new problems. In *In re A.C.* the U.S. Court ruled that the right to discontinue pregnancy does not include a concomitant right to willfully harm the fetus. In hospitals this can mean that women are assigned to social workers early in their pregnancy on the basis of their drug habits or other problems. They can choose to discontinue pregnancy without interference, but if they elect to bear the child in an environment that is dangerous to the child, steps may be taken in advance toward removing the future child at birth from the care of the mother.

The paradigm for such remarkable steps is the broad social consensus about the need to protect young and vulnerable children from dangers against which they cannot protect themselves. Parents who abuse or neglect children, who refuse to educate children, or who will not provide their children with medical care (like vaccinations) can lose their parental roles. In this important sense, parenthood has always been both a responsibility and a privilege, rather than right, from the view of the pediatric model.

Arguments of the National Bioethics Advisory Commission and others that clinical human cloning should be prohibited have relied on the pediatric model. Two kinds of claims have been made—first that cloning would be physiologically unsafe for any human clone, and second that cloning would deprive a child of its identity or in other ways rob it of freedom. In the first case, it is clear that the claim is pediatric in character. Just as parents are forbidden from intentionally exposing their children to great, preventable risks, it is argued that parents ought not to expose future children to the sorts of hazards experienced by the first offspring in animal human cloning experiments. This duty obtains especially in early trials, when parents could have little or no confidence that their actions would be safe for resultant offspring.

In the second case, the argument of Dena Davis and others that children have "a right to an open future"[6] is also based on a social commitment to ensure that those who make children participate in certain pursuits taken by the community to be essential for the development of children. It is required in many nations that children be educated. The failure to provide children with clothing or a home safe from extreme violence is punishable throughout the world. In this regard it is feared that cloning might put children in an untenable family relationship or rob them of skills necessary for flourishing. The young clone might grow up with his or her progenitor as a "living" genetic test, knowing early on what is in store for his or her own future.

The litmus test for human cloning, from the pediatric perspective, is the interest of the clone. If it can be argued that the human child born through a new reproductive technology will be significantly imperiled in a preventable way, those who argue for the interests of the clone will hold that the procedure was unwarranted.

While arguments in the pediatric model seem very valuable to us, neither the pediatric nor reproductive rights model speaks to the question of how to regulate or debate human reproductive technology. Thus while we may agree with advocates of reproductive liberty that parents ought to have wide latitude in their sexual and reproductive choices, it is unclear how one would recognize any compelling interest that merits restricting that latitude. And while we may agree that the cloning of humans does not take sufficient account of the interests of the clone, it is unclear how to prevent similar tragedies from taking place in low-tech parenthood, or how to regulate new reproductive technologies so that disaster is averted.

One significant impediment to dialogue between those who argue for reproductive rights and those who argue for the interests of the child is the dilemma described by Derek Parfit. Because there is no child actually born at the time of the request for clinical human cloning, it at first seems odd to ask whether "the child" is well served by that procedure. One can only with difficulty protect the interests or rights of an organism that does not yet exist. Some even maintain that the debate about the interests of future generations must always be framed in terms of whether or not the future child would be better off never having existed. It is an apparent dilemma. However, there is one area of social policy where the gap between reproductive rights and the interests of children has been nicely bridged, resulting in significant consensus about how to protect children from dangerous situations.

Children have been adopted for thousands of years, and relationships between adoptive families and children have taken many forms and been articulated in many ways. The enormous institutional wisdom accumulated in what we call the adoption model can be very important for bridging the gap between reproductive liberty and pediatrics. The adoption model can move the debate about cloning and new reproductive technologies from its present, highly politicized rancor into a more constructive arena in which interdisciplinary and bipartisan consensus may be possible.

Parents who seek to adopt children are required, in virtually every nation, to seek prior approval from a regional authority or court. In many nations applicants are required to undergo psychological testing, home visits or other pre-screening. In most cases these pre-screens take place before a particular child has been identified for adoption; in many cases the pre-screen is independent and antecedent to the identification of a pregnant birth parent.

From the reproductive rights model, it might seem odd that such gross oversight is permitted. After all, fertile parents are not pre-screened before the state permits pregnancy. It could be argued that the screening of applicants for adoption is a manifest invasion of reproductive privacy and an incursion on the rights of parents to reproduce in the manner they desire. We might very well have converted adoption to the model of reproductive rights, following for example the U.S. precedent of leaving surrogacy and egg and sperm donation to the marketplace. Why, when we tolerate a virtual free market in all donor-assisted reproduction, with no pre-screen or judicial oversight, do we insist that adoption be so closely monitored?

The answer is that adoption, in many respects, embodies the best features of both the reproductive rights and pediatric models. Adoption law is framed out of a recognition that the adoption of a child is an unusual way to enter into a family, devoid of pregnancy and birth and textured by its own social and moral features. The adoption process cannot replace these elements of gestation and preparation for childbirth. However, in an important sense it gives communal imprimatur to the creation of a family, drawing on other social rituals for sealing a permanent and loving commitment (i.e. marriage).

The adoptive parents are not screened in search of perfect parents, only with the aim of determining whether or not this particular set of parents can provide some bare minimum features of parenthood that have been historically important in the adoption setting. In this respect the adoption judge is much like the divorce court judge. When parents split up, a judge is in the unusual position of determining what sort of family is best for a particular child given some set of exigencies. What appears to us to be Solomon's wisdom embodied by such judges is actually the product of long-term study of human families in a particular communal context. While their decisions are imperfect, the ethical responsibility of the judge is identified with the representation that the judge makes for the community and for the laws of the state or nation as they apply to adoption.

The adoption judge or magistrate is in an important sense a community historian for the dimensions of family, tracking some of the important features of the community so that they can be accounted for in matching parents and children. Parents who are not judged to be good candidates for adoption may plead their case, but are finally at the mercy of the community leaders.

The adoption model for human family making is predicated on several simple and profound assumptions. First, where unorthodox parenting arrangements (as in adoption or divorce) pose special challenges, the responsibility of the community to provide counsel and oversight is compelling. Second, where arrangements for parenting have not worked or are likely to present special problems, the court and community ought to be empowered to enact short- or long-term restrictions on certain kinds of family-making. Just as regional governments decide how marriage will work, who may inherit, and what kinds of schools provide sufficient education, the family courts have a quite proper jurisdiction in prohibiting certain kinds of family relationships (e.g., incest, cloning, and polygamy). Third, the formation of a family is both a deeply personal and profoundly social act. The interests of children who are adopted or made through new reproductive technologies are best served when a spirit of openness and honesty about the meaning of the process is demonstrated.

It is already clear that we join dozens of other ethicists and scientists in favoring a short-term ban on clinical human cloning. The purpose of this paper however is to argue for a way in which human cloning restrictions might take shape. In their haste to pass legislation, many have settled for a simple, totalitarian approach to a cloning ban. We propose a more democratic, consensus-oriented model that entrusts the community to develop and enforce rules for the protection of children. Even those who disagree with our model will need to argue not only for restrictions on cloning but for the most sensible and careful way to frame such law.

The adoption model can be easily adapted to a variety of reproductive technologies.[7] Our purpose here is not to argue for specific policies. We have explicated the framing of the debate both about human cloning and reproductive technology more generally, holding that while new reproductive technology can be discussed in terms of either reproductive rights or pediatric interests, the two kinds of arguments can seem incommensurable.

Adoption as a model integrates both the importance of the rights of parents and the importance of the interests of children, even those children who have not yet been born or even conceived. Where unorthodox parenting and family making is concerned, the community should draw on much richer metaphors than simple analysis of rights. The conflict between reproductive rights and interests of the child is deceptively simple, reflecting more general debates in society about the role of the state in personal life.

By contrast, the making of children is as complex and confusing an area as exists in human inquiry and human life. In adoption, somehow consensus has been reached that children of new and unusual techniques merit special protection, but such protection ought not to be onerous for parents once the parental relationship is consecrated. Moreover, by applying the adoption model to the problem of human cloning, it becomes immediately clear how difficult it would be for any of the test cases described above to meet the high standards for use of such a risky technology. Parents who present with requests that would either excessively stylize children or place them in harm's way ought not to be allowed to proceed. In the short term this will doubtless mean that under an adoption model, sponsored by state or regional governments, cloning ought to be proscribed. At the same time, unlike other larger plans designed to restrict a broad swath of scientific research, the adoption model is a more limited endeavor whose scope is the making of families.

Notes

[1] Greg Pence, *Who's Afraid of Human Cloning* (New York 1998).
[2] See the recommendations of the National Bioethics Advisory Commission report, included herein. We note too that restric-

tions on cloning must be crafted carefully so as to ensure free-dom in scientific research not intended to produce human children.

[3] McGee makes this argument in *The Perfect Baby: A Pragmatic Approach to Genetics* (New York 1997), epilogue; it has been made by Wilmut and others as well.

[4] Cf. Arthur Caplan, *Am I My Brother's Keeper* (Indianapolis 1998).

[5] See especially Lee Silver, *Remaking Eden: cloning and beyond in a brave new world* (New York 1997) and Philip Kitcher, *The Lives to Come* (New York 1997).

[6] Dena Davis, "The Right to an Open Future," *Hastings Center Report*, March–April 1997, pp. 34–40.

[7] See, e.g., Glenn McGee and Daniel McGee, "Nuclear Meltdown: Ethics of the Need to Transfer Genes," *Politics and the Life Sciences*, March 1998, pp. 72–76.

Justine Burley and John Harris

Human Cloning and Child Welfare

Introduction

Debate over the moral permissibility of human cloning was much enlivened by the news that the first mammal, Dolly the sheep, had been successfully created from the transfer of an already differentiated adult cell nucleus into an enucleated egg[1], a technique popularly referred to as cloning.

Now that doubts about Dolly's genetic origins have, for the most part, been dispelled,[2] and that three other species, including the mouse,[3] have been cloned, the prospect that a human may also be cloned appears ever more likely.[4]

There is a broad, albeit loose, consensus among members of the lay public, various legislative bodies, and the scientific community that human *reproductive*[5] cloning should be banned because there is something deeply immoral about it *in principle* (i.e. something above and

234

beyond the fact that it would be wholly unacceptable to attempt it in humans until it appears reasonably safe). Precisely what this is, however, continues to elude even the most committed of critics[6] These opponents are not short of reasons for their anti-human cloning stance, indeed, such reasons, more often than not couched in mysterious appeals to human rights and human dignity, flow freely.[7] But none of the objections to the practice of human cloning have so far proved sound or convincing. In this paper we address one of the few intelligible (as opposed to persuasive) objections to human cloning that have been advanced: the objection which appeals to the welfare of the child. The form of this objection varies according to the sort of harm it is anticipated the clone will suffer. The three formulations of it that we will consider are:

1 . Clones will be harmed by the fearful or prejudicial attitudes people may have about or towards them. (HI);
2. Clones will be harmed by the demands and expectations of parents or genotvpe donors (H2);
3 . Clones will be harmed by their own awareness of their origins, for example the knowledge that the genetic donor is a stranger. (H3).

Below we aim to show why these three versions of the child welfare objection do *not* supply compelling reasons to ban human reproductive cloning, The claim that we will develop and defend in the course of our discussion is that even if it is the case that a cloned child will suffer harms of the type HI–H3, it is none the less permissible to conceive by gso long as these cloning-induced welfare deficits are not such as to blight the existence of the resultant child, whoever this may be.

Our article is divided into four main parts. We begin by outlining what Derek Parfit has called the "non-identity problem."[8] As we will demonstrate, this problem, when explored and understood properly, shows that those who object to human cloning on the grounds that it would have compromising effects on a *particular* child's welfare are making an error in reasoning.We then go on to outline Derek Parfit's principled solution to the non-identity problem and, in the ensuing three sections, we will argue agamst each of the three objections to human cloning from child welfare identified above, in turn, by reference to this solution. Once it is seen that Parfit's principle in unqualified form is what informs these objections it becomes clear that people who object to human cloning for reasons of child welfare are impaled on the horns of a dilemma: either they must concede that their position entails a whole host of morally unpalatable restrictions on both artificial and natural procreation or they must accept that their arguments are insufficient to support the view that human cloning is immoral in any strong sense and so should be prohibited.

I. Child welfare and the non-identity problem

One of the chief philosophical problems raised by human cloning is the question of how we should respond to the interests of people not yet in existence. Objections to human cloning from child welfare are objections relating to harms future clones might come to suffer and they may all be captured by the claim: a child who is cloned would, *for that reason or for reasons related but not intrinsic to it,* suffer a deficit in wellbeing relative to someone conceived through natural means.

Typical in discussions of this claim is the notion that the harms and benefits which concern us, occur to the same child. However, as exploration of the non-identity problem will now make clear, claims of this kind cannot explain what it is that might be thought problematic about a decision which results in a clone being harmed in any way at all.

To give shape to the non-identity problem we will now consider the following two cases. The first is Parfit's and involves a 14-year-old prospective mother:

This girl chooses to have a child. Because she is so young, she gives her child a bad start in life. Though this will have bad effects throughout the child's life, his or her life will, predictably, be worth. living. If this girl had waited for several years, she would have'had a different child, to whom she would have given a better start in life.[9]

Our analogue to this case is:

A woman chooses to have a child through cloning. Because she chooses to conceive in this way, she gives the child a bad start in life. Though this will have bad effects throughout the child's life, his or her life will, predictably; be worth living. If this woman had chosen to procreate by alternative means, she would have had a different child, to whom she would have given a better start in life.

In both cases, two courses of action are open to the prospective mother. In criticising these women's pursuit of the first option available (i.e. conception at 14 and reproductive cloning respectively) people might claim that each mother's decisions will probably be worse for *her child*.[10] However, as Parfit notes, while people can make this claim about the decisions taken it does not *explain* what they believe is objectionable about them. It fails to explain this because neither decision can be worse for the particular children born; *the alternative for both of them was never to have existed at all.* If the 14-year-old waits to conceive, a completely different child will be born. Likewise, if the woman chooses not to clone and instead conceives by natural procreative means the child born will be a completely different one. Thus claims about the badness of pursuing the first option in both of the above cases cannot be claims about why *these children* have been harmed. It is better for *these* children that they live than not live at all.

Parfit's solution to the non-identity problem is to posit claim "Q", which says that: "If in either of two possible outcomes the same number of people would ever live, it would be worse if those who live are worse off, or have a lower quality of life, than those who would have lived."[11] This claim, unlike the claim about the welfare of a particular child, can explain the goodness and badness of the procreative decisions that might be taken by the two women in the above cases because it avoids the problem of non-identity.

With respect to the two cases we have been examining Q implies that the 14-year-old girl should wait and that the woman should not use cloning technology. This is not necessarily Parfit's last word on the matter. He does qualify Q: he argues that some things may matter more than sub-optimal outcomes.[12] For example, a society might believe that the pursuit of equality is more valuable than promoting economic growth. Parfit, then, is a pluralist. He believes that Q is a helpful principle with which to evaluate moral judgments, but he does not think that this principle should necessarily be used to the exclusion of all others. It is, however, something very like Parfit's principle in its unqualified form (henceforth Q(U)) to which those who object to human cloning from child welfare are appealing, i.e. the idea that principle factor that should weigh in decision making about who should be brought into existence is the question of who will enjoy the highest level of welfare. We will now make explicit why we believe that this approach is gravely mistaken through an examination of objections 1–3 as stated above.

II. Cloning, societal prejudice

The first objection to human cloning from child welfare we will address says that human cloning should be disallowed because clones will be harmed by the fearful and/or prejudicial attitudes other people have about or towards them (H1).[13] The chairman of the Human Fertilisation and Embryology Authority (HFEA), Ruth Deech, offers paradigmatic examples of this objection in a recent comment on the subject:

"Would cloned children be the butt of jibes and/or be discriminated against? Would they become a sub-caste who would have to keep to each other? Would they be exploited? Would they become media objects (not an unlikely scenario given that Louise Brown, the first test-tube baby, is still in the media some 20 years after her conception)?"[14].

Deech's objection here gives primacy to the wellbeing of future clones. Cloning is thought undesirable because of H1 type harms that they might suffer. Her view appears to be informed by Q(U), according to which, the decision to clone should not be taken as any resulting child, other things being equal, would have a worse life than a child produced by natural means.

But, it is utterly crucial that we do not lose sight of the reason why in this case the clone's life would be the worse one, namely, that other members of society are prejudiced against him or her. Q(U) as applied by Deech entails morally repugnant conclusions. Deech's deployment of Q(U) reasoning does not show that parents who chose to clone would be acting immorally. The source of the harm is not the clone's parents, it is not they who do something wrong by cloning the child, rather it is other members of society who commit a moral wrong. Think of inter-racial marriage in a society hostile to mixed-race unions.

The following example involving Tom, Dick and Harry illustrates our point here. Suppose that a woman called Jane can conceive a child with either Tom, Dick or Harry, and that for her (not others) the only relevant difference between these men is that Tom, predictably, will be the better father; if either Dick or Harry were, predictably, the better father, she would choose one of them as her mate instead. Deech is committed to saying that Jane ought to choose Tom, as, if chosen, the resulting child will, other things being equal, have a higher level of wellbeing than any child parented by Dick or Harry. Let us more fully describe this scenario. Assume that the reasons Tom will be the "better" father is that the society in which all four of these individuals live is predominantly populated by white people, a fair number of whom are racist and that of Tom, Dick and Harry, only Tom is white. He is the; "better" father because, in this racist society, his skin color and cultural background afford him better employment and other life-enhancing opportunities and therefore he is better able to provide for any child that he and Jane (also white) conceive. Moreover, it is the case that if Jane selects Tom, they will not have a mixed-race child (as would occur were she to pair up with Dick or Harry instead), and therefore, because of the prevailing climate of racial prejudice any child born to Jane and Tom will lead a better life than any child born to Jane and Dick or Jane and Harry.

Q(U) recommends Jane's choice of Tom because the children Jane might have with Dick or Harry would lead worse lives *because of the prejudice of others*. However, to reject cloning on the grounds of this variant of the objection from child welfare is morally discreditable. It is true that we could prevent this sort of harm being done to a future child by avoiding human cloning altogether. But we should not prevent human cloning in the face of this sort of sub-optimality, rather we should concentrate on combating the prejudices and attitudes that are the source of harm to the clone. Those who embrace liberty and respect autonomy will prefer this approach and reject assaults on human freedom and dignity of the kind Deech suggests would be perpetrated on clones. Plainly, it is inappropriate to countenance any diminution in reproductive autonomy when attempts to diminish prejudice and tyranny are all the more consonant with human dignity.

III. Cloning, "life in the shadow"

It has been claimed by a number of critics that a clone might be harmed because of the expectations and demands of his or her parents or genotype donor (H2) and therefore reproductive cloning should be proscribed. Soren Holm, for example, argues that one reason that we have not to clone a human is that the clone will be living "a life in the shadow" of the person from whose genes he or she was cloned—the clone would not have a life that was fully his or her own.[15] Holm's argument may be stated in brief as follows: people are wedded to a belief in genetic essentialism (i.e. they misunderstand the relationship between genetics and personality), for that reason a clone's parent(s) may treat him or her such that the clone will not lead an autonomous life, he or she will always be *living in the shadow* of another (i.e. the genetic donor)—incessantly compared to the donor—therefore human cloning should not be allowed.[16] It is unclear from what Holm has said what, specifically, he believes the relationship between autonomy and wellbeing to be. If, like prominent liberal thinkers such as Ronald Dworkin, he thinks that autonomy is part of wellbeing, then his objections to human cloning is an objection about the welfare of the child. If, on the other hand, he, like Kant, understands autonomy as an independent principle, then the objection is not, per se, one about the welfare of the child. We shall respond to Holm as though he is advancing the former sort of objection.[17]

Note that the claim on which Holm's argument is premised (he calls it the "true" premise) is that the public harbour misunderstandings about genetic essentialism, i.e., they make a factual error. It is this crucial factual premise in Holm's argument which undermines its major normative force. Holm concedes that were the public to be disabused of its views about genetic essentialism the life-in-the-shadow argument would fall flat.[17] But, he insists, such a change in public understanding about genetics is unlikely.[17] Apart from the fact that we do not share Holm's dim view of what the lay public is likely to understand about genetics, the life-in-the-shadow argument is lacking in a different important way. It is morally problematic to limit human freedom on the basis of false beliefs of this character. Were we to apply the logic of Holm's argument to other factual errors parents might make or false beliefs they might have which would affect the wellbeing of possible children it would have pernicious implications. For example, parents might falsely believe that certain physical deformities implied intellectual impairment and this would lead them to treat children so deformed in a way which undermined their autonomy. Should such people be denied the freedom to procreate whenever it was known that they might conceive such a child? Likewise, parents might believe that female children were less intelligent than males and, in grooming them for marriage from birth, deny them an autonomous existence. Should such parents only be allowed to have male offspring? Holm's argument against human cloning appears also to commit him to restrictive procreative policies like these which undoubtedly,would adversely impact, for the most part, on people who are ill-educated/ill-informed (or genetically unlucky). If human cloning is banned because future people might suffer harms caused by the mistaken beliefs of parents about genetics then it follows that so too might natural procreation whenever prospective parents do not possess adequate factual information to ensure any future child's wellbeing in other ways. We reject this conclusion and propose that the preferable strategy for dealing with the problem Holm highlights is one which involves educating people about genetics.

Holm rightly signals that the moral basis for arguments about respect for autonomy is a claim about the fundamental importance or value of having control over the pursuit of one's own projects, plans and attachments. The ideal of autonomy is used by liberal theorists to defend a particular role for the state, namely, the creation and maintenance of the social, economic and political conditions under which people may learn about different aspects and ways of life, reflect critically on them, and embrace a set of values and aims which they believe give life meaning. While it may be true that the autonomy of a clone who lived her life in the shadow of another would be adversely affected this is not sufficient to curtail a would-be cloner's reproductive freedom. Holm fails adequately to appreciate that the liberal ideal of autonomy to which he appeals requires, amongst other things, that compelling reasons (construed as reasons which squarely locate a deeply immoral outcome) must be given to limit individual freedom. Holm champions impediments to autonomous living as a sufficient reason to ban cloning but he is surely mistaken.[18] In failing to distinguish between his idea of a clone living a life in the shadow and the degree of the harm which that entails from other acts of procreation involving equally, if not more severe, autonomy-affecting consequences, Holm invites highly illiberal restrictions on procreation. Freedom is costly—affording it to individuals will, in many cases, produce suboptimal outcomes but unless these outcomes involve a moral wrong so serious that freedom must be sacrificed to prevent it, the liberal view insists that freedom prevail and that other means be found to combat any resulting harms.

Holm's objection to human cloning is more sophisticated than the one we considered in II above. It implies that parents who elect to clone, who do not understand the distinction between genotype and phenotype, are committing a moral wrong of some kind. But how serious is this moral wrong? What Q(U) reasoning in this case shows is that this principle is useful conditionally on the severity of. the harm inflicted. We maintain that unless it is shown convincingly that "living in the shadow" is somehow both horrendous and more autonomy-compromising than the plethora of other widely accepted and permitted upbringings a child might be "forced" to undergo, the liberal principle of freedom in matters relating to procreation overrides the concern about autonomy-related welfare deficits that will be suffered by clones.

IV. Cloning and awareness of origins

The final objection to human cloning from child welfare we shall explore concerns instances of psychological harms caused by a clone's own awareness of his or her genetic origins (H3). According to this objection, a clone who knew his or her genetic donor was, for example, a randomly chosen stranger, or a distant, much older relative, or even someone now deceased, would be psychologically damaged by that information. (14) Is this plausible? We doubt that knowledge of peculiar genetic origins would *necessarily* be harmful. Indeed, it might even be beneficial in certain cases. In making this claim we have in mind children who are the product of in vitro fertilisation, (which need not always involve the genetic material of both the parents) who report that they feel "special" (as opposed to alienated) for having been brought into being in this way. Presumably this has much to do with the extent to which they feel loved by the parents they do have, as well as societal acceptance of IVF as a procreative method.

However, let us assume that it would be the case that a clone would be traumatised to some extent by his or her genetic origins. Is this sufficient reason to disallow cloning? If H3 harms are both very great and highly probable then, yes, this is a sufficient reason; but we judge this scenario to be a remote possibility. Consider that there are many possible sources of analogous H3-type traumas a child created by natural means might suffer: the realisation that your parent committed a criminal act earlier in his/her life, or is a drug addict or prostitute, or fought for an army established to advance a dictator's master plan for domination. Our intuition is that it would be far easier to cope with the knowledge that one's nurturing parents so desired a child that they were even prepared to use cloning technology to bring one into existence than to cope with the knowledge of, for example, a parent's collusion with the Nazis' systematic extermination of the Jews or Stalin's political re-education programmes in the Siberian gulags. These examples are admittedly provocative, but they are not isolated ones, and that is the point that merits stressing. If psychological distress about one's genenc origins is sufficient to ban cloning then it follows that people who fall into the aforementioned groups and others ought also to be (or to have been) prevented from procreating.

Thus undiscriminating adherence to Q(U) reasoning invites the response that this objection from child welfare, like the preceding two, logically entails other draconian restrictions on procreative freedom which the objector would hardly endorse. Even if such critics were prepared to go that far, their view should not be tolerated in any society which aims to promote freedom of the individual. Most people believe, and they do so rightly, that we :should be concerned about the sorts of lives that future people will lead, but that, at the same time, this concern should not be our sole one. If H3 harms were of exclusive import, we would have grounds for saying that a huge number of people in the world today are morally blameworthy in some strong sense for having brought children into the world.

Conclusion

We argued above that the objections that have been voiced about human cloning and child welfare are misleading. While we are sympathetic to what motivates them—society both does and should have an interest in the wellbeing of future people—we do not believe that the formulations of the anti-cloning arguments from child welfare that we have addressed are persuasive. We conceded that cloned individuals might indeed suffer welfare deficits (relative to a non-clone) but argued that even the likely occurrence of them is not sufficient to warrant state interference with the procreative choices of people who wish to clone their genes (or those of others, providing consent to their use in this way has been given).

Our examination of the objections 1–3 which respectively embody reference to harms HI–H3 are informed, we have suggested, by something very like Parfit's solution to the non-identity problem in unqualified form. Our discussion of these objections confronts those who object to human cloning for reasons of child welfare with a dilemma: either they must endorse the morally discreditable outcomes entailed by the principle guiding their view or they must admit that Q(U), as they have deployed it, does not provide sufficient reasons for branding reproductive cloning immoral either at all or in any strong sense of that term.

Where considerations of the welfare of the child are invoked in reproduction, including in the case of reproductive cloning, we need constantly to bear in mind the following questions and the distinctions they encapsulate: is it clear that the child who may result from cloning will be so adversely affected that it will be seriously wronged by the decision? Or rather is it the case that we have general anxieties about the likely advantages and disadvantages of being cloned, for example, that disincline us to look on it with much favour? Where it is rational to judge that an individual would not have a worthwhile life if he or she were to be brought into being in particular circumstances, then we have not only powerful reasons not to make such choices ourselves but also powerful moral reasons for preventing others from so

doing if we can—by legislation or regulation if necessary.
However, where we judge the circumstances of a future
person to be less than ideal but not so bad as to deprive
that individual of a worthwhile existence, then we lack
the moral justification to impose our ideals on others.
The difference we are looking for is the difference between considerations which would clearly blight the life
of the resulting child, and considerations that would
merely make existence suboptimal in some sense. We
may be entitled to prevent people from acting in ways
which will result in blighted lives. We are surely on less
firm, and less clearly morally respectable, grounds when
we attempt to impose our ideals and preferences about
the specifics of how future lives should go.

Q(U), as we have shown, has troublesome practical
implications for a whole range of policies concerning
procreation, both natural and artificial. We argued that
the reasons why a future clone's, or, for that matter, a
future non-clone's life might go badly (relative to someone else), command attention. If we allow considerations
like marginalisation, discrimination, impediments to
autonomy, etc, to outweigh all other considerations when
deliberating over the moral permissibility of human cloning, we, at the same time, court numerous other unacceptably illiberal outcomes. There are, of course, many
cases where it is true that the morally superior of two
otherwise identical procreative acts will be the one that
maximises child welfare. The crucial issue is what follows from this. Many people believe that the child welfare card trumps all, that once they have shown that some
procreative choice or technology can lead to suboptimal
circumstances for the resulting children this constitutes
a knock-down argument against any claimed freedom to
procreate in that way or using that technology. This
seems to us not only implausible but palpably morally

unacceptable.

References and notes

[1] Wilmut I, Schnieke AE, McWhir J, Kind AJ, Campbell KHS. Viable offspring derived from fetal and adult mammalian cells. Nature 1987;385:810–13.

[2] See Ashworth D, Bishop M, Campbell K, Colman A, Kind A, Schnieke A *et al.* DNA microsatellite analysis of Dolly. *Nature* 1998;394: 329 and Signer EN, Dubrova YE, Jeffreys AJ, Wilde C, Finch LMB, Wells M *et al.* DNA fingerprinting Dolly. *Nature* 1998; 394: 330.

[3] Wakayama T, Perry ACF, Zuccottis M, Johnson KR, Yanagimachi R. Full-term development of mice from enucleated oocytes injected with cumulus cell nuclei. *Nature* 1998;394:369–73. This development in nuclear transfer technology is significant for the case of human cloning because mice possess a reproductive physiology closer to that of human beings than animals like sheep and cows.

[4] This view is echoed in the opinion section of *Nature*1998; 394.

[5] Two main uses of cloning by nuclear transfer have been distinguished: therapeutic and reproductive. Therapeutic cloning is understood as any instance of cell nucleus replacement aimed at creating cell lines and/or for the treatment of disease. Reproductive cloning, by contrast, is any instance of cloning which is not motivated by the desire to avoid disease or disability. We have chosen to concentrate on reproductive uses of nuclear transfer technology because they are more controversial.

[6] For discussion of why it may be difficult to pinpoint the source of people's discomfort with human cloning see Kass LR, Chapter 5.

[7] For a critique of these see Harris J. "Goodbye Dolly"? The ethics of human cloning. *Journal of Medical Ethics* 1997;23:353–60.

[8] Parfit D. *Reasons and persons* (Oxford 1984), ch. 16.

[9] See reference 8: 358.

[10] This is Parfit's point made here in the plural. Reference 8: 359.

[11] See reference 8: 360.

[12] See Parfit's discussion of Jane's choice: reference 8: 375–7.

[13] We do *not* mean by the term prejudicial attitudes here *formal discrimination,* i.e. rights violations.

[14] Deech R. Human cloning and public policy. In: Burley J, ed.

The genetic revolution and human rights (Oxford, forthcoming) ch. 4.

[15] Holm S. A life in shadows: one reason why we should not clone humans. *Cambridge Quarterly of Healthcare Ethics* 1998;7:160–2. Other formulations of the objection may be found in: Wilmut I. Dolly: the age of biological control. In: Burley J, ed. *The genetic revolution and human rights*: ch 1 (see reference 14), and Klotzco AJ. Voices from Roslin: the creators of Dolly discuss science, ethics and social responsibility. *Cambridge Quarterly of Healthcare Ethics* 1998;7: especially, 137–9.

[16] See reference 15: Holm S: 162.

[17] Holm's own remarks suggest that this is appropriate. See reference 15: Holm S: 162.

[18] Matthew Clayton has developed an ingenious argument in support of the claim that the very act of choosing the genes of a child, irrespective of the consequences, is, in a non-person-affecting sense, a violation of its autonomy. See Procreative autonomy and genetics. In: Burley J, Harris J, eds. *A companion to genetics* (Oxford 1999).

Jonathan R. Cohen

In God's Garden: Creation and Cloning in Jewish Thought

The possibility of cloning human beings challenges Western beliefs about creation and our relationship to God. If we understand God as the Creator and creation as a completed act, cloning will be a transgression. If, however, we understand God as the Power of Creation and creation as a transformative process, we may find a role for human participation, sharing that power as beings created in the image of God

Some scientific revolutions change what people believe about the world. The Copernican and Darwinian revolutions, while not significantly changing what people could then use science to achieve, forced people to re-examine their understanding of the universe, of humanity and its place in the universe, and of God's agency within the universe. Other scientific revolutions, like Faraday and Maxwell's work on the physics of electric fields, pose little challenge to fundamental beliefs but dramatically change society through their technological application. We are now in the midst of a genetic revolution that may both profoundly influence our beliefs and dramatically change how society functions. Will designing our offspring someday be as easy and common as "cut and paste" on a word processor? Are we on the cusp of an evolutionary advance toward being an "autocreative" species, or in attempting to "play God" has our hubris reached its zenith? Such are the questions we face.

My purpose here is to explore how the genetic revolution could affect our beliefs. My strategy is to examine several challenges that human cloning and, to a lesser extent, genetic engineering raise for certain basic Jewish beliefs—though by no means exclusively Jewish beliefs—about humans and God, using as a lens for my thoughts the Biblical account of creation presented in the first few chapters of Genesis.[1] Not only are many basic Jewish beliefs about humans and God embedded in that account, but even if one believes that Genesis is inaccurate as a literal account of the world's creation, or even if one does not believe in God, Genesis provides an excellent framework for addressing some of the existential challenges posed by the genetic revolution. Although I address challenges human cloning presents for certain basic Jewish beliefs, such Biblically-rooted beliefs influence much Christian and Western thought. Moreover, such beliefs play an important part in developing public policy toward human cloning. For example, the National Bioethics Advisory Commission devoted roughly one quarter of its report on human cloning to religious views, focusing in particular on the Biblical account of creation.

The Biblical account is open to two different interpretations, of creation as a completed act and creation as a transformative process, which carry quite different implications for human cloning. Understanding creation in these different ways suggests different answers to how human cloning might impinge on our beliefs about the worth of a human life, about God's role as Creator and Sovereign, and about how meaning can be found in a human life. I want to suggest that if its implications are properly understood, human cloning can be integrated with many of our basic beliefs and can encourage us to view God's act of creation as a transformative process.

This is not to advocate that human cloning be permitted—that is a very different question. However, the possibility of human cloning challenges our beliefs irrespective of whether we ultimately permit or ban such practice, or of whether human cloning actually occurs.

A note before I begin. Although for simplicity I use terms such as "Jewish beliefs" and "Jewish thought," I do not mean to suggest that all Jews do hold or should hold similar beliefs about these topics or that Judaism requires one to hold a particular view about these topics. Indeed, I pretend no special expertise in Jewish thought, but speak as a lay Jew who seeks to make some existential "sense" out of the possibility of human cloning.

Completed Act or Transformative Process?

The Bible begins, *"Bereshit bara Elohim et hashamayim v'et haaretz..."* It is a mysterious phrase. Under one common interpretation, it is translated as a declarative sentence—"In the beginning, God created the heavens and the earth." The import is that God created the universe out of nothing, and essentially all at once. In this reading, God engages in two primary activities in Genesis: bringing into existence various elements, and dividing them from one another, each to have a distinct role. Light is separated from darkness; land is separated from sea; birds are to fly in the sky while fish are to swim in the sea. The patterns of reproduction also appear Divinely set. Each form of vegetation is to produce offspring of its own type, and there are two genders of humans, with reproduction to occur through the union of a male and a female.[2] We are also told that by the seventh day, "The heavens and the earth and all their hosts were complete" (Gen. 2:1). The structure of the universe had been set. Creation is essentially completed.

From such an interpretation, an argument arises: if God created the structure of our world, who are we to tamper with it? Further, the Bible describes humans as created "in God's image" (Gen. 1: 27). If "in God's image" means "after God's likeness," how could that likeness be improved upon? If "in God's image" means "in accordance with God's plan," who are we to create a better plan?

If God's stamp in creating the world and the life within it alone does not lead one to think that the structure of the world should be left as is, other sources might. The Bible depicts transgressing the boundaries God gave as the paradigm of sin. Eating the forbidden fruit leads to the expulsion from Eden, and the commingling of divine and human beings precedes the flood. Sex between humans and animals is prohibited, as is sex between two men (Lev. 18: 22–24; 20: 12, 15–16). So too crossbreeding animals and planting a field with different types of seed (Lev. 19: 19; Deut. 22: 9). The concern for nature's structure is even applied to clothing: it is forbidden to construct a garment of both linen and wool (Lev. 19: 19, Deut. 22: 12). Conversely, many Biblical passages, especially in Leviticus, indicate that holiness can be found by respecting boundaries. As Mary Douglas has argued, "Holiness requires that individuals shall conform to the class to which they belong. And holiness requires that different classes of things shall not be confused."[3]

Against such a reading of the Bible, human cloning would be wrong. Although human cloning would not bring into existence a new species-a potential criticism of transgenic activities such as making hybrid plants or animals—it would transgress the structure of sexual reproduction that God created. Human cloning supplants the structure by which God designed humans to reproduce. Our current genetic quandary might be cast as a second fall from Eden. Driven by our lust for Godlike power, we have picked of the tempting fruit of the tree of genetic knowledge. We ought not to use that knowledge to pervert the structure of the world.[4]

Like most great literature, however, the Biblical account of creation can be interpreted in different ways. A second, contrasting interpretation of Genesis may be offered that has quite different implications for how we view human cloning. Often the opening phrase of Genesis is translated not as a declarative sentence, but as a constructive clause—"When God began creating the heavens and the earth..." or "At the beginning of God's creation of the heavens and the earth..."[5] So construed, creation may be seen not as a completed act cast in a particular structure, but as a transformative process.[6] In this interpretation, the miracle of creation is not the specific world God produced, but rather God's moving the world from a chaotic nothingness to an ordered, light-filled, life-bearing place. Further, one might point to the Bible's repeated emphasis that God created things called "good" and "very good." Put differently, the miracle was that God improved what existed. Good purpose, rather than a particular form, lies at the heart of creation.[7]

If God is seen as Creator, and if we are created in the image of God, then might we not have a role to play as creators ourselves?[8] Abraham is viewed as praiseworthy when, exercising an independent conception of what is moral, he argues with God over the fate of Sodom and Gomorrah.[9] Might we be praiseworthy if we put our technology to work to pursue our independently formed conception of the good?[10] People get sick naturally, and yet most feel that medical intervention to aid the sick is morally permissible, perhaps even obligatory, as in Jewish law. God, rather than nature, is to be worshipped.

If creation is a transformative process of bettering our world in which humans are to play a part, then in assessing human cloning the normative focus would turn to whether we use human cloning to do good or evil. As Rabbi Elliot Dorff has written, "Cloning, like all other technologies, is morally neutral. Its moral valence depends on how we use it."[11] It is in this respect like our use of drugs: when used to improve health, they are a blessing; when taken by addicts, a curse. And some think that the use of human cloning would sometimes be merited, even obliged. Rabbi Moshe Tendler has declared, "Show me a young man who is sterile, whose family was wiped out in the Holocaust, and [who] is the last of a genetic line [and] I would certainly done him."[12] Other candidates include more common cases of infertility, such as parents who could not otherwise reproduce and want to done their recently deceased newborn, or of saving someone's life, such as cloning an infant who has suffered severe kidney damage in the hope that the clone might someday willingly donate a kidney to the clonee.[13]

In sum, different interpretations of Genesis have quite different implications for how we judge human cloning. If we believe structuring our world a particular way lies at the heart of God's creation, then we will likely view human cloning as transgressing that structure. In contrast, if we believe that transforming what exists for the better lies at the heart of creation, then our view of human cloning will likely depend on whether we use human cloning to accomplish good or evil.

Cloning and Humanity

Central to the Western conception of human nature is the Biblical view that we were created by God and "in God's image." The idea has been historically as well as philosophically important, for it has done much to protect and elevate the status of humans. Yet the genetic revolution, and especially the possibility of human cloning, deeply challenges that view. While humans have long produced other humans through traditional reproduction, they have never been able to control the exact genetic structure of their offspring. Traditional conception has always involved much randomness and uncertainty. Seeing God's hand in the uncertain and mysterious is relatively easy; seeing God's hand in what we can control may be difficult. Cloning and genetic engineering offer the prospect of removing that randomness and uncertainty, and so threaten to undermine the belief that humans are created by God, in God's image.

Commenting on the Biblical account of creation, the Mishnaic Rabbis (c. 200 CE) explained:

> For this reason was man created alone, to teach you that whoever destroys a single soul of Israel, Scripture imputes (guilt) to him as though he had destroyed a complete world; and whosoever preserves a single soul of Israel, Scripture ascribes (merit) to him as though he had preserved a complete world. Furthermore, (he was created alone) for the sake of peace among men, that one might not say to his fellow, "My father was greater than thine", ...[and] to proclaim the greatness of The Holy One, Blessed be He: for if a man strikes many coins from one mould, they all resemble one another, but The Supreme King of Kings, The Holy One, Blessed be He, fashioned every man in the

stamp of the first man, and yet not one of them resembles his fellow.[14]

The commentary exemplifies the traditional Jewish view that three central values are imputed by the Biblical account of creation to every human life: pricelessness, uniqueness, and equality. Arguably, cloning could undermine each of these values.

Consider pricelessness tint. Belief in the pricelessness of human life seems to fall naturally out of the belief that humans are created in God's image, for if each of us is created in God's image, then each of us is of infinite worth, indeed is sacred. The worry is that if we clone our offspring, then rather than seeing them as created in the Divine image, we might come to see them as mere objects of production, genetically replaceable like other products. The art market provides analogies: An original oil painting is typically much more valuable than copies of it, and objects that can be readily duplicated, such as photographs, usually sell for far less than those that cannot. In economic language, cloning increases the potential "supply" of each of us and so might cause our value to decline.

Yet this fear should not be overstated. If someone were cloned a thousand times over, perhaps it would be hard to see each as a priceless being. But such use seems unlikely. In contrast, if cloning were used to make only one or two "copies" of a person, maintaining the belief that each has infinite worth would be much easier. Few would argue that natural genetic twins have diminished worth.[15]

As interpreted by the Mishnaic Rabbis, the fact that God began by creating not a group of people but the individual Adam also shows that every human being is unique.[16] To this day, a belief in individual uniqueness has played an important part in Jewish thought. As was expressed by Rabbi Zusya of Anipol shortly before his death, "In the world to come I shall not be asked: 'Why were you not Moses?' Rather I shall be asked: 'Why were you not Zusya?' "[17] Martin Buber also put great weight on the concept of human uniqueness:

> Every person born into this world represents something new, something that never existed before, something original and unique... Every man's foremost task is the actualization of his unique, unprecedented and never-recurring potentialities, and not the repetition of something that another, and be it even the greatest, has already achieved. (p. 17)

To many (myself included), the thought of being cloned is frightening. Indeed, the very thought that one could be cloned may be disturbing. If I can be copied, what is so special about me?

Of course, as many have pointed out, two clones would not really be identical. Raised in different environments, perhaps at different times, they will become different people. Even if physically identical, each will have a different character—a different soul. Yet for many, this observation only ducks the question; even if a clone will not be in all ways identical to the one cloned, he or she will be similar in many ways and identical in one fundamental way—namely, in having the same genetic composition.

Ultimately, cloning challenges us to consider how important our genetic structure is to our sense of self. Specifically, it challenges us to consider to what extent a person is more than a physical being-or, to the degree that behavior is genetically influenced, more than just a set of particular behaviors. The less one's sense of identity is based on physical being, the less threatening cloning becomes. If when one looks in the mirror one sees only one's physical being, then a genetic duplicate might destroy one's sense of uniqueness.

Cloning also forces one to ask how important uniqueness is to one's sense of self. Why should one be a lesser person simply because there are copies of one? Contra Buber's view, perhaps a person's foremost task is not the actualization of his or her "unique, unprecedented and never-recurring potentialities," but simply the actualization of his or her potentialities, whether or not others possess those potentialities as well.

When first exposed to photography, some people refused to be photographed for fear that a photograph—an inanimate, two-dimensional copy—would "capture their souls." Over time, most of us have learned to tolerate the camera. For those who do not mind being photographed but are repulsed at the thought of being cloned, a useful thought experiment is to ask at what point our repulsion toward cloning begins. Would we be repulsed by an inanimate, three-dimensional copy—a statue? A three-dimensional copy that is mechanically animated? That is biologically animated? That can think?

The third lesson often tied in the Jewish tradition to the Biblical account of human creation is that of equality. If God initially created one person (Adam), and we are all descended from Adam, then we must all be equal.[18] Our common descent implies our equality.

What are the implications of cloning—and of genetic engineering—for equality? Would lesser people be squeezed out? Would we produce a basketball team of Michael Jordans or a university of Albert Einsteins? Would neo-Nazis produce their "master" race? Would we breed docile workers? Would the rich become genetically advantaged? Would we see people produced by genetic engineering as better or worse than those produced by traditional means?

Yet the challenge to equality, like the challenges to pricelessness and uniqueness, is also conceptually no greater than challenges we already face. Already there are significant genetic differences between people, and yet we view all people as equal. Already identical twins exist, and yet we view each as priceless and unique. Human choice, rather than genetic structure, has long determined the values we attach to human life.

Theological Implications

Just as the possibility of human cloning challenges our belief that humans are created in God's image, it also challenges our image of God as our Creator—our "Parent" or "Father." Of course, advances in genetic knowledge will not solve the great mystery of where the universe in toto came from, but because it suggests that we can "autocreate," it does seem likely to affect our own relationship to the creative power of God.

Again, it seems, we could turn to the transformative view of creation, augmented by the view that we participate in the creation. And perhaps it can be admitted that we participate in the transformation. Perhaps, instead of seeing God as an agent who acted in the distant past, we will see God as the Power of Creation, and hold that we too share in that Power.[19] If asked whether we are "playing God" by engaging in human cloning, we might respond, "Yes, for God is in us too." We might even stress that creation lies not merely in changing the world, but in changing it for the better.

A similar point holds for our image of God as Sovereign—as "Ruler" or "King." Under the view that creation is a completed act, our autocreativity seems to usurp

God's sovereignty. But if our understanding of God's sovereignty can parallel the changed understanding of our relationship to God's creative power, it need not. If creation involves changing the world for the better, not merely tampering with it, then we might see God's sovereignty as requiring the responsible exercise of the Godliness within ourselves.

Perhaps all this seems arrogant, but I do not find it so. Recognizing that responsibilities attach to the powers we have, and accepting those responsibilities, may form the basis of a more mature understanding of ourselves and of God and God's sovereignty. Children must eventually become adults, and works of art must stand on their own.

Death and the Search for Meaning

The Biblical account of creation concludes with expulsion. As punishment for eating the forbidden fruit of the tree of knowledge, Adam and Eve are expelled from Eden and blocked from eating the fruit of the tree of (eternal) life, lest they, like God, become immortal (Gen. 3: 22). Despite a presumed desire for immortality, death awaits, and Adam and Eve must live in its shadow.

Some might think that cloning (and perhaps other new genetic technologies, such as those derived by replicating embryonic stem cells) offers a way to escape death— a way to make themselves "immortal." Through cloning a person might try to ensure that he or she does not really die; indeed, one might suppose it possible to achieve immortality by spawning a series of clones over time. Others might seek immortality of a different sort by producing multiple replicates all at once, so as to spread their genes as widely as possible and ensure their perpetuation in the human stock. Or one might try to preserve oneself by creating clones to supply genetically identical, but more youthful, body parts.

Of course, there are a variety of specific reasons that such attempts either must fail or are morally abhorrent. A general response is also available, however. As the author of Ecclesiastes asked, what point is there in living, if death awaits us all (Eccles. 3: 18–19)? Yet even if, *arguendo*, immortality or near immortality could be achieved through human cloning, rather than asking, "What point is there in living if death awaits?" a simpler question would remain, namely, "What point is there in living?"

The Biblical author was well acquainted with the human search for meaning and well aware that personal immortality can be a seductive, yet fruitless, goal in that search. In contradistinction to other Near Eastern religions concerned with death and immortality (as seen, for example, in Egyptian embalmment and mummification), the Bible strictly limited contact with the dead (Numbers 19: 11–16). The approach advocated in the Hebrew Bible is to live in connection with the Eternal in the life one leads, rather than to seek eternal life. Indeed, death was later taken as an impetus for spiritual growth. As the Psalmist expressed, "Teach us to number our days so that we may maintain a heart of wisdom" (Psalms 90: 12).

For many, the greatest human existential dilemma is not death but isolation and loneliness, and the greatest source of meaning comes from finding a mate and having children. In the Biblical narrative, shortly after Adam's creation but before Eve's creation—and before Adam's mortality or immortality is clearly established—God offers a rare comment on the human condition: "It is not good for man to be alone" (Gen. 2: 18). God then creates Eve to be Adam's counterpart.

Cloning would be a poor substitute for what is achieved

through mating, understood in the richest sense, as involving bonding with another and sharing of life's joys and sorrows, and joining with that other to create an original and genetically intertwined life. By contrast, in cloning oneself one would be focused primarily on one's own life, trapped within one's own ego.

Perhaps the Biblical verb used to indicate sexual relations—*yodeah* (to know)—hints at the deep role that bonding with another person, including joining physically and genetically, may play in finding meaning in life. At its best, joining with another to create a child is an act not merely of reproduction, but of love. While there are many sources of meaning in life, it is hard to imagine one greater than love.

Wild Strains and Cultivars

A Jerusalem rabbi once shared with me a story that I have found helpful, indeed comforting, in thinking about the genetic revolution. I had asked this rabbi about raising my children, may I someday be so blessed, in the United States, versus raising them in Israel. Would one option provide a better life for them as Jews than the other? He responded with a story that he attributed to the Ba'al Shem Toy, the mythical, eighteenth-century founder of Hassidic Judaism. The Ba'al Shem Toy taught that there are two types of fruit in the world: fruit that grows in vineyards, and fruit that grows in the wild. Usually, fruit that grows in vineyards is large, shapely, tasty, and consistent. Fruit that grows in the wild often has blemishes or defects, and much of it is lost to insects and disease. However, it may be quite strong in flavor. How do these two types of fruit compare? Both are pleasing in God's eyes.

In time, we may well see a world in which many people will be cloned or genetically engineered, while others will be created through traditional means. Perhaps both will be pleasing in God's eyes.

References

[1] For an overview of religious issues raised by the possibility of human cloning, see National Bioethics Advisory Commission, *Cloning Human Beings: Report and Recommendations of the National Bioethics Advisory Commission* (Rockville MD, 1997); Ethics and Theology: A Continuation of the National Discussion on Human Cloning: Hearing Before the Subcommittee on Public Health and Safety of the Senate Committee on Labor and Human Resources, 105th Cong. (1997). For analyses of genetic engineering from a Jewish perspective before the "Dolly" breakthrough, see Azriel Rosenfeld, "Judaism and Gene Design," and Fred Rosner, "Genetic Engineering and Judaism," both in *Jewish Bioethics*, ed. Fred Rosner and J. David Bleich (New York 1979), pp. 401–408 and 409–420, respectively. For Christian perspectives on human cloning, see Ronald Cole-Turner, ed., *Human Cloning: Religious Responses* (Louisville 1997).

[2] Arguably, different accounts of how the genders arise can be found in the first and the second chapters of Genesis, which many have observed appear to provide not one but two accounts of creation. Traditional commentators have sought to reconcile these accounts (and thereby defend the view that the entire Bible is the word of God as transcribed by Moses). For one such recent work, see Joseph B. Soloveitchik, *The Lonely Man of Faith* (New York 1992). For the view that the Bible is composed of many documents, see E. A. Spieser, *Anchor Bible: Genesis* (New York 1962), pp. xx–xxii, 3–28.

[3] Mary Douglas, "The Abominations of Leviticus," in *Purity and Danger: An Analysis of the Concepts of Pollution and Taboo* (London 1984), pp. 41–57, at 53.

[4] A parallel argument can be made in evolutionary terms. The genetic structure of our world evolved over billions of years into an interwoven and equilibrated system. While we often use science to modify nature, such modifications function within an existing evolutionary structure. In contrast, human

cloning (and genetic engineering more generally) changes the very rules of the game of genetic evolution. Such a profound shift may shatter the entire system.

[5] See, for example, *Torah* (New York: Jewish Publication Society, 1962); Everett Fox, *Five Books of Moses* (New York 1995); and Robert Alter, *Genesis* (New York 1996). Under this second translation, a formless and void earth might, though need not necessarily, be supposed to have existed before God first acted by creating light.

[6] For a similar argument from a Christian perspective, see Ted Peters, *Playing God? Genetic Determinism and Human Freedom* (New York 1997), p. 14, distinguishing between *creatio ex nihilo* and *creatio continua*; and Philip Hefner, "The Evolution of the Created Co-Creator," in *Cosmos as Creation: Science and Theology in Consonance*, ed. Ted Peters (Nashville 1989), pp. 212–33.

[7] To explain the textual claim that by the seventh day God had completed the structure of the universe, various points might be made. For example, the text stresses that God rested from the work he had completed (Gen. 2: 2–3), but does not explicitly say that God did not engage in further work later. Indeed, the second chapter of Genesis proceeds to offer a second account of creation.

[8] When describing Divine creation, the Bible uses two verbs: bara (to bring into existence) and yatzar (to form or shape). However, when describing creation by humans, the Bible uses only one verb: yatzar. Some might feel that even if we humans should view ourselves as creators, we should limit ourselves to yatzar, a category that might exclude human cloning. The questions would then become: (1) What does one mean by bara and yatzar? and (2) Where on that spectrum do the various uses of genetic technology fall? I do not seek to resolve these questions here, but I do believe that how one resolves them depends in part on the extent to which one views creation as a completed act versus a transformative process.

[9] Arguing with God is a recurrent theme in Jewish thought. See Anson Laytner, *Arguing with God: A Jewish Tradition* (Northvale NJ, 1990).

[10] Some may ask whether creation by humans should be judged differently from creation by God. If God created something, then we can presume that something to be good; but if humans create, we can make no such presumption, the argument would run. Yet the Biblical text supports a different view. The

Bible suggests that the merits of God's creations must also be judged and cannot simply be deduced from their source or fully foreseen in advance. See Gen. 1: 3, 10, 12, 18, 21, 25, and 30, where God assesses God's own creations as "good" and "very good." See also Gen. 5: 5–13, especially 12, where God's destroys most of the world by flood after assessing the earth as corrupt. Similarly, one might think that the merits of human creation cannot be fully foreseen but must await later assessment.

[11] Elliot Dorff, "Human Cloning: A Jewish Perspective," Testimony before the National Bioethics Advisory Commission (14 March 1997), p. 5. Contrast J. M. Haas, Letter from the Pope John Center, submitted to the Nation Bioethics Advisory Commission (31 March 1997), p. 4.

[12] Rabbi Moshe Tendler, Testimony before the National Bioethics Advisory Commission (14 March 1997), 10–11, at 10.

[13] See James F. Childress, "The Challenges of Public Ethics: Reflections on NBAC's Report," *Hastings Center Report* 27, no. 5 (1997): 9–11, at 10.

[14] Babylonian Talmud: Seder Nezikin, vol. 1, tr. Isidore Epstein (London, 1935), pp. 233–234 (Sanhedrin 37a). Epstein points out that the term "of Israel" is omitted in some versions (p. 234, note 2). No doubt the editors of those versions were aware of the tension the phrase "of Israel" created with the ensuing verse proclaiming human equality.

[15] However, natural genetic twins, unlike clones, are not produced with the intention of achieving genetic identicalness.

[16] In one interpretation, God did not begin human creation with a single individual. See particularly Gen. 1: 26–28.

[17] Quoted in Martin Buber, *The Way of Man* (Chicago 1951), p. 18.

[18] Scholars debate whether the Biblical accounts of creation reflect men and women as equal. See Gen. 2: 16.

[19] For such an approach, see Mordecai M. Kaplan, *The Meaning of God in Modern Jewish Religion* (New York 1937), pp. 25–29, 51–57, and 62.

Gilbert Meilaender

Human Cloning Would Violate the Dignity of Children

The following remarks were presented to the National Bioethics Advisory Commission on March 13, 1997.

I have been invited, as I understand it, to speak today specifically as a Protestant theologian. I have tried to take that charge seriously, and I have chosen my concerns accordingly. I do not suppose, therefore, that the issues I address are the only issues to which you ought to give your attention. Thus, for example, I will not address the question of whether we could rightly conduct the first experiments in human cloning, given the likelihood that such experiments would not at first fully succeed. That is an important moral question, but I will not take it up. Nor do I suppose that I can represent Protestants generally. There is no such beast. Indeed, Protestants are specialists in the art of fragmentation. In my own tradition, which is Lutheran, we commonly understand ourselves as quite content to be Catholic except when, on certain questions, we are compelled to disagree. Other Protestants might think of themselves differently.

More important, however, is this point: Attempting to take my charge seriously, I will speak theologically—not just in the standard language of bioethics or public policy. I do not think of this, however, simply as an opportunity for the "Protestant interest group" to weigh in at your deliberations. On the contrary, this theological language has sought to uncover what is universal and human. It begins epistemologically from a particular place, but it opens up ontologically a vision of the human. The unease about human cloning that I will express is widely shared. I aim to get at some of the theological underpinnings of that unease in language that may seem unfamiliar or even unwelcome, but it is language that is grounded in important Christian affirmations that seek to understand the child as our equal—one who is a gift and not a product. In any case, I will do you the honor of assuming that you are interested in hearing what those who speak such a language have to say, and I will also suppose that a faith which seeks understanding may sometimes find it.

Lacking an accepted teaching office within the church, Protestants had to find some way to provide authoritative moral guidance. They turned from the church as interpreter of Scripture to the biblical texts themselves. That characteristic Protestant move is not likely, of course, to provide any very immediate guidance on a subject such as human cloning. But it does teach something about the connection of marriage and parenthood. The creation story in the first chapter of Genesis depicts the creation of humankind as male and female, sexually differentiated and enjoined by God's grace to sustain human life through procreation.

The biblical significance of marriage and children

Hence, there is given in creation a connection between the differentiation of the sexes and the begetting of a child. We begin with that connection, making our way indirectly toward the subject of cloning. It is from the vantage point of this connection that our theological tradition has addressed two questions that are both profound and mysterious in their simplicity: What is the meaning of a child? And what is good for a child? These questions are, as you know, at the heart of many problems in our society today, and it is against the background of such questions that I want to reflect upon the significance of human cloning. What Protestants found in the Bible was a normative view: namely, that the sexual differentiation is ordered toward the creation of offspring, and children should be conceived within the marital union. By God's grace the child is a gift who springs from the giving and receiving of love. Marriage and parenthood are connected—held together in a basic form of humanity.

To this depiction of the connection between sexual differentiation and childbearing as normative, it is, as Anglican theologian Oliver O'Donovan has argued, possible to respond in different ways. We may welcome the connection and find in it humane wisdom to guide our conduct. We may resent it as a limit to our freedom and seek to transcend it. We did not need modern scientific breakthroughs to know that it is possible—and sometimes seemingly desirable—to sever the connection between marriage and begetting children. The possibility of human cloning is striking only because it breaks the connection so emphatically. It aims directly at the heart of the mystery that is a child. Part of the mystery here is that we will always be hard-pressed to explain why the connection of sexual differentiation and procreation should not be broken. Precisely to the degree that it is a basic form of humanity, it will be hard to give more fundamental reasons why the connection should be welcomed and honored when, in our freedom, we need not do so. But moral argument must begin somewhere. To see through everything is, as C.S. Lewis once put it, the same as not to see at all.

If we cannot argue to this starting point, however, we can argue from it. If we cannot entirely explain the mystery, we can explicate it. And the explication comes from two angles. Maintaining the connection between procreation and the sexual relationship of a man and woman is good both for that relationship and for children.

It is good, first, for the relation of the man and woman. No doubt the motives of those who beget children coitally are often mixed, and they may be uncertain about the full significance of what they do. But if they are willing to shape their intentions in accord with the norm I have outlined, they may be freed from self-absorption. The act of love is not simply a personal project undertaken to satisfy one's own needs, and procreation, as the fruit of coitus, reminds us of that. Even when the relation of a man and woman does not or cannot give rise to offspring, they can understand their embrace as more than their personal project in the world, as their participation in a form of life that carries its own inner meaning and has its telos established in the creation. The meaning of what we do then is not determined simply by our desire or will. As Oliver O'Donovan has noted, some understanding like this is needed if the sexual relation of a man and woman is to be more than "simply a profound form of play."

And when the sexual act becomes only a personal project, so does the child. No longer then is the bearing and rearing of children thought of as a task we should take up or as a return we make for the gift of life; instead, it is a project we undertake if it promises to meet

our needs and desires. Those people—both learned commentators and ordinary folk—who in recent days have
described cloning as narcissistic or as replication of one's
self see something important. Even if we grant that a
clone, reared in different circumstances than its immediate ancestor, might turn out to be quite a different person in some respects, the point of that person's existence would be grounded in our will and desire.

Hence, retaining the tie that unites procreation with the
sexual relation of a man and woman is also good for children. Even when a man and woman deeply desire a child,
the act of love itself cannot take the child as its primary
object. They must give themselves to each other, setting
aside their projects, and the child becomes the natural fruition of their shared love—something quite different from a
chosen project. The child is therefore always a gift—one
like them who springs from their embrace, not a being
whom they have made and whose destiny they should determine. This is light-years away from the notion that we
all have a right to have children—in whatever way we see
fit, whenever it serves our purposes. Our children begin
with a kind of genetic independence of us, their parents.
They replicate neither their father nor their mother. That
is a reminder of the independence that we must eventually
grant to them and for which it is our duty to prepare them.
To lose, even in principle, this sense of the child as a gift
entrusted to us will not be good for children.

The distinction between making and begetting

I will press this point still further by making one more
theological move. When Christians tried to tell the story
of Jesus as they found it in their Scriptures, they were
driven to some rather complex formulations. They
wanted to say that Jesus was truly one with that God
whom he called Father, lest it should seem that what he

had accomplished did not really overcome the gulf that separates us from God. Thus, while distinguishing the persons of Father and Son, they wanted to say that Jesus is truly God—of one being with the Father. And the language in which they did this (in the fourth-century Nicene Creed, one of the two most important creeds that antedate the division of the church in the West at the Reformation) is language which describes the Son of the Father as "begotten, not made." Oliver O'Donovan has noted that this distinction between making and begetting, crucial for Christians' understanding of God, carries considerable moral significance.

What the language of the Nicene Creed wanted to say was that the Son is God just as the Father is God. It was intended to assert an equality of being. And for that what was needed was a language other than the language of making. What we beget is like ourselves. What we make is not; it is the product of our free decision, and its destiny is ours to determine. Of course, on this Christian understanding human beings are not begotten in the absolute sense that the Son is said to be begotten of the Father. They are made—but made by God through human begetting. Hence, although we are not God's equal, we are of equal dignity with each other. And we are not at each other's disposal. If it is, in fact, human begetting that expresses our equal dignity, we should not lightly set it aside in a manner as decisive as cloning.

I am well aware, of course, that other advances in what we are pleased to call reproductive technology have already strained the connection between the sexual relationship of a man and woman and the birth of a child. Clearly, procreation has to some extent become reproduction, making rather than doing. I am far from thinking that all this has been done well or wisely, and sometimes we may only come to understand the nature of the road we are on when we have already traveled fairly far along it. But whatever we say of that, surely human cloning would be a new and decisive turn on this road—far more emphatically a kind of production, far less a surrender to the mystery of the genetic lottery which is the mystery of the child who replicates neither father nor mother but incarnates their union, far more an understanding of the child as a product of human will.

I am also aware that we can all imagine circumstances in which we ourselves might—were the technology available—be tempted to turn to cloning. Parents who lose a young child in an accident and want to "replace" her. A seriously ill person in need of embryonic stem cells to repair damaged tissue. A person in need of organs for transplant. A person who is infertile and wants, in some sense, to reproduce. Once the child becomes a project or product, such temptations become almost irresistible. There is no end of good causes in the world, and they would sorely tempt us even if we did not live in a society for which the pursuit of health has become a god, justifying almost anything.

As theologian and bioethicist William F. May has often noted, we are preoccupied with death and the destructive powers of our world. But without in any way glorifying suffering or pretending that it is not evil, Christians worship a God who wills to be with us in our dependence, teaching us "attentiveness before a good and nurturant God." We learn therefore that what matters is how we live, not only how long—that we are responsible to do as much good as we can, but this means, as much as we can within the limits morality sets for us.

I am also aware, finally, that we might for now approve human cloning but only in restricted circumstances—as, for example, the cloning of preimplantation embryos (up to fourteen days) for experimental use. That would, of course, mean the creation solely for purposes of research of human embryos—human subjects who are not really best described as preimplantation embryos. They are unimplanted embryos—a locution that makes clear the extent to which their being and destiny are the product of human will alone. If we are genuinely baffled about how best to describe the moral status of that human subject who is the unimplanted embryo, we should not go forward in a way that peculiarly combines metaphysical bewilderment with practical certitude by approving even such limited cloning for experimental purposes.

Protestants are often pictured—erroneously in many respects—as stout defenders of human freedom. But whatever the accuracy of that depiction, they have not had in mind a freedom without limit, without even the limit that is God. They have not located the dignity of human beings in a self-modifying freedom that knows no limit and that need never respect a limit which it can, in principle, transgress. It is the meaning of the child— offspring of a man and woman, but a replication of neither; their offspring, but not their product whose meaning and destiny they might determine—that, I think, constitutes such a limit to our freedom to make and remake ourselves.

John Haas

A Catholic View of Cloning

The following testimony was delivered before the Senate
Subcommittee on Health and Public Safety on June 17, 1997

It may be instructive to point out that the Catholic intellectual tradition sees no conflict between science and
religion. The beginning of the third chapter of the Report of the National Bioethics Advisory Commission entitled "Cloning Human Beings" indicates that some "de-
pict the debate over the prospects of cloning humans as
a classical confrontation between science and religion."
Catholics believe both science and religion have the same
ultimate source which is God, the author of all truth. It is
not generally known that Gregor Johann Mendel, who
discovered the basic laws of heredity on which the modern science of genetics is based, was a Catholic monk.
Nicholas Copernicus, the astronomer who first proposed
the theory that the earth revolved around the sun, was a
Catholic priest. The papacy has frequently been a pa-

tron not only of the arts but of the sciences as well and maintains the Pontifical Academy for Science.

In the area of morality the Catholic Church works principally out of the natural law tradition, which is to say, the Church maintains that its moral positions should be accessible to all of open minds, to those of "right reason and good will." It does not mean that the moral positions of the Church are immediately self-evident. But Catholics do believe that its moral positions can at least be demonstrated to be reasonable. We as Catholics do indeed believe that God has revealed to us truths which we could not know without His revelation—such as our belief that Jesus was God come as man—but in the area of morality we believe that what God reveals confirms us, with complete certitude, in the truths to which we might come with some difficulty merely through the use of our reason.

In discussing the possibility of cloning human beings, we are reflecting as a nation on what we believe it means to be human. The decisions we make about the moral or legal permissibility of human cloning will have a profound impact on how we treat all human life. Over centuries we as a civilization have developed a profound respect for human life so that laws were developed which protected innocent members of society from direct assault. "Thou shalt do no murder." You shall not directly kill innocent human life. This is virtually a universal moral prohibition, which, since it is transcultural, certainly ought to be viewed as capable of engendering general assent also within a pluralistic society.

Our society periodically expresses its concern for human rights violations in other countries and thereby we acknowledge that respect for human dignity is not merely our preference, but something that is universally required from each person for all others. When all the bishops of the Catholic Church from around the world gathered in a general council in the mid 1960s, they spoke of "the sublime dignity of the human person, who stands above all things and whose rights and duties are universal and inviolable" (*Gaudium et spes*, no. 26). It is always shameful when our nation or any nation fails to show respect for that "sublime dignity of the human person". Indeed, regard for human life has been so great that societies have invariably extended their respect of it even to the "institutional manner" in which it is transmitted. Virtually all societies, by custom or by law, have insisted that the activity by which human life is transmitted be restricted to the man and woman who have committed themselves to one another and to the common task of engendering and raising children.

The principal reason the state attempts to regulate the sexual activity of its citizens is because such activity results in offspring who have inviolable dignity and inalienable rights. Also when the parents are not previously committed to one another in a permanent bond, they are far less prone to assume their responsibility toward their children, the offspring. When life is transmitted in ways other than within the context of marriage and family the personal and social costs are high. The Catholic Church's position on restricting sexual activity—one could better say, the activity which engenders human life—to the institution of marriage is not based on an uneasiness with sexual activity, nor is it based on an esoteric datum of divine revelation; it can be seen to be based fundamentally on common sense, the insights of which come to be confirmed by revelation.

However, this respect for the divine plan in which human life is transmitted goes beyond the institution of marriage to include respect for the act within marriage by which life is passed on, that is, personal sexual intercourse. In the words of a recent Church document, "attempts to produce a human being without any connection with sexuality through twin fission, cloning or parthenogenesis are to be considered contrary to the moral law, since they are in opposition to the dignity both of human procreation and of the conjugal union" (*Donum vitae*, 1987, I, 6). Only in and through the personal act of marital intercourse is the new life engendered best served. The child will be better nurtured if the parents are committed to one another, to their children and to their common social task, the raising of a family. Furthermore, children often suffer emotionally when they do not know who their actual, biological parents are, causing them often to feel isolated, disconnected and not truly belonging.

If a human being were cloned it would be deprived of the nurture of its own parents. The cloned individual would carry the genetic material of the one who provided the nuclear genetic material as well as some of the mitochondrial genetic material of the one who supplied the denucleated egg. But the one who provided the nuclear genetic material would be more the older twin of the cloned individual than the biological parent. The Church insists that human beings have a right to be engendered by parents in a loving committed relationship in which the parents are jointly committed to the nurture of their child, the embodiment of their love. In the Church document quoted above, it is maintained that it is objectionable when medical science "appropriates to itself the procreative function and thus contradicts the dignity and the inalienable rights of the spouses and of the child to be born" (*Donum vitae*, II, 7).

If an individual did manage to clone himself, the resultant cloned child would be deprived of the normal, nurturing relationship with engendering parents. The child might relate to the one who supplied the nuclear genetic material as a "parent" but as stated earlier, in reality the one who supplied the nucleus would be more similar to an older twin. However, that person would be only similar to what might be understood as an older twin, since the cloned child would also have mitochondrial genetic material from the donor of the egg. And the child would be deprived of the opportunity to bond with a parent or an older sibling. Its "engenderer" would be neither.

The Commission report expressed reservations about laws against cloning infringing on a person's private, individual choice about "reproduction." But it might well be asked whether we are speaking here of procreation as it has generally been understood. The cloned human being would not actually be the "child" of the one who had supplied the cell for cloning. Therefore, what rights and obligations would the supplier of the cell for cloning actually have toward the one who was cloned? Who would have primary responsibility for the one who had been cloned? Furthermore, no one has questioned the right of the state to deny marriage to blood brothers and sisters because of potentially deleterious personal and social consequences, the principal ones being those which would result from inbreeding. But cloning would give "inbreeding" a profoundly new meaning! It certainly would not diminish the concerns which all societies have had toward the breeding of siblings. Would the state have to begin making decisions about the quality of one's own genetic make-up before allowing that person to have himself or herself cloned?

Cloning also raises the specter of using others for personal gain. As a society we must always beware of dehumanizing and using for our purposes our fellow human beings. Within our western medical moral tradition we never perform any invasive procedure (unless in an emergency) without the individual's informed consent. This principle is consonant with our societal conviction that each individual is inviolable in his or her dignity. This should also be true for the person as he or she comes into being. A human person is not a product, a commodity, or something manufactured and subject to quality control. Unconscionable horrors have occurred in this century because one group of individuals has reduced others to the mere status of being things.

Some of the language of the Commission Report is terribly ambiguous. What the Commission explicitly rejects as "cloning human beings" is somatic cell transfer "with the intent of introducing the product of that transfer into a woman's womb or in any other way creating a human being." It appears the Commission would allow the engendering of new human life as long as it was destroyed or permitted to die. This hardly manifests the kind of respect which ought to be due every human being, even as he or she comes into being. There ought to be federal bans against engendering life through cloning or through *in vitro* fertilization, or any other laboratory technique, particularly when such life is used for experimentation and research and then discarded. In fact, both cloning and *in vitro* fertilization subject the emerging life to the absolute power of another and establish a relationship of inevitably abusive power of one group of people over another. As one analyst has noted of the Commission's Report: "This is not a ban on human cloning but a (temporary) ban on letting cloned human embryos survive."

Again, the Commission expressed reservation about infringing on personal reproductive rights. Suggestions have already surfaced about parents cloning a dying child. But how would the parents' "reproductive rights" embrace even the engendering of new life from cells of a dying child? What of the inviolable right to bodily integrity of the dying child? Cloning would seem inevitably to lead to human beings using other human beings as things, as manufactured products, with the intimate, personal and yet profoundly social act of marital intercourse being displaced by a manufacturing technique. One aspect of the Commission's report that was particularly unsettling was the frequency with which it referred to "creating" human beings, whether through cloning, reproductive technologies or intercourse. Simply by using such language the Commission appears to have made a judgment of the most profound implications, a judgment about the nature of human life, indeed, a judgment about the existence of God! I hardly think the Commission intended to do so.

Human beings do not create human beings, even utilizing procedures such as cloning, if it is possible, and *in vitro* fertilization. They merely manipulate material that already exists and find ways of initiating spontaneous growth thereafter. The Commission report ought more accurately to speak of "engendering life" through cloning, or "initiating its growth", rather than to speak of "creation." That act belongs to God alone.

There is a way in which we rightly speak of married couples "making love" not "making babies." As they make love, that is, give intimate, physical expression to their commitment to one another, children are often engendered. We generally say that offspring are begotten, not made. The language used is not inconsequential, and the Commission's references to humans creating humans truly need correcting.

We do not speak properly even if we refer to human beings reproducing. Lower animals reproduce; human beings procreate. Human beings are not the only ones involved in the process of engendering new human life.

Without the creative intervention of God in the activity of the couple—or in the activity of the manipulating laboratory technicians—children would not be engendered. This is why we speak of procreation rather than creation when we speak of the passing on of life by human beings.

It is not as though those who attempt the cloning of human beings are "playing God." No one can play God. In such cases, scientists are not elevating themselves to be more like God. Rather they are degrading and lowering themselves by treating human beings in their very coming into being as though they were objects, rather than individuals of sublime and inviolable dignity.

A federal ban against the attempted cloning of human beings would certainly be consonant with Catholic moral teaching. But it must be an honest ban. Human life must be protected from its very beginnings, as soon as there is interior, spontaneous growth.

The Commission Report may appear at first reading to reflect the moral sentiments of the American people about cloning humans. They are against it, as is the Catholic Church. However, it appears that when the Commission speaks of its opposition to the cloning of humans, they are actually referring only to a procedure which would involve transferring embryonic life to a woman's uterus. Obviously the Commission needs to broaden its opposition to cloning to include engendering human life for any research or experimental purposes.

The Commission stated: "We believe (human cloning) would violate important ethical obligations were clinicians or researchers to attempt to create a child using these particular technologies, which are likely to involve substantial risk to the fetus and/or potential child" (pg. iii). However, in a society in which access to the abortion of fetuses and/or potential children is virtually un-

limited, and in a government in which the National Institutes of Health's Human Embryo Research Panel recommended the engendering of new life in the laboratory for purposes of experimentation, such articulated
moral reservations ring hollow: indeed, the words cannot even mean what they seem to mean.

As said at the beginning of this testimony, the discussion regarding cloning will help define our societal understanding of the very nature of human life. If the discussion helps to rekindle a sense of reverential awe before the sublime dignity of human life from its very beginning and helps lead to the protection of innocent life
in all arenas of human activity on contemporary society, then we will have much for which to be grateful. As
said recently by His Eminence, Anthony Cardinal
Bevilacqua, Archbishop of Philadelphia, on the subject
of attempts to clone humans: "We are all aware of things
that we can do, but for the sake of morality ought not do.
Science itself is not exempt from that same obligation."

Geshe Michael Roach *et al.*

Buddhists on Cloning

Geshe Michael Roach
Abbot, Diamond Abbey, New York NY

It's a different mindstream. But other than that, what's the problem? I'm not sure there's a conflict with Buddhist ethics here. It may even be a virtue to create more life. By having collected similar karma, the clone's mindstream would seem to be similar, to be the same person. But it's two different beings.

William LaFleur
Professor of Japanese Studies and Fellow at the Center for Bioethics at the University of Pennsylvania, Philadelphia PA

Buddhists, I think have a viewpoint different from the theistic religions when it comes to issues of what may and may not be done in science. To them the risks of "playing God" by cloning will not be crucial. More important for Buddhists would be the sense that we avoid research likely to result in cruelty to individuals or in more general misery than already exists in our world. It's the compassion matter again.

Ravi Ravindra
Professor of Comparative Religion and Physics at Dalhousie University, Halifax, Canada

In a certain way, psychologically and socially, we humans clone ourselves. Look at teenagers, they all wish to be the same way, to imitate each other. That to me is a more serious issue—how our propaganda, our social-psychological manipulation through the media, actually makes people behave as if they were clones.

Work in this field can't really be stopped. This research will be carried on underground—in much the same way that chemical warfare technology and nuclear research have been. There are people with enough knowledge to do this all over the world. Enough knowledge, but maybe not enough conscience. Like the Buddha himself said, we are all driven by fear and desire.

I am not overly worried about these developments. But we need the development of conscience among the scientists and political leaders. As our knowledge grows, it is not accompanied by conscience or compassion, and I think that is a serious need. This new development only points this need out more. Even the underlying philosophy of science research doesn't make any room for conscience.

So sooner or later, this will blow up in our faces. It is knowledge without conscience. There are, of course, exceptions—some scientists have great consciences. But spiritual training of the scientist, in general, is what we need.

Judith Simmer-Brown
Chair, Religious Studies at Naropa Institute Boulder CO

Cloning, per se, is an interesting prospect with no real philosophical problem for Buddhists, since we know that there is no such thing as two identical, existent beings, and that the genetic makeup is only an outer physical manifestation of the person. Mind is always fresh and unique. As for the uses of cloning, it all depends upon one's motivation. If we have the benefit of others in our hearts, such as healing or extending life, cloning could be quite helpful. If we wish to become rich and famous, or to extend our own personal agendas or lives, there could be quite a problem.

Rita M. Gross
Professor of Comparative Studies in Religion at the University of Wisconsin–Eau Claire, Eau Claire WI

This time, instead of focusing on the question "Can we do it?" let's focus on the question "Should we do it?" Why would anyone want a genetic clone? In any case, a genetic clone would not have the same karma as its genetic double, and the fact of all-pervasive impermanence would still apply both to the genetic original and to its double.

Sojun Mel Weitsman
Abbot, Berkeley Zen Center, Berkeley CA

Scientific, technological curiosity cannot be squelched. You cannot put the genie back into the bottle. But whatever is produced we'll have to be dealt with. Although replicas bear certain identical characteristics, it is not clear how something can be exactly duplicated in this non-repeatable universe, especially such a complete organism as a human being. Although a human may start out with the same identical genetic patterning as someone else, his conditioning will most likely develop a unique personality. It brings up the question: If I had my life to live all over again, would I do it in exactly the same way? Or, is my clone's experience the same as mine? When my clone drinks wine, do I get drunk?

Munawar Ahmad Anees

Human Clones and God's Trust: The Islamic View

A specter haunts our future. It is the phantom of our phylogenetic past that has been decoded by science and used to replicate human life. What for all previous human cultures had been the unknown has come to be known through the act of human cloning. What are the implications of this audacious act by man? How should it be regarded by Muslims?

We are not looking here at simply another newfangled technique. Through the prism of replicating cells, we are peering into the past, and the future. Only three decades ago, the so-called genetic code was discovered as a sequence of four bases across the helical structure of DNA. Today, we are engaged in a gigantic endeavor to map the entire genetic makeup of man through the Human Genome Project. It is for biology what the Manhattan Project, which devised the nuclear bomb, was for physics.

Terrible secrets are being unlocked. Already in this short span of time many a taboo stands obliterated: artificial insemination by donor, *in vitro* fertilization and surrogate motherhood to name just a few variations on the theme. Lest we baptize the first human clone with the fluid truths of postmodern casuistry, that is to say clever but false arguments, let us be honest about what this foreshadows. With reproductive technology there is no going back; its habit is propulsive, to advance ever further, evolving into a technique of ever greater instrumental value and refined efficacy.

A Bundle of Tissues

There is an inherent contradiction in human cloning: the very process is an exercise in dehumanization. By negating the inviolability of the human body, cloning is an intrusion into the *primum mobile* of the genetic ecosystem. The invasive vigor of this procedure will reach a truly awesome level when computers are placed in the service of cloning.

The moral and ethical impasse born out of cloning has many layers. Like the test tube baby that accomplishes human reproduction without sexual intercourse, cloning replaces procreation with replication and further confuses the functions of the human family.

Cloning raises all the age-old questions about life, but in a new mold. Is our body only a bundle of genes, tissues and organs? What is a person? What is the relation of the body to the spirit? In the Cartesian duality of mind and matter, how far can one go denying the link between organic composition and existential identity? Most worrisome of all, cloning forecloses genetic variability. It reinforces the values of genetic determinism because it poses a threat to individuality and diversity through identical replication.

Here the good old nature-nurture debate is in for a real shock! Cloning imposes a deterministic blueprint of bodily development, but cannot furnish the nurturing component of the person. In no small measure genetic determinism is the antithesis of moral and ethical choice. Where, with cloning, is the boundary between nature and nurture when the pre-selective hand of man reaches into the variety of combinant possibilities and makes his choice?

Choice brings us to the much-contested debate on parental vs. fetal rights. The issue gets even murkier than with the early stages of embryonic development when the long arm of *in utero* genetic manipulation becomes part of the picture. For instance, we can be nothing but mute on the risk of inherited disorders and the ability to fight disease in a person born of a frozen-and-thawed cloned embryo. Similarly, do parents have a right to deliberately alter the genetic endowment of a future child? Will that future child make a retroactive claim for damages inflicted through pre-birth genetic selection?

And what about the market? In the biological bazaar, one is naggingly familiar with shopping for commodities like blood, sperm, ovum, or organs. Cloning gives a new meaning to the human body as merchandise. Instead of being content with the organ parts it would acquire novel techniques for wholesaling, packaging, and marketing made-to-order clones. In its instrumental mode, cloning will become an agent of commercial exploitation very much like the rent-a-womb syndrome from which we already suffer.

If success with the transgenic animals—where defective genes have been replaced so as to prevent the symptoms of an inherited disease—is any yardstick, then there is nothing whimsical about the idea of conducting business through a mail-order catalog where the genetic map of possibilities offers wide consumer choice. The only question is, cash or charge?

The Qur'an on Clones

In the Muslim consciousness the body is the medial, or middle ground, where the world of spirit and matter meet. It is the pivot around which one's world revolves. In Islam, there is neither an idea of "rights" over one's body nor an "ownership" of the body in the Western sense of the word. For a Muslim, the body is a trust from God. It is neither a solely owned property nor a disposable commodity: hence the interdiction against suicide. The temporary possession of the body does not imply its ownership by the possessor. The ritual prayer one recites at the death of a person comes as a vivid reminder: "He alone grants life and deals death; and unto Him you all must return"(*Qur'an 10:56*).

Notwithstanding some Muslims whose mislaid zeal appears to portray the Qur'an as a book of human embryology, there are verses aplenty that point to a *normative* guidance on human creation. Let us read a sample: "We have created [every one of] you out of dust, then out of a drop of sperm, then out of a germ cell, then out of an embryonic lump complete [in itself] and yet incomplete, so that We might make [your origin] clear unto you. And whatever We will [to be born] We cause to rest in the [mother's] womb for a term set [by Us]" (*Qur'an 22:5*). Another verse reads: "Was he not once a [mere] drop of a sperm that had been split, and thereafter became a germ-cell—whereupon He created and formed [it] in accordance with what [it] was meant to be, and fashioned out of the two sexes, the male and the female? (*Qur'an 75:37-8*).

The Quranic paradigm of human creation, it would appear, preempts any move toward cloning. From the moment of birth to the point of death, the entire cycle is a divine act. Humankind is simply an agent, a trustee of God. The body is a trust from God. In the absence of a

ined long-standing religious traditions that often
ence and guide citizens' responses to new technolo-
Religious positions on human cloning are pluralis-
their premises, modes of argument, and conclu-
Nevertheless, several major themes are prominent
vish, Roman Catholic, Protestant, and Islamic posi-
including responsible human dominion over na-
human dignity and destiny, procreation and fam-
e. Some religious thinkers argue that the use of so-
cell nuclear transfer cloning to create a child would
trinsically immoral and thus could never be mor-
ustified; they usually propose a ban on such human
ng. Other religious thinkers contend that human
ng to create a child could be morally justified under
circumstances but hold that it should be strictly
lated in order to prevent abuses.

e public policies recommended with respect to the
tion of a child using somatic cell nuclear transfer
ct the Commission's best judgments about both the
s of attempting such an experiment and its view of
tions regarding limitations on individual actions in
name of the common good. At present, the use of
technique to create a child would be a premature
riment that exposes the developing child to unac-
able risks. This in itself might be sufficient to justify
hibition on cloning human beings at this time, even
ch efforts were to be characterized as the exercise of
ndamental right to attempt to procreate. More specu-
e psychological harms to the child, and effects on
moral, religious, and cultural values of society may
nough to justify continued prohibitions in the fu-
, but more time is needed for discussion and evalua-
of these concerns.

eyond the issue of the safety of the procedure, how-
r, NBAC found that concerns relating to the potential

Quranic axiom on body as property, genetic intervention would appear to be quite unethical.

On the utilitarian side of the corporeal possession,
Muslims are exhorted—as a ritualistic obligation—to keep
this trust in good shape. Given that cloning is an asexual
experience (in the sense that it is performed within the
legal marital bonds; no extramarital genetic boundaries
are crossed and the genetic endowment is only from the
spouses), its prohibition must be judged against Islamic
ethical norms. For instance, unlike Catholic strictures,
Islam sanctions therapeutic abortion in cases of a genuine clinical condition, that is, impending danger to a
mother's life.

Would cloning offer an analogous condition? We can
think of only one possible scenario: prenatal corrective
genetic intervention, provided there exists a clinical justification. Our reasoning for this assertion takes root in
the body-as-trust paradigm and the ensuing responsibility for its care as the duty of every Muslim woman and
man.

The arrogance of Western science has never been
greater than when it crossed the boundary of cloning.
Does cloning represent the malevolence of the rebellious?
Is it the vengeful self-perpetuation of those who would
defy God? The human body is God's property, not man's
laboratory. To abuse God's trust will only lead to a trav-
esty of the human essence.

National Bioethics Advisory Commission

Recommendations

With the announcement that an apparently quite normal sheep had been born in Scotland as a result of somatic cell nuclear transfer cloning came the realization that, as a society, we must yet again collectively decide whether and how to use what appeared to be a dramatic new technological power. The promise and the peril of this scientific advance was noted immediately around the world, but the prospects of creating human beings through this technique mainly elicited widespread resistance and/or concern. Despite this reaction, the scientific significance of the accomplishment, in terms of improved understanding of cell development and cell differentiation, should not be lost. The challenge to public policy is to support the myriad beneficial applications of this new technology, while simultaneously guarding against its more questionable uses.

Much of the negative reaction to the potential applica-

tion of such cloning in humans car[...] about harms to the children who m[...] psychological harms associated w[...] ished sense of individuality and per[...] ers express concern about a degrad[...] parenting and family life. And virt[...] that the current risks of physical h[...] ciated with somatic cell nuclear tra[...] justify a prohibition at this time o[...] tion.

In addition to concerns about sp[...] dren, people have frequently express[...] spread practice of somatic cell nucl[...] would undermine important social va[...] door to a form of eugenics or by ter[...] nipulate others as if they were obje[...] sons. Arrayed against these concerr[...] tant social values, such as protectin[...] particularly in matters pertaining to p[...] rearing, maintaining privacy and the[...] tific inquiry, and encouraging the pos[...] of new biomedical breakthroughs.

As somatic cell nuclear transfer cl[...] sent a means of human reproduction[...] limitations on that choice must be m[...] societal benefits of prohibition clearly[...] of maintaining the private nature of su[...] decisions. Especially in light of some[...] ling cases for attempting to clone a h[...] somatic cell nuclear transfer, the ethics[...] must strike a balance between the valu[...] to reflect and issues of privacy and the[...] vidual choice.

To arrive at its recommendations co[...] of somatic cell nuclear transfer techn[...]

psychological harms to children and effects on the moral, religious, and cultural values of society merited further reflection and deliberation. Whether upon such further deliberation our nation will conclude that the use of cloning techniques to create children should be allowed or permanently banned is, for the moment, an open question. Time is an ally in this regard, allowing for the accrual of further data from animal experimentation, enabling an assessment of the prospective safety and efficacy of the procedure in humans, as well as granting a period of fuller national debate on ethical and social concerns. The Commission therefore concluded that there should be imposed a period of time in which no attempt is made to create a child using somatic cell nuclear transfer.

Within this overall framework the Commission came to the following conclusions and recommendations:

I. The Commission concludes that at this time it is morally unacceptable for anyone in the public or private sector, whether in a research or clinical setting, to attempt to create a child using somatic cell nuclear transfer cloning. The Commission reached a consensus on this point because current scientific information indicates that this technique is not safe to use in humans at this time. Indeed, the Commission believes it would violate important ethical obligations were clinicians or researchers to attempt to create a child using these particular technologies, which are likely to involve unacceptable risks to the fetus and/or potential child. Moreover, in addition to safety concerns, many other serious ethical concerns have been identified, which require much more widespread and careful public deliberation before this technology may be used.

The Commission, therefore, recommends the following for immediate action:

- A continuation of the current moratorium on the use of federal funding in support of any attempt to create a child by somatic cell nuclear transfer.

- An immediate request to all firms, clinicians, investigators, and professional societies in the private and non-federally funded sectors to comply voluntarily with the intent of the federal moratorium. Professional and scientific societies should make clear that any attempt to create a child by somatic cell nuclear transfer and implantation into a woman's body would at this time be an irresponsible, unethical, and unprofessional act.

II. The Commission further recommends that:

Federal legislation should be enacted to prohibit anyone from attempting, whether in a research or clinical setting, to create a child through somatic cell nuclear transfer cloning. It is critical, however, that such legislation include a sunset clause to ensure that Congress will review the issue after a specified time period (three to five years) in order to decide whether the prohibition continues to be needed. If state legislation is enacted, it should also contain such a sunset provision. Any such legislation or associated regulation also ought to require that at some point prior to the expiration of the sunset period, an appropriate oversight body will evaluate and report on the current status of somatic cell nuclear trans fer technology and on the ethical and social issues that its potential use to create human beings would raise in light of public understandings at that time.

III. The Commission also concludes that:

- Any regulatory or legislative actions undertaken to effect the foregoing prohibition on creating a child by somatic cell nuclear transfer should be carefully written so as not to interfere with other important areas of scientific research. In particular, no new regulations are required regarding the cloning of human DNA sequences and cell lines, since neither activity raises the scientific and ethical issues that arise from the attempt to create children through somatic cell nuclear transfer, and these fields of research have already provided important scientific and biomedical advances. Likewise, research on cloning animals by somatic cell nuclear transfer does not raise the issues implicated in attempting to use this technique for human cloning, and its continuation should only be subject to existing regulations regarding the humane use of animals and review by institution-based animal protection committees.

• If a legislative ban is not enacted, or if a legislative ban is ever lifted, clinical use of somatic cell nuclear transfer techniques to create a child should be preceded by research trials that are governed by the twin protections of independent review and informed consent, consistent with existing norms of human subjects protection.

• The United States Government should cooperate with other nations and international organizations to enforce any common aspects of their respective policies on the cloning of human beings.

IV. The Commission also concludes that different ethical and religious perspectives and traditions are divided on many of the important moral issues that surround any attempt to create a child using somatic cell nuclear transfer techniques. Therefore, the Commission recommends that:

The federal government, and all interested and concerned parties, encourage widespread and continuing deliberation on these issues in order to further our understanding of the ethical and social implications of this technology and to enable society to produce appropriate long-term policies regarding this technology should the time come when present concerns about safety have been addressed.

V. Finally, because scientific knowledge is essential for all citizens to participate in a full and informed fashion in the governance of our complex society, the Commission recommends that:

Federal departments and agencies concerned with science should cooperate in seeking out and supporting opportunities to provide information and education to the public in the area of genetics, and on other developments in the biomedical sciences, especially where these affect important cultural practices, values, and beliefs.

Contributors

Munawar Ahmad Anees is Editor-in-Chief of *Periodica Islamica.*

Ronald Bailey is a writer and television producer in Washington D.C. He is a contributing editor of *Reason* magazine.

Justine Burley is Simon Fellow in the Department of Government and a Fellow of the Institute of Medicine, Law and Bioethics, University of Manchester.

Arthur Caplan has authored *Am I My Brother's Keeper, Due Consideration,* and other books. He is Professor of Molecular and Cellular Engineering and Professor of Philosophy at the University of Pennsylvania. He is also Director of the Penn Center for Bioethics, and Trustee Professor of Bioethics.

Jonathan R. Cohen is Assistant Professor of Law in the Levin College of Law, University of Florida.

LEON EISENBERG is Professor Emeritus of Social Medicine at Harvard Medical School and editor most recently of *Implications of Genetics for Health Professional Education.*

JOHN HAAS, Ph.D., S.T.L., is President of the Pope John Center for the Study of Ethics in Health Care.

JOHN HARRIS is Sir David Alliance Professor of Bioethics, and a Director of the Centre for Social Ethics and Policy and of the Institute of Medicine, Law and Bioethics, University of Manchester.

LEON KASS is the Addie Clark Harding Professor in the College and The Committee on Social Thought at the University of Chicago.

PHILIP KITCHER is the author of *The Lives to Come, Abusing Science,* and other books. He is Presidential Professor of Philosophy at the University of California, San Diego.

RICHARD LEWONTIN is author of *Biology As Ideology: The Doctrine of DNA, Human Diversity,* and other books. He is Professor in the Department of Organismic and Evolutionary Biology at Harvard University.

GLENN MCGEE is author of *The Perfect Baby: A Pragmatic Approach to Genetics,* and of many articles in the field of bioethics. He is Assistant Professor and Associate Director for Education at the University of Pennsylvania Center for Bioethics.

GILBERT MEILAENDER holds the Board of Directors Chair in Theological Ethics at Valparaiso University in Indiana.

TIMOTHY F. MURPHY is the author of *Gay Science: The Ethics of Sexual Orientation Research.*

STEPHEN POST is associate professor of bioethics at the Center for Biomedical Ethics, Case Western Reserve University.

JOHN ROBERTSON has written widely on law and bioethics issues, including the book *Children of Choice: Freedom and the New Reproductive Technologies.* He holds the Vinson & Elkins Chair in Law at the University of Texas, Austin.

CARSON STRONG is the author of *Ethics in Reproductive and Perinatal Medicine: A New Framework.*

POTTER WICKWARE writes extensively on biotechnology for *Nature, Nature Medicine, The New York Times,* and other publications. He has degrees in English and Molecular Biology, and makes his home in northern California.

IAN WILMUT is a researcher at the Roslin Institute in Scotland and co-author with A. E. Schnieke, J. McWhir, A. J. Kind, and K. H. S. Campbell of "Viable offspring derived from fetal and adult mammalian cells", *Nature* vol. 385 (6619), February 27, 1997, pp. 810–13.

Acknowledgements

"Cloning as a Reproductive Right" excerpted from "Liberty, Identity, and Human Cloning", published originally in 76 *Texas Law Review* 1371 (1998). Copyright 1998 by the Texas Law Review Association. Reprinted by permission.

Parts of "If Ethics Won't Work Here, Where?" previously appeared in "Can ethics help guide the future of biomedicine?", in: Robert Baker, Arthur Caplan, Linda Emanuel, Stephen Latham (eds.), *The American Medical Ethics Revolution: Sesquicentennial Reflections on the AMA's Code of Medical Ethic* (Baltimore: The Johns Hopkins University Press, 1998).

"The Wisdom of Repugnance: Why We Should Ban the Cloning of Humans" reprinted by permission of *The New Republic*. © 1997, The New Republic, Inc.

"The Twin Paradox: What Exactly is Wrong with Cloning People" reprinted, with permission, from the May 1997 issue of *Reason* Magazine. © 1997 by the Reason Foundation, 3415 S Sepulveda Blvd, Suite 400, Los Angeles CA 90034.

"Ban Cloning? Why NBAC Is Wrong" reprinted courtesy of Susan M. Wolf and the Hastings Center Report

"The Uncertain Art: Narcissus Looks Into the Laboratory" reprinted from *The American Scholar* Autumn 1998. Copyright © by Sherwin B. Nuland.

304

"Human Cloning" originally appeared as "Postscript" in *The Lives to Come: The Genetic Revolution and Human Possibilities* (New York: Simon & Schuster). Reprinted by permission.

"The Confusion over Cloning" reprinted with permission from *The New York Review of Books*. Copyright © 1997 NYREV, Inc.

"Would Cloned Humans Really Be Like Sheep" reprinted from *The New England Journal of Medicine* 340.6 (2/11/99), 471–475. Copyright © 1999 Massachusetts Medical Society. All rights reserved.

"Cloning and Infertility" reprinted from the *Cambridge Quarterly of Healthcare Ethics* 7 (1998). Copyright © 1998 Cambridge University Press. Reprinted with the permission of Cambridge University Press.

"Response to 'Cloning and Infertility' by Carson Strong" reprinted from the *Cambridge Quarterly of Healthcare Ethics* 8 (1999). Copyright © 1998 Cambridge University Press. Reprinted with the permission of Cambridge University Press.

"Human Cloning and Child Welfare" reprinted from the *Journal of Medical Ethics* 25 (1999), 108–113, with permission from the BMJ Publishing Group.

"In God's Garden: Creation and Cloning in Jewish Thought" reprinted courtesy of Jonathan R. Cohen and *The Hastings Center Report*.

"A Protestant Perspective on Cloning" reprinted with kind permission from *First Things* (June/July 1997, pp. 41–43).

"A Catholic Perspective on Cloning" reprinted courtesy of the Pope John Center.

"Buddhists on Cloning" reprinted with permission from *Tricycle* magazine (Summer 1997).